JEWISH LIFE AFTER THE USSR

JEWISH LIFE AFTER THE USSR

Edited by Zvi Gitelman

WITH

Musya Glants and Marshall I. Goldman

INDIANA University Press

Bloomington & Indianapolis

Published with the assistance of
the Davis Center for Russian Studies, Harvard University

This book is a publication of

Indiana University Press
601 North Morton Street
Bloomington, IN 47404-3797 USA

http://iupress.indiana.edu

Telephone orders   800-842-6796
Fax orders   812-855-7931
Orders by e-mail   iuporder@indiana.edu

The paper used in this publication meets the minimum requirements of American National Standard for Information Sciences—Permanence of Paper for Printed Library Materials, ANSI Z39.48-1984.

Manufactured in the United States of America

Library of Congress Cataloging-in-Publication Data

Jewish life after the USSR / edited by Zvi Gitelman
with Musya Glants and Marshall I. Goldman.
p. cm.
Includes bibliographical references and index.
ISBN 0-253-34162-0 (cloth : alk paper) — ISBN 0-253-21556-0 (pbk. : alk paper)
1. Jews—Russia—Identity. 2. Jews—Russia—Politics and government—
20th century. 3. Jews—Russia—Social conditions 20th century.
4. Russia—Ethnic relations.
I. Gitelman, Zvi Y. II. Glants, Musya, date III. Goldman, Marshall I.
DS135.R92 J4635 2003
305.892'4047—dc21
                                        2002007645

1 2 3 4 5 08 07 06 05 04 03

CONTENTS

Acknowledgments

This volume includes essays originally presented at a conference in 1999 sponsored by the Davis Center for Russian Studies, Harvard University. We would like to express our gratitude to the Center and its director, Professor Timothy Colton, for their contributions. Our discussions benefited from the participation of the following people: Ralph Goldman, American Jewish Joint Distribution Committee; David Harris, American Jewish Committee; Rabbi Shmuel Kaminetsky, Dnepropetrovsk, Ukraine; Professor Samuel Kassow, Trinity College, Hartford; Gideon Meyer, World ORT; Dr. Benjamin Sachs, Harvard Medical School; Rabbi David Wilfond, Kiev and Wellesley, Mass. All have worked with Jews in the former Soviet Union and their practical experience shed much light on our deliberations.

We are grateful to a wide circle of supporters who made the conference possible. They include the Barrington Foundation; Combined Jewish Philanthropies of Boston; the de Gunzburg family and the Minda de Gunzburg Center for European Studies, Harvard University; the Jean and Samuel Frankel Center for Judaic Studies, University of Michigan; Susan Gardos and Howard Bleich; Guido Goldman; Steve Grossman; Lucius Littauer Foundation; Manitoba Foundation; Mandell and Madeline Berman Foundation; Richard and Claire Morse; Arthur S. Obermayer; David E. Powell.

We hope they will take as much pride in this volume as we do.

Zvi Gitelman
Musya Glants
Marshall I. Goldman

JEWISH LIFE AFTER THE USSR

ZVI GITELMAN

Introduction

Since the late 1980s, one of the world's largest Jewish populations has faced a unique dilemma: at the very same time that it has gained unprecedented freedoms, Soviet and post-Soviet Jews have encountered political uncertainty, economic instability, resurgent antisemitism, and the option of immigrating, almost at will, to Israel. Thus, Jews in the former Soviet Union and their concerned co-ethnics and co-religionists have had to decide whether to take advantage of the new opportunity to revive Jewish life and rebuild Jewish communities, disappear as Jews and live in the newly established states, or abandon their homelands to immigrate to Israel or elsewhere.

This volume analyzes the situation of post-Soviet Jewry in depth, providing knowledge and understanding to those who are studying or wrestling with these dilemmas. It will serve as a guide to policy planners and those working to reconstruct Jewish communal life in the former Soviet Union. Students and scholars will find careful analyses of demographic, cultural, political, and ethnic processes among the post-Soviet populations, and will gain insights into larger developments in the post-Soviet states.

As happened so often to them throughout the twentieth century, Jews in the Soviet Union experienced radical upheavals in the late 1980s, culminating with the dissolution of the world's largest empire in 1991. This collapse created new opportunities and challenges to what was, at that point, the third largest Jewish population in the world. The erosion and eventual demise of the Soviet system did away with the official restrictions that had nearly killed off Jewish culture and had severely constricted the life chances of Soviet Jews. Today Jews are no longer barred from high office nor are they restricted in their movement or expression. However, the very freedoms that accompanied the collapse of Communism and the emergence of new political and economic orders in the USSR's successor states also permitted unbridled expressions of antisemitism. Moreover, the successor states have proved unable to provide the welfare and educational services to which the Soviet peoples had become accustomed. This has both impoverished segments of the Jewish population and bred social and economic resentments that Jews sometimes express through the act of migration. Among non-Jews, the resentment is sometimes expressed in antisemitism. Over the course of the last twenty years, no other Jewish population in the world has migrated in such large numbers, engaged in such massive attempts at cultural and communal reconstruction, and wrestled with so many thorny issues of identity as they determine their places in the societies they inhabit.

In this collection of essays, leading scholars of Soviet and post-Soviet Jewry present to the scholarly and attentive lay communities alike a rounded picture of important Jewish communities whose actions are having a direct impact on the two largest concentrations of Jews, those in Israel and the United States. The picture that emerges is of a population teetering simultaneously on the edges of decline and revival. Demographic decline, decades of acculturation, and ongoing and massive emigration threaten Jewish communities that are nevertheless reconstituting themselves institutionally, financially, culturally, and spiritually. On the one hand, no dramatic religious revival is taking place among post-Soviet Jews, contrary to what some religious organizations in the West would like us to believe. These Jews define their Jewishness in radically secular terms. Yet there is a strong sense of belonging to an ethnic group that has been defined by descent, shared feelings of belonging, and by the perceptions of non-Jews. It has been easier to revive and construct Jewish communal institutions than to revive religious adherence. Local organizations have been markedly more stable and successful than regional or national ones. The latter have been plagued, particularly in Russia and Ukraine, by internal disputes, personal rivalries, and financial difficulties. On the other hand, foreign Jewish organizations, based mainly in Israel and the United States, have had considerable success in aiding the reconstruction of Jewish public life and Jewish education at several levels. However, the efforts of such bodies are sometimes seen as paternalistic interference that does not address the most pressing needs of the Jews.

Another radically new development in the post-Soviet states is the near disappearance of state-sponsored antisemitism; however, this disappearance is counteracted by the surfacing of the grassroots variety, the latter especially visible in Russia, West Ukraine, and Lithuania. New political freedoms have assured the ability of Jews to organize and express themselves, but have also allowed antisemites to do the same. In assessing their position and deciding whether to cast their lots with the emergent states or seek their futures elsewhere, Jews in the former Soviet space have to take all of the consequences of their new freedom into account.

The complex interplay of larger domestic political, economic, and social developments with internal developments among the Jews—all influenced by events and trends in the West and in Israel—will yield the answer to the question, "Whither post-Soviet Jewry?" The contributors to this volume cannot answer that question definitively, but they have provided the fullest analysis available of the factors that will play major roles in this interplay. Reflecting the complexity of the issues, some of the authors sketch or hint at different scenarios and outcomes. It is up to the reader to assess which of them are more likely to describe the future of Jews in the former Soviet Union.

The book is arranged in four parts. Part I, Jews and the Soviet Regime, provides the political and historical background necessary for understanding post-Soviet Jewry. Part II, Politics, Identity, and Society, establishes the context for subsequent sections, and focuses on broadly conceived political developments in Russia and Ukraine, where the vast majority of the Jews reside. The chapters also examine how Russian and Ukrainian Jews conceive of themselves and how others in Russia and Ukraine regard them. Part III, Reconstructing Jewish Communities, includes essays on specific regions and communities, as well as analyses of attempts at communal reconstruction. It also surveys the drastically changing demographic structure of post-Soviet Jewry. The last part, Jews and Russian Culture, examines cultural developments since the collapse of the USSR, an area of study hitherto completely unexplored in Western studies.

We begin by identifying the main policies of the Soviet state toward the Jews. Ted Friedgut demonstrates that "Soviet nationalities policy was a bundle of contradictions from the outset. It negated nationalism, but preserved national identity through ethno-federalist structures." Policies toward Jews were equally contradictory, though the overall tendency from the 1930s to the late 1980s was to treat the Jews as second-class citizens. While there was much acculturation and some assimilation (loss of Jewish identity) among Soviet Jews, state and grassroots antisemitism constrained assimilation and provided the impetus for emigration. By the 1980s, relations between the Jews and the Soviet government had been damaged beyond repair. Denied both identity and opportunity, Soviet Jews in increasing numbers exercised the option of emigration, an alternative that maintains its momentum even today, more than a decade after the collapse of the USSR. As Friedgut observes, "a Jewish identity remained alive in the USSR both because of and in spite of Soviet policy."

Some of the impetus to preserve Jewish identity emanated from the secularized customs of Jewish traditions and attachment to the State of Israel. Yaacov Ro'i sees the latter as a major stimulant of Jewish consciousness. The national consciousness of Soviet Jews had been stimulated by the Holocaust, the establishment of the State of Israel, and Soviet antisemitism. It swelled into what can be called a Jewish movement in the wake of the Six Day War between Israel and the Arab states, and bred the unprecedented emigration wave of the 1970s. Israel's military and scientific achievements became a source of pride for a people who were generally made to feel insecure and ashamed of their ethnicity by Soviet society and the state that managed it.

How politics shape ethnic identity is discussed in the next four chapters. While the Soviet system shaped the way most Jews in the USSR regarded themselves and others, for over a decade now they have been free to find their own ways. External organizations have attempted to direct them along paths they could not take previously. Two of the chapters in Part II explore how post-Soviet Jews see themselves as Jews in the states in which they live. Based on the most extensive surveys ever taken of Russian and Ukrainian Jews, Gitelman, Chervyakov, and Shapiro conclude that in the minds of Russian and Ukrainian Jews being Jewish is not fundamentally about Judaism, traditional customs, Jewish languages, or communal participation and activity. Rather, most Jews in Russia and Ukraine conceive of their Jewishness as a matter of descent, belonging to a "nationality" (ethnic group), and holding subjective feelings of belonging to a group. Jewish identity is understood in the way the Soviet state defined it, as membership in an ethnic group (a "nationality"). Yet this sense of belonging to a distinct group is quite powerful for most respondents. Gitelman observes, "for most Russian and Ukrainian Jews sentiment and biology have largely replaced faith, Jewish law and lore, and Jewish customs as the foundations of Jewishness." He raises the issue of whether a secular Jewish identity based on "thin culture" can be effectively transmitted across generations and from one country to another.

The fact that understandings about Jewishness in Russia and Ukraine are very different from those found in the rest of the Diaspora and Israel has profound implications for those who would assist a "Jewish revival" in the former Soviet Union (FSU) as well as for Jews who migrate to the West or to Israel to discover that their Jewishness is often questioned or perceived as non-normative.

Marshall Goldman's chapter on Russian Jews in business examines the much commented on but little understood sudden rise of Jews to prominence in the country's post-Soviet economy. The high proportion of Jews among the "oligarchs," who seemed to exercise a great deal of economic and political power when Boris Yeltsin was president, and who have been the target of sustained attacks by his successor Vladimir Putin, has often been commented upon but never as keenly analyzed as in Goldman's chapter. Goldman traces the careers of several "oligarchs," illustrating concretely and dramatically how these Jews, previously operating at the margins of Soviet society, gained wealth and power, only to see it diminished since 2000. The author cautions, "if Russian history provides any lesson, it is that the incredible success enjoyed by those who only a short time earlier had been part of a marginal group may not endure." The very fact that so many of the newly rich are Jews, and that even before the economic collapse they were resented as a new, often extravagant class, can make Jews a convenient target.

Robert Brym analyzes how Russian society regards Jews and whether attitudes have changed in the post-Soviet era. He deals with the contradictory and complex findings of opinion surveys regarding Jews and argues that people who had earlier kept their antisemitic attitudes less visible became more outspoken following General Albert Makashov's antisemitic outbursts in parliament and in the media in 1998. To an unprecedented degree, both those who expressed antisemitic feelings and those who did not aligned themselves with particular political parties and personalities in late 1998 and thereafter.

Citing historical precedent, Brym concludes, "The fate of Russian Jewry depends less on the level of anti-Jewish sentiment in the general population than on the policies and perceived needs of the people who control the Duma and especially the presidency. Just like the Soviet-era leadership, Russian political leaders today can choose to dry up the country's ample reservoir of anti-Jewish sentiment or can draw on it for their own sustenance."

Part III deals with the reconstruction of Jewish communities. In the last decade or so, hundreds of schools and cultural organizations have been established; newspapers are being published; and social, political and cultural organizations have emerged. At the same time, over a million Jews have left the FSU permanently. Is the investment in Jewish communal revival worthwhile? Will it achieve lasting results? To what extent should external organizations be involved? What are the most effective ways to reconstruct Jewish communities and public life?

The authors in Part III present different answers to these questions, allowing the reader to ponder the complexities of communal reconstruction in an era of great demographic flux and decline. Martin Horwitz, an American activist who has worked closely with local Jewish communities, many of them small, documents the explosive growth of Jewish communal and educational activity in the FSU. He proposes that external observers and activists reorient their thinking to absorb these new realities and focus their efforts on analyzing the consciousness of post-Soviet Jews. Another American activist, Sarai Brachman Shoup, takes a more skeptical view of communal reconstruction: "Despite significant efforts by distant funders and on-the-ground organizations alike," she claims, "there is no definitive Jewish community or Jewish leadership in Russia." While there are "strong pockets of involved Jews in a multitude of Jewish projects," the majority of Russian Jews do not feel a part of a Jewish community and "a good number are even suspicious of the motivations of the organized Jewish bodies."

Western Jewish organizations that wish to stimulate communal development must take into account the unique Soviet and pre-Soviet traditions of organization and community building that are quite different from Western models. At the same time, Shoup argues, younger FSU Jews, now cross-pressured by local and imported models of Jewish identity, may develop their own styles and structures that will not conform to Western conceptions. A major issue, raised in the earlier chapters on Jewish identity, is determining the boundaries of Jewishness, a highly salient issue among many Jews around the world. Who is in the Jewish community and who is not is a thorny issue. Shoup suggests that Russian Jews be given the freedom to define Jewishness in their own ways, and to form their own movements and organizations. "The alternative may in fact be no Jewish community at all."

Anthropologist Alanna Cooper tackles the complex relationship, discussed in the two previous chapters, between local Jewish communities and external sponsors and supporters. She focuses on the "Bukharan" Jews of Uzbekistan who were able to maintain their traditional Judaism far longer than their Ashkenazic brethren but who are now challenged by external Jewish organizations to bring their practices in line with norms prevailing elsewhere. Cooper weaves a fascinating story of how mourning rituals, far more extensive than those in other Jewish communities, were instrumental in preserving Jewish identity and traditions among Bukharan Jews.

As Central Asian Jews migrate to Israel and the United States, they face an unusual challenge. "Before the break-up of the Soviet Union, the Bukharan Jews' definitions of Judaism had been woven into the local social fabric and into the norms particular to Central Asia." They did not see their version of Judaism as a particular variant of Judaism but as the authentic form. Since their reunion with the wider Jewish world, the few Bukharan Jews who remain in Central Asia, and all who have immigrated, have had to confront the challenge presented by newly introduced global definitions of Judaism.

The chapter by Yohanan Petrovsky-Shtern, on the revival of academic studies of Judaica in Ukraine, provides a vivid insight into a very different Jewish community, the second largest in the FSU. Petrovsky-Shtern focuses on the development of academic Jewish studies in the post-Soviet period to illustrate the achievements and difficulties, rivalries and cooperative efforts that have involved mostly domestic but also foreign personalities and organizations. He traces the rise and fall of several Jewish institutions of learning and delves into the politics and economics behind their shifting fortunes. He laments the growing disconnection between academic Judaica and Jewish communal activity. In Petrovsky-Shtern's view, Russia "has produced a new generation of Jewish leadership able to assume responsibility for local communal and cultural development, [but] Ukrainian Jewish leadership has failed to do this." He adds that "Communal and religious leaders remain aloof from or ignorant of developments in Ukrainian or even Russian cultures; and the Jewish intellectuals remain largely ignorant of Jewish traditions and culture." Younger Jews in Ukraine are not interested as much in Judaic study and scholarship as they are in "applied Judaism" and in the social opportunities that Jewish communities offer. Massive emigration, the gap between scholarship and communal activity, and disinterest on the part of the young do not bode well for Jewish scholarship in Ukraine.

For Jewish communities to be viable, Jewish populations must obviously be of sufficient size and vitality. Detailed analysis of the demographic trends among FSU Jews leads to the conclusion that the viability of these populations is doubtful. Mark Tolts believes that the number of "core" Jews—those who define themselves as Jews in the census—is now about 540,000 in the entire FSU, while the number of "peripheral" Jews—those eligible for immigration under the Israeli Law of Return—is far greater. Trends such as low fertility, high intermarriage rates, and increasingly aged populations began at least half a century ago, but have accelerated dramatically since 1989.

Between 1989 and 1998, about 1.2 million Soviet Jews and their non-Jewish close relatives left the FSU. Nearly 800,000 immigrated to Israel.

About 290,000 went to the United States, about 110,000 to Germany—which has become the second largest receiving country of Soviet Jewish émigrés after Israel. Younger people were overrepresented in this migration. This phenomenon has a major impact on the viability of the population remaining in the FSU.

The rate of marriages between Jews and non-Jews has risen very high. About four out of five marriages of Jews in the 1990s in Russia, Ukraine, and Latvia were to non-Jews. The great majority of the offspring of these intermarriages do not identify primarily as Jews. Tolts draws the sobering conclusion that we are witnessing the "demographic collapse" of Jews in the FSU, though the Russian Jewish population benefits somewhat from Jewish migration from other successor states. Jews have moved to Russia from post-Soviet states where economic conditions are worse and ethnic tensions greater than in Russia.

The last section of the book, Part IV, deals with culture, an area neglected in most studies of Jews in the FSU (these other studies tend to focus instead on Jewish religion, politics, economics, and social relations). Russian culture remains vitally important to most Jews of this region. Since the demise of the USSR, both religious life and cultural expression have been freed from state regulation. Judith Deutsch Kornblatt's chapter examines the incidence of Jews who become Russian Orthodox Christians, perhaps as an outcome of their involvement in Russian culture and their ignorance of Judaism, as well as out of their desire to escape the "mental vacuum" of the USSR. Most of these converts insist that they remain ethnically Jewish. This phenomenon highlights the points made by Chervyakov et al. and Gitelman about the secular nature of Jewish identity and the divorce of Judaism from Jewishness in the former Soviet Union.

The other chapters in the last part of this text analyze post-Soviet literature and art, showing how Jews participate in them both as producers and subjects. Musya Glants observes that Jews were prominent among artists who did not conform to the strictures of "socialist realism" during the Soviet era. Antisemitic reactions to their work only strengthened their Jewish consciousness and led some to use Jewish themes explicitly. Biblical themes and the Holocaust became prominent in the work of some Jewish artists. The peak of interest in their work came in the early 1990s, but ongoing emigration and the withdrawal of state support for art projects have led to a declining audience for Jewish art. Jewish artists, like others, are now more responsive to the market and their subjects are increasingly dictated by what sells.

Finally, Mikhail Krutikov analyzes literature, traditionally one of the most valued components of Jewish and Russian cultures. Krutikov focuses on the search for Jewish identity in Russian Jewish writing over the past thirty years. Jewish identity and emigration are major themes in a large number of works of fiction. "Russian Jewish identity is increasingly defined not by the memory of the *shtetl* but by the eclectic gamut of contemporary forms of religious, cultural, and political life." Krutikov predicts, however, that descriptions of Soviet reality and of Jews' places within it are bound to become less common themes in Russian fiction.

Ambiguity, ambivalence, and uncertainty are the hallmarks of post-Soviet Jewry, just as they are of many of the successor states to the Soviet Union. Clearly, the Jews of the former Soviet Union are in transition. Though we know their origins and the experience from which they have emerged, few would dare predict even their short-term destination. This volume is a fine-grained and richly detailed snapshot of one of the world's great Jewish centers. It will provide some guidance to those who would like to understand the present and future of the people who inhabit this vast region.

JEWS AND THE
SOVIET REGIME

Part One

ONE

❦

YAACOV RO'I

Religion, Israel, and the Development of Soviet Jewry's National Consciousness, 1967–91

The struggle of Soviet Jews to leave the USSR and emigrate to Israel attracted considerable international attention in the early 1970s. Its appeal lay first and foremost in its political implications—the desire of a rather large number of Soviet citizens, many of them intelligentsia, to leave the Communist paradise was an indication of social unrest within the Soviet "monolith." The struggle, however, also had considerable emotional appeal, seeming to herald, as it did, the return to the fold of an oppressed and largely assimilated segment of the Jewish people that had been cut off from the main body of the nation for two generations. To those in the West who were not aware of the Soviet Jewish situation in previous years, or who had merely taken note of the Soviet policy of repressing its Jews and their national culture and heritage without heeding the rumblings of their awakening national consciousness,[1] the emigration movement that surfaced so dramatically with the aborted hijack attempt of 1970, where a small group of Jews unsuccessfully attempted to get to Israel by commandeering a Soviet civilian aircraft, was indeed a major turnabout.

In fact, as of World War II, significant numbers of Soviet Jews had begun shedding their previous Soviet patriotism and identification with the regime and its goals. Although many Jews had been brought to the verge of assimilation, others recognized the futility of giving up their Jewish identity. The

Holocaust and the attitude toward Jews of the non-Jewish population on one hand, and of the Soviet authorities on the other, which culminated in the Doctors' Plot—the official, trumped-up accusation that Jewish physicians in the pay of the West had attempted to medically murder Soviet leaders—on the eve of Stalin's death, brought home to Jews that try as they might to become an integral component of Soviet society and the Soviet body politic, the chances of achieving this status were meager and diminishing.

Another factor that played a major role in the development of Jewish national consciousness was the creation of the State of Israel through its successful war of independence in 1948, and the support given the new Jewish state by the Soviet government. It is impossible to gauge the numbers of those who identified in some way with Israel in its formative years, but there is evidence that many tens, and perhaps hundreds, of thousands were so affected, even if not all of them had the opportunity or the courage to give this sentiment public expression. It is important to bear in mind that as an ex-territorial minority in the Soviet Union, Jews were not equal to other ethnic groups, for the much vaunted "Leninist nationalities policy" acknowledged as a nation a people having a common territory and bestowed "national rights" on populations concentrated in their native territory or in administrative units where they comprised the eponymous nationality.[2] The creation of a Jewish state in a sense transformed the Jews of the Soviet Union into a nation by Soviet criteria. Those among them who identified as Jews, who sought to give their Jewishness a positive connotation, almost inevitably sensed an affiliation with the Jewish state. Nor did this association with Israel of individual Jews lessen over the years. While driven deep underground by the repression of Stalin's last years and the discouragement of Jewish nationalism under Khrushchev, Jewish identity was inspired by a number of events that brought interest in Israel to the surface: the international Youth Festival of 1957, tours in the first half of the 1960s of Israeli musicians and singers, and Israeli pavilions at a number of exhibitions in the middle of that decade. Soviet Jews took immense pride in Israel's technological and scientific progress and accomplishments. The appearance of Israeli embassy staff in different parts of the country also invariably attracted significant numbers of Jews.

There was, however, no way for Jews interested in Israel to demonstrate their sympathies on a regular basis, although in a number of cities small Zionist groups or cells maintained a clandestine existence. As of the mid-1950s, Jewish "concerts" of popular folk songs were allowed in many places, but there was no standing Jewish communal or collective activity of any sort. The only official Jewish organizations in the decades following World War

II and the liquidation of the last Jewish cultural institutions in the late 1940s were the few registered religious communities and synagogues. For the most part, synagogue services did not draw large crowds, except on a few festivals, specifically Yom Kippur (the Day of Atonement); Simhat Torah, which by the late 1950s was mustering many thousands, mostly youngsters; and Pesah (Passover), the traditional festival of freedom, denoting the redemption from bondage in ancient Egypt. The great majority of those who attended synagogue on these occasions were not observant Jews; they probably had not the slightest notion of the precepts of Judaism, nor much desire to learn, let alone observe, them, although many went to considerable lengths to try to acquire any relevant literature that might be available. They did not know Hebrew and so could not read the prayer book, even had those been available, which mostly they were not. Jews were attracted to the synagogue in order to meet other Jews, to identify publicly as Jews, and to register their protest against the anti-Jewish discrimination many of them were experiencing in universities, the workplace, and sometimes even the street.[3]

In addition to the registered communities, there were also *minyanim*, small groups that came together in private homes for collective prayer, again mainly on festivals, in many cities and towns. These groups seem to have consisted mostly of older people who were genuinely interested in preserving the practice of their faith, or at least a few of its tenets. Their existence, while noteworthy, is not relevant to the trends and developments that are the subject of this paper.

Some of the Jewish festivals continued to be observed, even if not entirely in accordance with all the particulars laid down by Jewish law. The most important of these was Passover, which had extra-religious, distinctly national connotations that seemed to have a special message in the Soviet context. Throughout the Soviet Union in the postwar period, even in the prison camps, there were Jews who baked and ate matzoh, the unleavened bread eaten by Jews as they left Egypt, and celebrated the *Seder,* the service where that event was retold with wine and song. By the latter half of the 1950s, collective *Seders* were beginning to be held. In the course of the following decades, these became a fairly widespread phenomenon and a manifestation of the link between religion and the growing national consciousness.[4]

The Six Day War of 1967 brought matters to a head. Perhaps even more than the war itself and Israel's spectacular victory, the three weeks that preceded the war had a tremendous effect on Soviet Jewish consciousness. When it seemed that Israel's very existence was in jeopardy, huge numbers of Jews felt that the threat bore on them directly, that their existence and lives would be adversely affected if something disastrous happened to the

State of Israel. Soviet Jews would revert to being a people without roots, without a homeland that, even if most of them did not really believe they would ever see it, had value as a dream. Jews all over the Soviet Union and from all walks of life found themselves glued to foreign radio stations, particularly Kol Israel. As the threat not only passed but became transformed into a major victory against superior odds, the anxiety of Soviet Jews turned into pride. Moreover, since Israel's enemies were armed with the most modern weapons of Soviet manufacture, many Jews felt estranged from the society in which they lived and the state to which they owed formal allegiance. The situation now was dissimilar to that which had pertained nineteen years before, when the Soviet Union supported Israel: then, young Jews who asked to be allowed to volunteer to fight for Israel in its war of independence had convinced themselves that there was no basic contradiction between their attachment to Israel and to the Soviet Union—even though this was not a feeling shared by the Soviet security apparatus. In 1967, by contrast, people felt that they had to decide between the two countries, for they manifestly stood on opposite sides of the fence. For this reason, the Six Day War was in many ways a watershed, and those Jews who consciously made the choice in Israel's favor realized that they had reached a point of no return.

At this juncture, many Jews drew the conclusion that Soviet authorities had arrived at long before. Since the Soviet regime brooked no alternative allegiances, but demanded total loyalty to itself and its ideology, Jews who entertained feelings of identity with Israel placed themselves outside the pale. In the wake of the Six Day War, the anti-Zionist, anti-Israel propaganda conducted by the regime became part of a virtual campaign. Hundreds of books in the country's various languages and many thousands of articles in newspapers at all levels were devoted to the "aggressive" and "imperialistic" nature of Zionism and were, inevitably, also opposed to the State of Israel.[5] By this time, the Communist Party's Central Committee Department of Propaganda and Agitation was channeling instructions to the organs directly responsible for the media, instructing them on themes to use to "expose Zionist propaganda."[6]

As Moscow relaxed somewhat its restrictions on emigration, and as emigration mounted significantly in 1971 and even more so in 1972 (with the help of détente and the pressure of the Soviet Jewry movement in the United States and elsewhere), a new category of leaders of the Jewish movement emerged: the "refuseniks" (*otkazniki*). In fact, this term was something of a misnomer that came to be used popularly for those active in the emigration movement in the 1970s, irrespective of whether their applications to leave were actually refused. Indisputably, those among the activists who became refuseniks made a stronger imprint on the movement than those who were able to leave swiftly, for the refuseniks remained active over a number of years—sometimes almost twenty. At the same time, not all refuseniks were active in the Jewish movement. Some were refused for reasons that had no relation to their Jewish activity. I have, therefore, opted for the most part for the term *activist*, rather than refusenik.

Since the mid-1950s, when in the framework of the post-Stalin "thaw" Jews began applying to go to Israel,[7] the majority of applications had been systematically rejected. Many people applied and were refused several times in the course of the ten or twelve years prior to the Six Day War, but on the whole they operated as individuals, continuing to go about their daily lives after receiving refusals and not coming together as a collective of any sort in order to apply pressure on the regime. There had been no way to publicize one's refusal, let alone to turn it into a reason to claim a special status, with a certain halo and pretensions of heroism (although in a way it might well be claimed that applying to leave was a more daring act when each individual had only his or her own resources and resourcefulness on which to rely).[8] By the beginning of the 1970s, however, the entire constellation was different. There was a clear rise in the incidence of dissident activity in the country, at least in Moscow, Leningrad, and the capital cities of a number of the union republics. Various national movements—the Ukrainian, Lithuanian, and Georgian, to take the most strident examples—were staging demonstrations and strikes, even though these events were given minimum, or no, publicity. Some political (nationalist and other) dissenters maintained illicit literary activity known as *samizdat*.

Jewish activists, in other words, did not exist in a vacuum. Not a few of them, moreover, had been involved in the Democratic Movement. In fact, these people had become active in the Jewish national movement in reaction to the disillusionment so many Soviet intellectuals had felt following the trial of dissident "underground" authors Iulii Daniel and Andrei Siniavskii in 1966 and the frustration of those inclined to promote political reform after there had been no significant protest in face of the Soviet invasion of Czechoslovakia in 1968. It was thus inevitable that, as they entered on a collision course with the regime, or, to be more precise, at the point where the authorities doomed them to a well-nigh untenable existence by issuing them refusals, they would adopt the methods of dissident activity then in use. Earlier, the most ardent Jewish nationalist feeling and activity had been in the "Western territories," those parts annexed by the Soviet Union in the course and context of World War II.[9] These regional differences persisted, with the Western territories—and Georgia—boasting an unduly high proportion of those who emigrated to Israel in the 1970s. When increasing proportions of emigrants chose not to go to Israel, correspondingly few *"noshrim"* (dropouts— the pejorative Israeli term for those who did not immigrate to Israel) came from the Western territories and Georgia.[10] Now the leadership of the movement transferred to Moscow. Perhaps this was the result of a sense that in an atmosphere of détente, the chances of exerting influence on the regime were markedly greater than had traditionally been the case; with such a situation, Moscow was where pressure would be most effective. Moreover, Moscow was the base of a rather large contingent of foreign correspondents who were showing a keen interest in all dissident activity and could be relied upon to transmit its message to the outside world, thus increasing leverage on the decision-makers in the Soviet capital. The beginnings of détente and the interest in the West in what happened to Soviet Jews made every development in the *aliyah* movement newsworthy and sensitized the Soviet leadership to Western pressure. Foreign tourists, too, were coming to Moscow in meaningful numbers. Many of them brought literature, which was so essential to the movement. In the course of the 1970s, visitors also brought provisions and other goods that refuseniks needed to maintain themselves in a period when many were unemployed. Finally, because Moscow was the country's capital, people from all over the Soviet Union could visit the city with relative ease, so that the activists there were able to establish and maintain links with like-minded Jews in other cities.

The refuseniks were, a priori, a disjointed group. While some could hardly have expected that their applications would be accepted, others seemed to have become refuseniks by chance, the authorities never explaining the criteria by which an emigration application would be accepted or rejected. They were not a group that had prepared in any way for the role of leadership of the Jewish movement; indeed, the majority had not previously felt connected to it. Nevertheless, brought together by a common destiny— the fact of being refused an exit permit with all the concomitant deprivations —those among them whose Jewish consciousness was more acute, or who felt perhaps that they possessed leadership qualities, quickly became part of a struggle that had been conducted for a number of years by an earlier generation of activists, who had meanwhile emigrated, as a result of the authorities' endeavor to deprive it of its leaders. The new leaders thus inherited a legacy of struggle and the skeleton of an organization. Many of them were intellectuals and scientists, some of them eminent people in their field, accustomed to expressing themselves publicly, often with some contact with the outside world. As Jews who had reached senior positions despite discrimination, they had already demonstrated their stamina and determination. Acutely aware of the opportunities their new circumstances generated, the new leaders not only differed in their professional standing and expertise from their predecessors but also developed different instruments for the conduct of the struggle.

A first sociological survey of *aliyah* activists, made in the mid-1970s in Israel, demonstrated that their national consciousness had been aroused by a variety of factors.[11] Some of these were "negative" personal experiences of antisemitism and anti-Jewish discrimination; others were "positive" desires to become acquainted with Jewish tradition, culture, and religion. The survey covered some three hundred individuals who had been active in the years 1968–73 (unfortunately, it drew no distinctions between those who had been active prior to 1968 and those who joined the movement in the years when it went public). All had been attracted to Israel, until 1973 almost the sole outlet of the emigration movement and the natural focus of most, if not all, Jewish nationalist activity. Given these circumstances it was a moot question whether the identification with Israel was the consequence of Israel's pull, or objective magnetism, or of the Soviet Union's push, the urge to leave the country of their birth. Even in the latter case, however, it can fairly be stated that Jewish national consciousness was influenced directly by Israel, if only by the fact of Israel's existence as a refuge for all oppressed Jews and its commitment to persecuted Jewish communities the world over, rather than by propaganda or any specific Israeli achievement.

Like the earlier activists, many of the refuseniks attended synagogue on the major Jewish festivals, or stood in the street outside the synagogue on the Sabbath to identify as Jews and meet fellow Jews.[12] True, most of the regular synagogue-goers were pensioners and simple people who had no message to hand on to the younger generation of intelligentsia, who looked askance upon the regular synagogue-goers as time-servers of the regime. At the same time, the synagogue itself seemed to transmit a sense of stability and continuity between a past about which the activists knew very little, yet felt distinctly connected to, and a future full of question marks. It was, as it were, a bastion of faith whose very durability and ability to withstand persistent regime pressure filled them with pride even though very few of them were, strictly speaking, observant Jews. (Here an exception has to be drawn regarding the situation in Georgia, where the synagogue had continued throughout the Soviet era to play a significant role in the community's life.)

Nor was Judaism restricted to the synagogue. The increasing quantity of available literature and the *ulpanim* (courses) for the study of Hebrew, which prepared cadres with some knowledge not only of the language, but also of history and literature, created enhanced opportunities to become acquainted with the national culture. Consequently, more people were better informed about the various facets of Judaism than had been possible before. Perhaps even more salient was the urge so many Jews felt as a result of what activist Aleksander Voronel called "the development of national feeling and the search for the roots of Jewish distinctiveness." In Voronel's view, "European education and the long experience of equality have affected the psychology of Soviet Jews in such a manner that they are more interested in their ancient history and biblical literature than in the culture of the recent past, reminding them of their humiliating situation in pre-revolutionary Russia." For Jews, Voronel went on, "the Bible is the foundation of the national tradition and the original source of history. It cannot be separated from secular Jewish culture and is superior to any other cultural value that might be counter to it. . . . A large part of the Jewish tradition evolved as the unique spiritualization of secular Jewish history and national life. To separate this national life from religion would be to impoverish it. It is impossible to separate the celebration of the historical liberation of the Jews at Passover, Purim and Hannukah from the religious content of these events." Finally, Voronel pointed out that although "in embarking on the search for national tradition and more profound spirituality, many go further and affiliate themselves formally with religion," the aspiration to "gather regularly at the synagogue, observe national holidays, try to understand the meaning and to observe the letter of Jewish customs," was "generally speaking . . . not identical with religious seekings."[13] Apart from the mainstream activists, there were a few who, as of the mid-1970s, began studying and teaching Torah, Mishnah, and even Talmud.[14]

Almost certainly, the attitude of the refuseniks to religion was not fundamentally different from that of other Jews, at least Jews of their own social standing—inhabitants of large cities, intellectuals—although we may safely assume that they were prepared to express their opinions more truthfully and openly than Jews who had not taken the step of filing applications to leave.[15] This is particularly pertinent given the negative attitude to religion of the Soviet regime. If we bear in mind that this attitude had characterized the regime since its earliest days and that Soviet education took pains to imbue people, young ones in particular, with anti-religious views, it becomes clear that many Jews had gone a long way to distance themselves from the ruling political ethos. At the same time, it is necessary to remember that this attitude did not apply only to Jews. Corresponding cohorts among other ethnic groups were similarly inclined. The intelligentsias of a number of the country's many nationalities, led by the Russians themselves, were identifying increasingly with their national religions in order to give greater force to their demands.[16] Like the Jewish activists, these national intelligentsias were on the whole secularly oriented people who, paradoxically, had in many cases arrived at their nationalist positions as a result of ruminating about and internalizing the theory behind Soviet nationalities policy, and their attachment to their various faiths was similarly cultural and secular. In other words, they, too, saw in religion a basic and central ingredient of their national heritage.

🌀 *National Consciousness and Emigration*

The activists' perception of Israel and religion was, then, largely a consequence of their experiences in the Soviet Union and reflected their adoption of ideas perpetrated by the Soviet system. Much the same can be said for their reaction to antisemitism. Could those who attained national consciousness as a result of negative factors be distinguished from those who did so because they were positively attracted by Israel, religion, Hebrew, or identification with Jewish culture and history? For example, were the former less likely to want to go to Israel, preferring to emigrate to the United States or other Western countries, once these options evolved as of 1974? In other words, did Jews who endeavored to leave because they felt discriminated against or who encountered more active antisemitism desire to leave the Jewish fold by going to the West, believing that there they could finally shake off their Jewish affiliation, and so accomplish something they had tried but failed to achieve in the Soviet Union? Or, again, would the emigration movement have slowed down markedly had Israel remained the sole destination after the first wave of emigration (1969–73) that embraced in great part those who were indisputably drawn to Israel?

Almost certainly, Israel could not have provided an answer for those whose main motivation to leave was economic or professional—their numbers undoubtedly rose in the 1970s—let alone for those who sought to reunite with family in the United States.

Some studies have shown that once in the United States, large numbers of Soviet Jewish emigrants showed an inclination to stay clear of any Jewish community affiliation, especially after the first period in which they were happy to receive material and moral aid from so organized and mobilized a support group.[17] But this is not necessarily an indicator of their motivation to leave the Soviet Union and, in particular, to leave specifically for the West. One study initiated by the Israeli Ministry of Absorption in the late 1970s, however, found that 84 percent of the *noshrim* (those who emigrated to the West), as against 29 percent of the *olim* (immigrants to Israel) maintained that for them antisemitism was "a very important factor" in their decision to emigrate. Similarly, whereas 23 percent of the latter said their prime motive in leaving was their aspiration to live "a Jewish life," this held for only a minute number of the former.[18] At the same time, the research determined that the Jewish identity of the two groups did not differ fundamentally either in intensity or substance. For both, the "Jewish experience" was highly composite, including the lot of being Jewish (which for them was connected to the Holocaust, the Doctors' Plot, the Six Day and Yom Kippur wars), a Jewish socio-cultural experience (a Jewish home, an attachment to Jewish culture and education), religion, and a national–Zionist experience. The first factor was the dominant one for the two groups—just over 60 percent—although the *noshrim* tended rather to stress its negative implications; the second was the most important for just under 30 percent in each category; and religion accounted for less than 10 percent in both. The main difference was, expectedly, that while the national–Zionist element was peripheral among *noshrim*, it was an essential ingredient in each of the other three components among those who had left for Israel.[19]

The policy of issuing refusals to a certain number of would-be emigrants and the criteria—or lack of them—for so doing did not change substantially over the years, although emigration figures plummeted in the years 1974–77 and rose to new heights in 1978 and 1979 for reasons that are extraneous to this essay. In the 1980s, however, it became increasingly difficult to get exit visas. The composition of the refusenik community, moreover, changed radically once the majority of those asking to leave desired to go to the West (these first exceeded the 50 percent mark in 1977 and continued to comprise the majority till 1989). The mass of refuseniks in the 1980s were no longer totally committed to achieving a goal for which they had suffered considerably, but simply people who happened to have filed their emigration application as of the last months of 1979, when the clampdown began.[20] Moreover, the new trend of issuing fewer visas was accompanied by a conscious policy of not alienating people who asked to leave, but rather enabling them to re-acclimatize and even to improve their general position in the hope of lessening pressures on the regime both at home and abroad. (This more lenient line toward refuseniks did not apply to the old-timers, the "leftovers" from the previous decade, who continued to be harassed and persecuted.)

Events proved that the dwindling number of emigrants was not a harbinger of any transformation in the Jews' sense that they would do well to depart from a country where they were largely unwanted and even hated, especially since they, unlike most Soviet citizens, had a viable alternative. With the onset of Gorbachev's perestroika and glasnost, pressures resumed, both domestic and foreign, to let Jews leave. Eventually the regime introduced changes in its laws about citizens desiring to leave for permanent residence abroad. As of 1989, emigration again took on large proportions—in just the two years 1990–91 considerably exceeding that of the entire 1970s. The motivation for the new emigration was probably more pragmatic than it had been in the early 1970s, although it, too, was directed almost solely to Israel, often willy-nilly, since few other countries would admit them in large numbers and the United States, possibly under Israeli pressure, restricted immigration significantly. Suffice it to state here that emigration was not connected to any changed or enhanced Israeli role in the Jewish national consciousness of the emigrants, and only marginally to an increase in the influence of religion.

We conclude, then, that the Soviet Jewish population was indisputably characterized by a growing national consciousness. There was ample evidence of this in the latter 1940s, particularly in the context of Israel's establishment, followed by some signs of it in the latter 1950s and early 1960s as well. The national consciousness swelled into what can be called a "Jewish movement" in the wake of the Six Day War and bred the unprecedented emigration wave of the 1970s. This Jewish awareness was the consequence of a combination of factors: on the one hand, there were purely Jewish considerations, while on the other, there was the impact of events and trends in Soviet society, where ethnicity was making its mark among most national groups. Regarding the two factors on which this chapter has focused, we can safely say that Israel's very existence was a major component in the development of Jewish consciousness in the Soviet Union and that its role was further enlarged by Israel's achievements, particularly its military and scientific ones. Religion, too, made a significant contribution, but—given the secular character of the actors—it did so as an inalienable part of the Jewish heritage and culture rather than as a way of life, system of faith and worship, or spiritual value.

A number of assertions seem to follow that have relevance to the post-Soviet situation, for while the country's political and economic circumstances have changed drastically, society has not, nor have many of the undercurrents that dominate it. In the first place, in the post-Soviet states, as in the former Soviet Union, national consciousness is rife among all ethnic groups; indeed, it has probably gained ground. This holds, too, for the Jews, almost paradoxically, given the high incidence of intermarriage and their essentially Russian culture. In the context of the general national consciousness, there are trends, moods, and developments in the surrounding population that inevitably have an impact upon the Jews, even when on the surface such factors do not relate to them directly. The Jews now, as in the 1970s, inevitably use language and other mechanisms that resemble those prevalent among other national groups. It is, perhaps, in this connection that one can attribute a certain growth in the appeal of the Jewish religion, particularly among young people, religion having among some sectors of the general population replaced Marxism-Leninism as the dominant ideology or belief system.

Secondly, although the arbitrary rule of the previous authoritarian regime has given way to a system that boasts the trappings of a parliamentary democracy, the uncertainties and fluctuations of life in the CIS have left its Jews very much in need of a link with the Jewish world outside. Perhaps even more crucial than actual assistance—save the various needy groups maintained by the American Jewish Joint Distribution Committee, for example—is the knowledge that the State of Israel and Jewish organizations in the West are there and ready to support them. For while many Jews in Russia today have important, even leading, positions in all walks of life and many have used their acumen and expertise to achieve considerable wealth, they continue to an extent to live there on sufferance, well aware that any political, economic, or social disaster may reverberate disastrously on them. Certainly Jews continue to follow with close attention the doings and fate of the State of Israel, which today, as twenty or thirty years ago, they perceive to be highly relevant to their own present and future. Indeed, Israel has become a far more tangible reality, what with daily direct flights between the two countries and so many Jews in the former USSR having close family there.

Once the Jews of the Soviet Union began to tread the path of national consciousness, it was hardly feasible for the Jews of the CIS as a community to return to the earlier goal and ideal of internationalism or of total assimilation and acculturation. This has not, of course, affected individual behavior, especially with regard to intermarriage (see the essay by Mark Tolts in this volume). This is particularly true so long as their neighbors of other ethnic groups stress their own national identities and heritage. In this way, the factors and instruments that shaped the formation of Jewish national awareness in the Soviet past persist in influencing it today.

NOTES

1. There had been a number of publications in earlier years that sought to bring the plight of Soviet Jewry and its implications to the attention of the outside world. The best

known of these was probably Elie Wiesel's account of his first visit to the Soviet Union in the mid-1960s, *The Jews of Silence,* first published in 1966.

2. True, the Jews were given an autonomous *oblast'* in Birobidzhan in the Far East, but it proved, and may well have been intended to be, irrelevant to the Jewish population as a whole.

3. See my article, "The Role of the Synagogue and Religion in the Jewish National Awakening," in Yaacov Ro'i and Avi Beker, eds., *Jewish Culture and Identity in the Soviet Union* (New York: New York University Press, 1991), 114–26.

4. See my article, "The Passover Holiday Versus the Soviet Regime," *Bar-Ilan,* Vol. 24–25 (1989): 173–95, especially 189–93.

5. Such propaganda had existed as early as the 1950s. In the first years of the decade, it took the form of a number of newspaper articles; toward its close, it was evident even in books, such as Konstantin Ivanov and Zinovii Sheinis, *Gosudarstvo Izrail', ego polozhenie i politika* (Moscow: Gospolitizdat, 1958), and Grigorii Plotkin, *Poezdka v Izrail'* (Moscow: Literaturnaya Gazeta, 1959). See also Aleksei Romanov to Central Committee Secretary Nuretdin Mukhitdinov, January 31, 1958, quoted in Boris Morozov, *Documents on Soviet Jewish Emigration* (London: Frank Cass, 1999), 34–36. In the mid-1960s, the number of newspaper articles grew markedly, whereas the coarse antisemitism of the best known in the litany of this genre, Trofim Kichko's *Iudaizm bez prikras* (Kiev, 1963), aroused such an outcry worldwide that the Soviet authorities instructed the publisher, the Ukrainian Academy of Sciences, to retract the book.

6. Following June 1967, anti-Zionist, anti-Israel literature became widespread. See Jonathan Frankel, "The Soviet Regime and Anti-Zionism: An Analysis," in Ro'i and Beker, eds., *Jewish Culture and Identity in the Soviet Union,* 310–54. Just in the years 1970–71, fifty-nine books with a print run of over two million were published in a number of languages. A. Iakovlev to the CPSU Central Committee, Nov. 29, 1971, quoted in Morozov, *Documents on Soviet Jewish Emigration,* 126–27.

7. Jews had applied to leave in 1948 as well, but then the rules of the game were very different. No applications were approved and those who asked for permission to leave were arrested and sent to camps. In the nearly five years from Israel's establishment until Stalin's death, just eighteen exit visas were granted and fewer than ten Jews actually left the Soviet Union for Israel. In the single year 1956, on the other hand, over 750 exit permits were issued.

8. For these early refuseniks, see Yaacov Ro'i, *The Struggle for Soviet Jewish Emigration, 1948–1967* (Cambridge: Cambridge University Press, 1991), 330–35. On the refuseniks of the 1970s, see Petrus Buwalda, *They Did Not Dwell Alone: Jewish Emigration from the Soviet Union, 1967–1990* (Washington, D.C., and Baltimore: Woodrow Wilson and Johns Hopkins, 1997), especially Chapter 4.

9. The Baltics, Western Ukraine and Belorussia, Northern Bukovina, Bessarabia, and Transcarpathia. Riga, in particular, was a center of intense Jewish nationalist activity.

10. See, for example, Z. Alexander, "Immigration to Israel from the USSR," *Israel Yearbook on Human Rights* 7 (1977): 268–335, Tables C, E, and I; and Benjamin Fain, "Background to the Present Jewish Cultural Movement in the Soviet Union," in Ro'i and Beker, eds., *Jewish Culture and Identity in the Soviet Union,* 237.

11. For this survey, see Yossi Goldstein, "The Jewish National Movement in the Soviet Union: A Profile," in Ro'i and Beker, eds., *Jewish Culture and Identity in the Soviet Union,* 27–41.

12. See my essay, "The Role of the Synagogue and Religion in the Jewish National Awakening," in Ro'i and Beker, eds., *Jewish Culture and Identity in the Soviet Union,* 126–29.

13. Aleksander Voronel, "The Social Pre-Conditions of the National Awakening of the Jews in the USSR," in A. Voronel and Viktor Yakhot, eds., *I Am a Jew: Essays on Jewish Identity in the Soviet Union* (New York: Academic Committee on Soviet Jewry and Anti-Defamation League of B'nai Brith, 1973), 33–35.

14. For one prominent refusenik who affiliated formally with Judaism (Voronel's terminology) and began teaching Torah in 1977, see Ilya Essas, "Jewish Life in the USSR: Emerging Opportunities and a Plan." This essay was prepared for the aborted symposium on Jewish culture, planned for Moscow in December 1976. It appeared in *Soviet Jewish Affairs* 10, no. 2 (May 1980): 48–50. See also "The Moscow Symposium: Ten Years Later," in Ro'i and Beker, eds., *Jewish Culture and Identity in the Soviet Union,* 262–65.

15. A sociological survey conducted in 1976 among 1,200 respondents who had not taken any steps to try to leave the country revealed that 53 percent respected religion although they did not believe, compared with 35 percent who entertained various negative positions—indifference (18 percent), not knowing "what religion means" (14 percent), and a conviction that religion had to be actively struggled against (3 percent). Eleven percent had more positive attitudes toward religion (7 percent being believers and another 4 percent hesitant). Benjamin Fain and Mervin F. Verbit, *Jewishness in the Soviet Union: Report of an Empirical Survey* (Jerusalem: Jerusalem Center for Public Affairs, 1984), 11 and Table 12. (The last category, being hesitant or vacillating regarding their belief, was one used regularly in Soviet sociological surveys that sought to gauge belief levels among different strata of the population.)

16. See my articles, "Religion as an Obstacle to *sblizhenie*: The Official Perception," *Soviet Union* 14, no. 2 (1987): 163–79, and "The Islamic Influence on Nationalism in Soviet Central Asia," *Problems of Communism* 29, no. 4 (July–August 1990), 49–64. Other scholars have reported similar findings: for example, Zvi Gitelman, *Immigration and Identity: The Resettlement and Impact of Soviet Immigrants on Israeli Politics and Society* (Los Angeles: Wilstein Institute, 1995), 32–33.

17. See, for example, Steven J. Gold, "Community Formation among Jews from the Former Soviet Union in the United States," in Noah Lewin-Epstein, Yaacov Ro'i, and Paul Ritterband, eds., *Russian Jews on Three Continents: Migration and Resettlement* (London: Frank Cass, 1997), 261–83.

18. Elazar Leshem, Yehudit Rosenbaum, and Orit Kahanov, *Tofa'at ha "neshira" bekerev yehudei Brit-Hamo'etsot,* Jerusalem, 1979, 45–46. The research found, too, that among *noshrim,* economic considerations also played a major role, and that in both groups some 15 percent gave the desire to reunite with their families as the dominant motive for their decision to leave.

19. Ibid., 62–80. For a summary of this study, see E. Leshem, Y. Rosenbaum, and O. Kahanov, "Drop-outs and Immigrants from the Soviet Union (Research Report)," in Tamar Horowitz, ed., *The Soviet Man in an Open Society* (Lanham, Md.: University Press of America, 1989), 57–63.

20. For a study of over 11,000 refuseniks in 1986, see Mordechai Altshuler, "Who Are the 'Refuseniks'? A Statistical and Demographic Analysis," *Soviet Jewish Affairs* 18, no. 1 (1988): 3–15.

TWO

❦

THEODORE H. FRIEDGUT

Nationalities Policy, the Soviet Regime, the Jews, and Emigration

Only in 1989, when after two years of debate and preparation, the Central Committee of the Communist Party of the Soviet Union adopted a new "Draft Nationalities Policy of the Party Under Present Conditions,"[1] was it officially admitted that "the nationalities question in the Soviet Union has become exceptionally acute recently." This admission came in the wake of three and a half turbulent, even violent, years of ethnic conflict that followed Gorbachev's declaration at the 27th Congress of the CPSU that the national question in the Soviet Union had been completely and permanently resolved, and that Soviet nationalities policy was "a contribution to world civilization."[2]

From the outset, Soviet nationalities policy was a mass of contradictory compromises, instrumental in nature, rather than an enshrinement of basic values. The Marxist view, informing the Bolsheviks' outlook, was that nations were of no intrinsic importance, but were an ephemeral phenomenon that would recede from the world stage with the advent of socialism. The Soviet regime, however, had seen the mobilizing potential of national feelings from close quarters and had utilized them during the Civil War. When it came time to determine the structure of the Soviet state, the compromise, as is well known, was a strictly centralized, unitary party in an ethno-federal state. Given the Leninist values that dominated, this immediately placed the Federation at a disadvantage as against the Partocracy.

Even at the highest point of national–cultural activity during the *ko-renizatsiia* ("nativization") period of the early to mid-1920s, the regime's intentions were instrumental. The Bolsheviks, well aware of their narrow social base, sought to mobilize indigenous cadres who could open avenues of communication for the Communist Party to the multitude of ethnic groups within the new state. However much the national cultures and histories were filtered to leave only a "socialist content," they still had the "national form," allowing those for whom nationality was important to maintain their identity and some part of their customs. The right to preserve a distinctive national culture was well-based in Soviet nationality theory, for the dialectics of development as expounded by Lenin placed the ultimate merging of national identities far in the future; meanwhile, there was to be a flowering of each individual culture. Nevertheless, the limits were clear from the outset. When Moyshe Rafes of the *Evsektsiia* (Jewish Sections of the Communist Party) declared in 1919: "We hate any social independence,"[3] his was the voice of the Communist Party, and he spoke to all ethnic minorities. Any activity outside the Communist ideological framework, or in competition with it would not be countenanced.

For the Jews as well as for most other minorities, most traditional roots, and in particular, religious roots, were cut from the Soviet version of national culture, alienating large sections of the population. However, the extraterritorial minorities suffered most from this, for one of the features of ethno-federalism was that most national minorities remained in their traditional territories, surrounded by the cultural and historical landmarks that supported the survival of their national identity. Germans and Jews, as well as a number of smaller groups, presented problems of national extraterritorial culture. Stalin, as theoretician of nationality policy, had postulated a common territory as an indispensable factor of national existence. As leader of the Soviet Union, he oversaw the creation of national–territorial units for those extraterritorial minorities deemed important enough (for either domestic or foreign reasons) to merit such honor.

The "Revolution from Above," begun in 1928, opened a second track of development. The turbulent urbanization and rapid spread of education were part of a forced-draft modernization that offered almost unlimited social mobility to those wishing to abandon the limits of the national community. For some Jews in particular, this appeared to be an advantageous tradeoff within the Soviet context. They left behind ideologically doubtful social origins and structures for the prospect of prestigious positions offering considerable economic benefits. For a few precious years there was a free choice between identity and opportunity, but in the mid-1930s, with institutionalization of the industrialization, and the spread of Stalin's mass purges into the broadest strata of society, national schools, churches, and cultural organizations outside the national territories were closed down.[4] This applied to Jewish cultural institutions in areas of Ukraine and Belorussia with large, compact Jewish populations, in which Jewish soviets, courts, and presses had been created and where there were Yiddish schools, newspapers, and theater groups. One of the two avenues of development open to Jews began to close, and this closure was completed under the traumatic circumstances of the "Black Years of Soviet Jewry," 1948–53, in which the remaining vestiges of Jewish national expression were done away with, the leading figures of these institutions were murdered, and a palpable threat was posed to the continuing physical existence of the main concentrations of Soviet Jews through a mass deportation similar to that to which the Volga Germans and a number of other nationalities had been subjected during World War II. At the same time, considerable numbers of Jews who had established themselves, not as Jews, but as professionals in various fields, had their "foreignness" thrown up to them in the context of the "anti-cosmopolitan campaign," and many were ousted from their positions. The second avenue of development for Soviet Jews began closing as well.

While much changed with Stalin's death, and most fundamentally, permission for a large-scale emigration was granted in the 1970s, the closure of these two avenues of development remained almost to the end of the Soviet period. In all the Soviet authorities' discussions of emigration that have been found in the archives, only one recognizes the influence of this period (coming as it did on the heels of the Holocaust and immediate postwar cases of antisemitism in the Soviet population) in forming the emigration-consciousness of Soviet Jews. L. Onikov, a consultant of the Central Committee Department of Propaganda, wrote a frank analysis of the emigration phenomenon.[5] In a memorandum written in September 1974, he points out that in the past, some Jews chose national identity while others attempted assimilation. "Today, both are impossible." He emphasizes the alienation of Jews who ask, "Who will guarantee that 1948 and 1952 will not return? Why was the last Party statement on the evil of antisemitism issued some ten years ago?" He concludes that some Jews, despite their material advantages, feel that socialism has betrayed their expectations of a "progressive solution to their national problems." While Onikov notes that a part of this may be due to "the well-known Jewish inferiority complex," some Jewish claims of discrimination in hiring and promotion are true. In addition, he notes "the gross errors" committed in some Soviet anti-Zionist publications, singling out the works of Trofim Kichko, Evgenyi Evseev, and Vladimir

Bol'shakov. Onikov wrote his analysis and recommendations for correcting the situation for the Central Committee Secretariat. Nine of the Party Secretaries initialed his report as having been read, and a general discussion was proposed. This was canceled after Mikhail Suslov, the Party's chief ideologist at the time, suggested that the report be removed from the agenda as "having lost its relevance."

🌼 The Soviet Regime and the Jews

How did the Soviet authorities relate to Jews as a nation and as a culture through the period 1956–91? Analysis of memoranda and discussions in the KGB, the various Communist Party Central Committee departments, and in the Politburo, reveals a spectrum of attitudes ranging from ignorant indifference through stereotyped folk prejudice, through almost paranoiac suspicion, to malicious anti-Jewish hatred. All of these attitudes are present in a varying mix and at different levels throughout the post-Stalin years. What attracts the researcher's eye in analyzing these documents is the paucity of discussion of nationalities policy. This area of policy appears to be either taken for granted as fully successful, as in Gorbachev's speech of 1986, or reserved as a topic for propaganda abroad. Apart from Onikov's exceptional memo, security and propaganda considerations, both domestic and foreign, are paramount. Where academic theorists express themselves on the subject of Jewish emigration, they generally bring forward the thesis set forth by Stalin in 1913, that there is no basis of community among the Jews of various countries, or Lenin's thesis from the early years of the twentieth century that Zionism is inherently a reactionary ideology, distracting Jews from the class struggle. Hence, any expressions of Jewish national identity tend toward Zionism and are considered reactionary. The more recent (1970s) Soviet position was that Zionism is the handmaiden of imperialism. These were themes put forward by two professors and two senior officials of the Ministry of Foreign Affairs in 1974, as a counter to criticism of one of Evseev's books (*Fascism under the Blue Star*) by the editor of the Yiddish-language monthly *Sovetish heimland,* Aaron Vergelis.[6]

Nikita Khrushchev, a complex and contradictory personality, who in his memoirs repeatedly denounces antisemitism and recounts occasions on which he acted on his abhorrence of discrimination, was responsible for more than one prominent Jewish Communist's resignation from European and North American Communist parties. His statements to socialist and Communist leaders in 1956, differentiating between Jews and the "indigenous peoples" of the Soviet Union, were redolent with antisemitic stereotypes.[7]

As First Secretary of the Communist Party of Ukraine in 1945, Khrushchev wrote a memo to Beria and Molotov noting the presence of large numbers of Jews in the Chernovtsy region who had asked to be allowed to emigrate to Romania. They had been residents of Northern Bukovina and had had Soviet citizenship "conferred" upon them in June 1940 when the USSR annexed this territory. Khrushchev writes that "the vast majority of them are merchants, craftsmen, people without definite occupation, etc., who have relatives living in Romania and other states."[8] In view of their being such unproductive types, and evidently considered unreliable and even potentially subversive, Khrushchev recommended that they be "permitted" to renounce their Soviet citizenship and be transferred to Romania. As a result, in the spring of 1946, some 23,000 Jews (only Jews were so treated) were transported to the Romanian border and handed over to the Romanian authorities. It is of interest to note that the only Soviet contact with the Romanians on this question was to inform the latter of the time and place of this transfer and to request that the means of transport be available.[9]

Khrushchev's policy of "affirmative action," setting higher education quotas in keeping with the proportion of each ethnic group in the population of any given republic, was not meant to discriminate against Jews, but nevertheless disadvantaged them as a minority group concentrated in the upper middle classes of the metropolitan urban population. Because of their status, Jews had a pronounced tendency to go on to higher education. In addition, the Jews were a widely scattered minority, and so had strict admission quotas no matter in which of the Soviet republics they applied for higher education. The economic trials of "speculators" and "embezzlers" of the early 1960s were also motivated mainly by the government's desire to offset the slowdown in economic growth. Nevertheless, the implementation of the death sentences, and the publicity surrounding these trials, gave them a distinctly anti-Jewish cast. Thus, during the Khrushchev period little or nothing was done to alleviate Jewish anxieties of the late Stalin years.

The regime of Brezhnev and Kosygin was marked by less overt anti-Jewish expression at the top, but a clear growth of hatred for and suspicion of the Jews in the apparatus of the Central Committee. Much, however, was done by oral instructions, without documentation. In March 1973, in the single Politburo session in which there was an extended discussion of Jewish emigration, Brezhnev, annoyed that questions of Jewish emigration were delaying both his scheduled visit to the United States and the granting of "Most Favored Nation" status to the USSR, urged the temporary suspending of the education tax and the granting of exit permits without payment to "a couple of engineers with higher education who have no connections to secrets, for instance from the food industry. Let those go, but not from defense industry. Let out some who don't earn their pay. This is a temporary tactical maneuver."[10] He then added: "But don't give any written instructions. Call in the officials and explain to them, because not everyone may understand and they may start blabbing about this being a tactical step."[11] In this same session, both Brezhnev and Kosygin showed considerable ignorance of Jewish matters. Brezhnev reveals that he had no idea that for over a decade there had been a Jewish monthly published in Moscow. Kosygin interjects, "What, in Russian?"[12] The reference of course is to the Yiddish-language monthly, *Sovetish heimland.* In the same context, Brezhnev muses aloud that no harm would come to the Soviet Union if the Jews of Moscow had their own theater, daily newspaper, and school where they could learn Yiddish, all under Party supervision and Soviet censorship: "Old Abramovich would read in Yiddish what Tass puts out."[13]

There were probably numerous reasons why the Soviet leaders were ignorant of and insensitive to Jewish matters. In all likelihood, when Onikov wrote of the "well-known Jewish inferiority complex," he expressed a widespread feeling. Soviet propaganda was neither hypocritical nor mendacious when it described the high level of education and high percentages of Jews in leading cultural and scientific occupations. It was simple for people who had grown up in a tradition of folk antisemitism to be blind to the effect that such envious-sounding remarks had on their Jewish compatriots. In addition, the mass removal of Jews from the top of the Party and governmental administrations from the time of Stalin's last years onward meant that these powerful decision-making centers were removed from close working contact with anyone from the Jewish public. As Brezhnev put it, "Our entire Jewish policy is based solely on [Deputy Prime Minister Veniamin] Dymshitz. When it is claimed that we discriminate against Jews we say, 'Look, here is Dymshitz, a Deputy Prime Minister!'"[14] Indeed, when the International Department and the Department of Propaganda (Vadim Zagladin and Vadim Medvedev) of the Central Committee Secretariat were asked to judge between Aaron Vergelis's critique of *Fascism Under a Blue Star* and the previously mentioned attack on Vergelis's alleged "Zionist-leaning errors," they found fault with both, and excused their own inability to forestall such errors by noting a sharp shortage of competent supervisory personnel in the field, adding that "Even in *Glavlit SSSR* [the central Soviet censorship bureau] the official responsible for supervising the journal [*Sovetish heimland*] does not know the language."[15]

Deputy Prime Minister Veniamin Dymshitz, the highest-ranking Soviet citizen of Jewish nationality after the 1957 expulsion of Lazar M. Kaganovich from the Politburo, is recorded as having addressed one memo in February 1971 to the Central Committee, dealing with Jewish matters. This was the period when the Jewish exodus movement had gone public, the Leningrad and Riga trials of Jewish emigration advocates were taking place, and there was rising concern both from the Soviet authorities and in world public opinion regarding Jewish emigration. Dymshitz's analysis of "anti-Soviet Zionist propaganda" and its motives is fairly standard, but in his memo, he shows that he was apparently bothered by the nature of official communications regarding those Jews who were leaving. He wrote: "Zionist propaganda cites numbers in the tens of thousands of individuals and families allegedly wanting to emigrate to Israel. This is hard to believe, but the question arises: has anyone clarified in detail and on the spot with the people applying for emigration, who they are, and on the basis of what information or propaganda they have come to such a wild decision as to emigrate from the Soviet Union to a capitalist country engaged in war with the Arabs for alien interests? What have they been promised, and what actually awaits them there? . . . Then it will be clear with whom, for what reasons, and with what number we are dealing, how to get along with them, and who should actually be let go so that they will not interfere with our life and work."[16] Dymshitz is one of the few who wraps his words in the banner of "the further strengthening of the Leninist nationality policy of the Party for the unifying of all the peoples of our country."

Dymshitz's memo included numerous suggestions that were already on the agenda, and it was he who headed the list of prominent Soviet Jewish personalities appearing at a press conference in Moscow in March 1971 denying all discrimination against Jews in the USSR. In addition, in his memo he had recommended various steps for the strengthening of Jewish culture in the USSR. The reply of the Central Committee Department of Propaganda came only a year later, and totally ignored the subject of Jewish cultural institutions.[17] The practice of ignoring suggestions for Jewish cultural revival may be noted in connection with suggestions proffered by Aaron Vergelis in November 1971.[18] In this case the answer took only two months to prepare, but here too, there is absolutely no response to suggestions about the field of Jewish culture.[19]

The hostility to Jewish culture that may be inferred from such behavior was sometimes explicit. In June 1959, a commission of the CC Department of Agitation and Propaganda examined sixteen basic Jewish religious publications—the Bible, the Talmud, and various prayer books, including one published in Moscow in 1956 (which was averred to be "the most reactionary prayer book published in the past 100 years"). It found them to be "imbued through and through with a spirit of militant nationalism, 'spiritual racism' often spilling over into biological and political racism. . . . Basing itself on this, contemporary Zionism has evolved the theory of the necessity of spiritual and political aggression of the imperialist state of Israel."[20] The commission also found that inasmuch as Jewish folk sayings, folk songs, and the like were drawn largely from biblical and religious writings, they too should be regarded as pernicious. In short, Jewish culture on the whole was to be regarded as subversive.

We have already mentioned the admission by the reviewers of the International Department and the Department of Propaganda that certain "errors" cropped up in anti-Zionist literature. Dymshitz by implication criticized the work done by those producing anti-Zionist literature when he noted that there is no scientific institution in the entire Soviet system that systematically studies all aspects of the problems involved in the refutation of Zionist propaganda. There were also instances of even sharper criticism. In 1977, two scholars of the Oriental Institute, Academy Member M. A. Korostovtsev, an Egyptologist, and Dr. L. A. Korneev, then a specialist in Malagasy language studies, sent a blistering letter of criticism against the level of scientific accuracy of Soviet anti-Zionist literature, which they characterized as "impossible to regard as meeting the demands of the task. . . . and often the scientific and popular works of this group contain attacks insulting to the Jews."[21] The two level the accusation that "the researchers in this particular group have set themselves the goal of stimulating the exodus of Jews from the Soviet Union, regarding them all as potential 'traitors.'"[22] Some doubt may be cast on the objectivity of their criticism, for they attach a manuscript written by Korneev entitled "Marxism-Leninism on the Jewish Question and on Zionism," suggesting that it be published. This attack was given a chilly reception in the Central Committee apparatus, which noted that the critics cited no specific examples to illustrate their criticisms. The response also rejected the Orientalists' accusation that official publications might contain attacks insulting to the Jews. The CC suggested awaiting a pending report from the Academy of Sciences' Permanent Commission for Coordinating the Scientific Criticism of Zionism (a body evidently established some time after the criticisms leveled by Dymshitz against the unorganized nature of Soviet anti-Zionist writings) before deciding anything. It remains only to be noted that in the years 1980–85, Lev Korneev became one of the most prolific, as well as one of the most vile and vicious, purveyors of antisemitic writings under the guise of anti-Zionism.[23]

In 1958, when a Central Committee commission chaired by N. Mukhitdinov examined questions of emigration and repatriation, the main line of propaganda suggested was to emphasize the harm that potential emigrants did to themselves and their families by leaving the Soviet Union for a harsh and uncertain future—whether in Poland, Spain, or Israel.[24] The documents attest to an interest in having emigrants return (both from Israel and from Spain), on a selective basis to be sure, and with an eye to using them for propaganda purposes, but the impression is created that the emigrants are officially regarded more in sorrow than in anger. At that time there were only about a thousand Jewish requests pending for exit permits. However, as the stream grew, and as the campaign for Soviet Jewry became more visible and vocal, popping up in all sectors of Soviet foreign relations, the Soviet response became more suspicious and ill-tempered, sometimes verging on paranoia. In November 1971, the Central Committee Department of Propaganda, in a memo signed by A. N. Yakovlev, the deputy director, reported on the publication of fifty-nine books and pamphlets in a total edition of two million copies in eight languages, "unmasking the reactionary anti-Soviet essence of contemporary Zionism."[25] This vast effort came, as has been noted, at a time when the same institutions that took part in the campaign studiously ignored far more modest suggestions for the strengthening of Jewish culture. In another incident in 1974, when Interior Minister Shchelokov raised the question in the Politburo of publicizing the fact that a number of Jewish families had applied to return to the USSR, Prime Minister Kosygin interjected: "Our people react very badly to returnees. They say that if they have gone out, don't take them back!"[26] The paranoid tendencies in regime thinking found expression in a KGB memo to the Central Committee in 1981. It stated that the sending of invitations to emigrate appeared to be directed purposefully at specialists working on current projects of the Ministry of Defense, the gas and oil industry, the radio industry, and light and heavy machine building—in short, in fields "of interest to the economies of Israel and a number of leading capitalist countries."[27] Here, as in numerous documents, Yuri Andropov, who in his time enjoyed a reputation for enlightened realism, appears as a harsh opponent of Jewish emigration.

For a variety of reasons connected with the degeneration of the Soviet regime during the Brezhnev period, with the polarization of international relations throughout the post–World War II period, and with the success of the Soviet-Jewish exodus movement in placing its cause prominently on the international agenda, and subjecting the Soviet authorities to embarrassing pressures, the Soviet regime and Soviet Jews became increasingly alienated from each other. Relations had deteriorated beyond repair by the time Brezhnev enunciated his doctrine of "neither Zionism nor antisemitism" at the

1981 Party Congress, a doctrine that supposedly removed much of the employment and educational discrimination that had been more and more oppressive to Jews. Even the 1989 Nationalities Policy Platform of the CPSU that offered the extraterritorial minorities free contact with their co-nationals abroad with whom "they have ties of common ethnic origin or cultural heritage"[28] could not restore any measure of confidence. Denied both identity and opportunity, Soviet Jews in increasing numbers created for themselves the third option of emigration, which maintains its momentum even today, more than a decade after the collapse of the USSR.

Emigration

Like nationalities policy, and perhaps even more so, emigration was seen instrumentally by the Soviet regime. For a variety of reasons, the Soviet Union throughout its existence was an introverted polity—particularly as concerned its citizens. Their loyalties, their energies, and their attentions were to be turned inwards to the building of Communism in the Soviet Union. Despite this basic principle, all four types of emigration noted by Pinkus—repatriation by unilateral or bilateral decision; expulsion; illegal emigration; and most importantly for our discussion, individual emigration[29] —existed almost continuously throughout the Soviet period. For Jews in the pre-Soviet and early Soviet periods, emigration was not an unusual choice. Between 1899 and 1914, 1,300,000 Jews had emigrated from the Russian Empire,[30] and virtually every Jewish family must have had relatives who had gone abroad. War and revolution diminished this stream, but could not dam it entirely.

Between 1919 and 1924, 20,000 Jews are said to have left Soviet territory for Palestine alone, some by individual permits, some by group arrangements between the *Yidgezkom* (Public Committee to Aid Victims of War, Pogroms and Natural Disasters) and the American Jewish Joint Distribution Committee, while others, particularly leading Zionist activists, were expelled by the Soviet authorities. It should be remembered that in this period mass expulsion was used against the "old-regime" intelligentsia as well. Though emigration slowed to a trickle in the 1930s, as all aspects of Soviet life were affected by Stalin's "revolution from above," the number of Jews leaving the USSR between 1917 and 1939 is said to have totaled 70,000.[31] A memoir of this period describes mass smuggling of emigrants across the Dniestr River into Romania in the early 1920s, a description highly similar to incidents from the late tsarist years.[32]

In the pre–World War II period, all the elements to be found in post-

Stalin emigrations were established—repatriation, family unification, international lobbying, even payments for release.[33] Pinkus notes the emigration of 20,000 Soviet Germans in the mid-1920s, mainly Mennonites, with the active support of the Mennonite communities of the United States and Canada.[34] One of the major contributions of the work of Heitman and of Pinkus is the revelation that in spite of all limitations, emigration and the internal pressure for emigration were continuous throughout the Soviet period. Heitman gives an estimate of 13 million emigrants and deportees from the USSR between 1917 and 1985, including the mass migrations of the period of the 1917 revolutions, and of the immediate post–World War II period.[35] Pinkus documents the existence of Zionist groups, however tenuous, and the desire to emigrate as continuous features of Soviet Jewish life,[36] and Ro'i notes a number of sources within Soviet Jewry in the early 1950s that estimated the emigration potential of Jews as ranging from 100,000 up to a million.[37]

We dwell upon these developments to correct the impression that a Jewish national awakening and the movement for emigration began only with the Six Day War in 1967. Perhaps the most dramatic demonstration of earlier emigration pressures was the letter of 1948 sent in the name of all the Jews of Zhmerinka, Ukraine, following the founding of the state of Israel, asking that they be allowed to emigrate "to our homeland . . . to create a large Jewish democratic state."[38] In the early and mid-1950s, thousands of Jews used the repatriations to Poland and to other "People's Democratic Republics" of Eastern Europe as a path to Israel, with full knowledge of the Soviet authorities.[39]

Even the central phenomenon with which we are concerned, the growth of individual emigration of Jews, began to take on mass character from the mid-1950s. As early as October 1951, the Minister-Counselor of the Israeli Embassy in Moscow, Shmuel Eliashiv, had broached the subject of family reunification with Soviet Deputy Foreign Minister Andrei Gromyko.[40] The Israeli proposals brought no response. Only in 1956 can we discern the beginning of a regularized mass individual Jewish emigration. In that year, 753 Jews emigrated to Israel, compared with only 174 between 1948 and 1955.[41] During these same years, while the numbers of Jewish emigrants were growing, and the number of applicants was growing faster still, the Soviet authorities initiated a series of trials in half a dozen cities against persons charged with disseminating "Zionist, anti-Soviet propaganda." In this connection, three members of the Israeli diplomatic mission in Moscow were expelled. Examination of these events yields two insights into the dynamics of the regime's relation to the exodus movement. First, it may be noted that as prospects for actual emigration increased, requests for emigration multiplied and spread geographically. The internal communication network of the Jewish population was efficient and widespread. The second insight is that whatever the policy line adopted, it was important to the regime that the government clearly assert its control over the process. Neither Jewish nor foreign pressure would set the parameters of emigration. Only Soviet state and Party interests would be decisive. The tentative exodus was interrupted by the Sinai War of 1956, and the numbers began to grow again only in 1960, passing 1,000 in 1965 and reaching nearly 2,000 in 1966.

The period of the mid-1950s was the height of the post-Stalin thaw, a propitious time for a change of policy regarding emigration. Agreements were made for repatriation of German prisoners of war who had been used as laborers in the USSR for ten years; for the repatriation of Spaniards; former Polish citizens (among them, as we have mentioned, some 14,000 Jews who continued on to Israel); Armenians; and a little later Greeks and Koreans. The results were assessed in terms of favorable public relations with the public in these various countries, and with fraternal Communist parties and other "progressive groups" in the world with whom the Soviet government was attempting to strengthen its relations to advance the Soviet-led peace movement.[42] It was also a period in which the Soviet Union was experiencing relative economic well-being, and perhaps for the first time in its history could feel a sense of confidence in the future.[43] Although the report of the Mukhitdinov Commission to the Central Committee in 1958 leaves the impression that the Soviet regime was then interested in the Jews remaining, and even recommends efforts to return some of those who have emigrated, it is not clear whether the motivation was to score propaganda points externally, or whether Jews were regarded as intrinsically valuable citizens.[44] It was in this period, however, that Khrushchev's "affirmative action" programs were initiated, causing problems, wittingly or unwittingly, for Jews as well as for other extraterritorial minorities.[45]

The Jewish emigration movement grew from several different roots. First was the repressed remnant of a traditional Jewish community that maintained some embers of Zionist and religious consciousness, a few books, stories of former Jewish life, memories of friends and relatives who had emigrated, whether to Palestine or to America, and were maintaining active Jewish lives there. These sources of living memory were strongly reinforced in 1939–40 when territories with dense Jewish populations and vibrant Jewish institutions were annexed to the USSR and many of their leading figures were dispersed throughout the Soviet Union. For a number of younger future emigration activists, a first systematic knowledge of Jewish affairs and Zionist ideas came in the labor camps, where the future protesters met and learned from the exiled activists of the Jewish communities of the Baltic states and Polish and Romanian territories.

The impact of the war, the Holocaust, and the antisemitism that flourished openly in Stalin's last years affected even convinced communists who had hitherto believed firmly in "Soviet internationalism," stimulating their Jewish identity.[46] Postwar antisemitism, and perhaps the war itself, appear to have been a turning point in the Jewish consciousness of the famous Soviet writer and war correspondent Il'ia Ehrenburg, among others. The Soviet regime's refusal to revive the Jewish cultural institutions that Stalin had destroyed, along with its denial of any particularly Jewish aspects of the Holocaust, only exacerbated the anxieties felt by Soviet Jews.[47] A KGB report in November 1959 stated that the burning of the synagogue in the Moscow suburb of Malakhovka and the murder of the caretaker had evoked fears in "a certain part of the Jewish public," and linked this incident to tendencies to emigrate.[48]

A little-discussed factor in maintaining Jewish identity in this difficult period is what may be called the "natural Jewish community." It was part of Soviet folklore that certain Soviet institutions were heavily Jewish. In its early days, the Soviet Foreign Ministry was dubbed, half-jokingly, half-maliciously, "the synagogue." The rapid social mobility of the Jews in the late 1920s and through the 1930s brought them into the middle and upper echelons of science, industry, and culture. Just how great these concentrations were is revealed in a 1979 report by Interior Minister of the Ukraine, I. K. Golovchenko, who, in a discussion of the impact of Jewish emigration, cites five industrial enterprises in Odessa in which Jews made up between 25 and 40 percent of the work collective.[49] Moscow and Leningrad were home to scientific institutes with similar concentrations of Jews. This meant that large numbers of Soviet Jews quite naturally shared intellectual and social lives, lived as neighbors, and sent their children to the same schools as other Jews. It was only natural that in such circles some remnants of Jewish holidays and traditions were marked, Jewish topics were frequently discussed, and Jewish symbols and culture was valued, much as old Russian icons were in other circles. All of this was in addition to the relatively newly Sovietized Jewish communities of the Baltics, West Ukraine and Belorussia, and Moldavia, and the still traditional communities of Georgia, Uzbekistan, and the East Caucasus. When emigration arose as a real possibility on the "Jewish agenda," the practice spread rapidly through this "natural community."

From the beginnings of the emigration, a delicate symbiosis was created between the internal response of the Jews to the possibility of emigration, and foreign pressures on their behalf. The will of a substantial part of the Jewish community to emigrate was the *sine qua non* of the entire movement, but Israel was committed, from its first diplomatic contacts with the USSR, to the maximum realization of such a will. As Ro'i discusses in detail,[50] initial inquiries in this direction were rebuffed and produced no substantial results. Zionism was both historically and politically anathema to the Soviet regime. But the environment of the late 1960s encouraged the Jews to "go public" in their activism on behalf of emigration. This was a period when the Democratic Movement of dissidents was openly demonstrating and petitioning for liberalization, the "Prague Spring" was taking shape, and it seemed as though the Soviet regime was mellowing with age. When, largely due to Soviet domestic evolution and a changing international climate, emigration appeared a real possibility, Israel's "Liaison Bureau," a special section under the Prime Minister's office, decided on an indirect strategy of lobbying through third parties. The first contacts chosen were the European and Latin American Socialist and Communist parties whose sympathy and support was then being actively sought by the USSR.[51] The Jewish question thus entered the USSR's foreign policy agenda, and, owing to activity by American and European Jewish organizations, grew steadily in salience to a climax in December 1987 when some 200,000 persons demonstrated in Washington for free Jewish emigration, bringing President Reagan to explain at length and in detail the political significance of the emigration issue before he would enter into negotiations with Gorbachev over the strategic and economic issues that were the official agenda of the summit meeting.[52]

Placing the question of emigration on the international agenda was a two-edged sword. Unable to ignore the issue, Soviet diplomats quickly learned to use it for something more substantial than the nebulous approbation of public opinion that was noted as having been achieved through the repatriation of Spaniards and others. In negotiating for credits and better trade conditions with the United States, Brezhnev told the Politburo, "We have supplied Comrade [Anatoly] Dobrynin [Soviet ambassador to the United States] with a fall-back position, which he will hold back until he gets agreement. . . . We have also discussed how to pull the Jewish question out of his pocket."[53] Richard Schifter, who was deeply involved in negotiations regarding emigration in the late Soviet period, writes that the USSR was clear on demanding a *quid pro quo* for any concessions on emigration and that "willingness to deal" was an essential part of the negotiation.[54] It may be said that by having ultimate control of the numbers of Jews or others permitted to emigrate, and holding the option of deciding whether the concessions offered were sufficient, the USSR maintained its control of the issue. What it would have been very happy to do, but was unable to, because of the successful combination of Soviet Jewish and outside pressures, was remove the issue from the international agenda. Instead, the Soviet regime was forced to negotiate the price of emigration with growingly informed and increasingly hostile international actors.

The handling of emigration was, like all Soviet life, highly bureaucratized. Numerous agencies were involved in the process of freeing an emigrant. Policy decisions were ultimately the responsibility of the Politburo and Secretariat, but were generally taken on the basis of information and recommendations supplied by the KGB. The decree of the Supreme Soviet dated February 17, 1967, automatically stripping Soviet Jewish emigrants of their citizenship, was taken on the basis of the KGB pointing out an anomaly in the phrasing of the law that allowed Jews to leave the USSR but still claim Soviet citizenship.[55] The recommendation to stop emigration to Israel after the 1967 war was made by the KGB, as was the recommendation (with concurrence of the Foreign Ministry) to renew it on a selective basis a year later.[56] Andropov, as chairman of the KGB, signed recommendations regarding individuals' emigration. For example, because of his "low moral and professional character" the film scenarist Efraim Sevela was granted permission to go.[57] In another case, in March 1971, Andropov recommended that public pressure be brought against the Smeliansky family of Moscow because of a "nationalist poem" one member of the family had written and sent to relatives in Israel; it was recommended that they be refused exit permits. Five Politburo members read and initialed the recommendation. In the Politburo meeting of 1973 cited extensively above, Brezhnev castigated Andropov for not immediately implementing a decision to suspend the education tax, clearly embarrassing the latter. This is only one of a number of examples of bureaucratic differences of opinion related to this question. The International Department of the Central Committee was sensitive to objections from the Arab countries over the issue of Jewish emigration. As a result, the department lobbied for sending a letter minimizing the numbers and qualities of Jewish emigrants from the USSR (compared to 600,000 emigrants from Arab countries) to thirteen Soviet embassies in Arab capitals, to be distributed to the local Communist Parties.[58] Schifter reports that during the period of perestroika, the Foreign Office was "way ahead of the rest of the Soviet bureaucracy in its willingness to cooperate with us." He writes also that the liberalization of emigration that took place from the beginning of 1987 resulted from Foreign Ministry pressure on other government agencies. [59]

Soviet nationalities policy was a bundle of contradictions from the outset. It negated nationalism, but preserved national identity through ethnofederalist structures. It praised internationalism and the equality of all peoples, but fell into recurrent bouts of Russification. As was the case in more than one field of policy, the Soviet officials believed their own propaganda about the success of their "Leninist-Soviet nationalities policy," until the flames of ethnic conflict were devouring the country. Finally, in 1989, when the national question was acknowledged as "acute," the Party decided on yet another impossibly contradictory course: satisfying the rightful complaints of minorities while remembering that "[t]he interests of all the peoples involved in the situation in question, the existing realities, and the likely consequences for people's lives must be taken into account in resolving such questions."[60] Essentially, this meant that the Volga Germans could not return to the portions of Saratov *oblast'* that had been theirs before June 1941, the Crimean Tatars could not claim their lands back from the Russians and Ukrainians who now worked them, and a number of other ethnic claims would remain unsatisfied.

The people charged with setting policy and its implementation were poorly equipped for the realization of any reforms. The history of the USSR consisted of a series of catastrophes that performed a reverse "natural selection" on the leadership of the Communist Party. These included the "Lenin enrollment" of 1924–26 that brought large numbers of half-proletarized peasants into the ranks of the Communist Party; the Stalinist blood purges that advanced these new recruits into positions of influence; World War II, in which a whole generation of activists was lost; and Brezhnev's "stability of cadres" policy, that brought forward the most mediocre, conformist, and ultimately the most corrupt elements in Communist Party ranks. The *apparat* sprang, essentially in a single generation, from a village society imbued with anti-Jewish stereotyped prejudices to responsible positions determining the life of Soviet Jews and other minorities. The inbred antisemitism of the *apparat* played no small part in the discrimination against Soviet Jews and their consequent alienation.

A Jewish identity remained alive in the USSR both because of and in spite of Soviet policy. As long as opportunity compensated for the loss of identity, the Jewish presence could be eroded by acculturation and ultimately assimilation. The prewar expansion of the USSR, the Holocaust experience, and the Black Years of Soviet Jewry that followed erased much of what the previous decades had done. Facing a blockage of opportunity, denial of identity, and a hostile regime, the Jews found a way to vault the barrier that stood in the way of emigration, and voted with their feet.

NOTES

1. *Pravda,* September 24, 1989, translated in FBIS Daily Report-SOV-89-104, September 25, 1989, 98–107.

2. M. S. Gorbachev, *Politicheskii doklad tsentral'nogo komiteta KPSS XXVII s'ezdu Kommunisticheskoi Partii Sovetskogo Soiuza* (Moscow: Politizdat, 1986), 66–68.

3. Zvi Y. Gitelman, *Jewish Nationality and Soviet Politics* (Princeton, N.J.: Princeton University Press, 1972), 271.

4. See Laurie P. Salitan, *Politics and Nationality in Contemporary Soviet-Jewish Emigration* (New York: St. Martin's Press, 1992), 74, for the Germans; Benjamin Pinkus, *The Soviet Government and the Jews, 1948–1967: A Documented Study* (Cambridge and New York: Cambridge University Press, 1984), 259–62, for Jewish schools.

5. Boris Morozov, ed., *Evreiskaia emigratsiia v svete novykh dokumentov* (Tel Aviv: Ivrus, 1998), document 57, 199 204.

6. Morozov, ed., doc. 53, 183–87.

7. Benjamin Pinkus, *The Soviet Government and the Jews: A Documented Study* (Cambridge and New York: Cambridge University Press, 1984), 58.

8. Mordechai Altshuler, "The Soviet 'Transfer' of Jews from Chernovtsy Province to Romania," *Jews in Eastern Europe* 2(36) (Fall 1998): 54–75.

9. Ibid., 62.

10. Morozov, ed., doc. 45, 166.

11. Ibid., 167.

12. Ibid., 166.

13. Ibid., 167.

14. Ibid., 167.

15. Ibid., doc. 53, 188.

16. Ibid., doc. 21, 91.

17. Ibid., 92–93.

18. Morozov, doc. 31, 117–19.

19. Ibid., 119–20.

20. Morozov, doc. 5, 37.

21. Morozov, doc. 65, 222–24.

22. Ibid., 222.

23. Theodore H. Friedgut, "Soviet Anti-Zionism and Antisemitism, Another Cycle," *Soviet Jewish Affairs* 14, no. 1 (1984): 8–11.

24. Morozov, doc. 2, 27–31.

25. Ibid., doc. 33, 122–23.

26. Ibid., doc. 45, 166.

27. Ibid., doc. 69, 231.

28. FBIS Daily Report-SOV-25, September 25, 1989, 104.

29. Benjamin Pinkus, *T'khiya ut'kuma leumit: hatsionut v'hatnuah hatsionit biVrit hamo-tsot, 1947–1987* (Beer Sheva: Ben Gurion University Press, 1993), 54.

30. Walter Z. Laqueur, *A History of Zionism* (New York: Schocken Books, 1978), 160.

31. Benjamin Pinkus, *The Jews of the Soviet Union*, 135.

32. Leah Trakhtman-Palkhan, *M'Tel Aviv haktanah l'Moskva* (Tel Aviv: Saar, 1989), 33–34.

33. *New York Times*, March 1, 1955, 10, reported from Rome that a "reliable source" in Italy had said the Soviet Union was willing to let some of its Jews emigrate to Israel for ransoms ranging from $2,000 to $3,000. It was stated there that American Jewish organizations had paid $1,000 each for the release of 197 Hungarian Jews in 1953. The following day, the Israeli newspaper *Ha'aretz*, p. 2, citing the story, reported that an Israeli Foreign Ministry spokesman denied the whole thing and commented that it was to be regretted that "a reporter for an authoritative newspaper permitted himself to refer to such a fantastic tale." It is known that in the 1970s there was payment for the release of Romanian Jews to Israel, but other than the short-lived attempt to levy the "diploma tax" on Jews emigrating, no post–World War II demands for or suggestions of payments to Russia are known to the author or to former Foreign Ministry personnel with whom he consulted. Pinkus, *The Jews of the Soviet Union*, writes that such payments were made in the 1930s (361, n. 105).

34. Benjamin Pinkus, "The Emigration of National Minorities from the USSR in the Post-Stalin Era," *Soviet Jewish Affairs* 13, no. 1 (February 1983): 5.

35. Sidney Heitman, *The Third Soviet Emigration: Jewish, German, and Armenian Emigration from the USSR since World War II* (Fort Collins: Colorado State University, 1986) (mimeograph), Table I, 10.

36. Benjamin Pinkus, *T'khiya ut'kuma leumit: Hatsionut v'hatnuah hatsionit biVrit hamo-tsot, 1947–1987*.

37. Yaacov Ro'i, *The Struggle for Soviet Jewish Emigration* (Cambridge and New York: Cambridge University Press, 1991), 285.

38. Shimon Redlich, *War, Holocaust, and Stalinism: A Documented Study of the Jewish Anti-Fascist Committee in the USSR* (Luxembourg: Harwood Academic Press, 1995), doc. 152, 401–404.

39. Morozov, doc. 2, 27.

40. Ro'i, *The Struggle for Soviet Jewish Emigration*, 91.

41. Heitman, *The Third Soviet Emigration*, Table 2, p. 21.

42. Morozov, doc. 2, p. 29.

43. Nikolai Shmelev, "Avansy i dolgi," *Novyi mir*, no. 6 (1987), as translated and excerpted in Alexander Dallin and Gail W. Lapidus, *The Soviet System: From Crisis to Collapse* (Boulder, Colo.: Westview Press, 1995), 263. Shmelev dates the end of Soviet economic hardships to the mid-1950s.

44. Morozov, doc. 2, pp. 27–30.

45. Salitan, *Politics and Nationality in Contemporary Soviet-Jewish Emigration*, 29–30.

46. See, for instance, Leah Trakhtman-Palkhan, *Arbaim shnot khaim shel Yisraelit bivrit hamotsot* (Jerusalem: n.p., 1996), 67, 73.

47. Salitan, 19.

48. Morozov, doc. 6, p. 41.

49. I. K. Golovchenko, Report of the Interior Ministry of the Ukrainian SSR for 1979; photocopy of typescript provided to the author by the Lookstein Center, Bar Ilan University, Ramat Gan, Israel.

50. Yaacov Ro'i, *The Struggle for Soviet Jewish Emigration*, chapter 1.

51. Nechemia Levanon, *Shem hakod, N'tiv* (Tel Aviv: Am Oved, 1995), 110, 168.

52. Ibid., 404–405.

53. Morozov, doc. 45, p. 165.

54. Richard Schifter, "The Impact of the United States on Soviet Emigration Policy," in Noah Lewin-Epstein, Yaacov Ro'i, and Paul Ritterband, eds., *Russian Jews on Three Continents: Migration and Resettlement* (London: Frank Cass, 1997), 95.

55. Morozov, doc. 11, p. 59.

56. Mordechai Altshuler, "How the Soviets Decided to Renew Emigration to Israel after the Six-Day War," *Jews in Eastern Europe* 1, no. 26 (Spring 1995): 59–60. For the Russian text of the documents see Morozov, doc. 13, 62–63.

57. Morozov, doc. 22, 95.

58. Ibid., doc. 37, 130.

59. Schifter, op. cit., 95, 110.

60. FBIS Daily Report-SOV-89–184, September 25, 1989, 105.

POLITICS, IDENTITY, AND SOCIETY

Part Two

THREE

ZVI GITELMAN

Thinking about Being Jewish in Russia and Ukraine

Ethnic groups are defined by content and boundaries. *Content* may be shared interests, shared institutions, or shared culture. After decades of forced and voluntary acculturation, during which they could not articulate or represent their shared interests, Jews in Russia and Ukraine hardly share any substantive or "thick" culture, and are only now rebuilding institutions and finding ways to defend their interests. But culture can also be a "common and distinct system of understandings and interpretations that constitute normative order and world view and provide strategic and stylistic guides to action."[1] I label this "thin culture," as opposed to "thick culture" that has tangible manifestations (language, customs, foods, clothing). The crucial issue for Russian and Ukrainian Jews—indeed, for Diaspora Jews generally—is whether without substantive, manifest "thick" cultural content Jewishness becomes merely "symbolic ethnicity," much like that of most Polish-Americans or Swedish-Americans; and whether "thin culture" is sufficiently substantive and sustainable to preserve a group's distinctiveness on more than a symbolic level.[2]

Not only the content but also the boundaries defining Jewishness are being pushed out and becoming more blurred. Groups set boundaries in order to define who belongs to the group and who does not.[3] In modern times, the two most salient components of the boundary of Jewishness were the prohibitions on marrying non-Jews and practicing a faith other than Judaism. The first prohibition is increasingly violated in the FSU and elsewhere, and the second is rejected by a fair number of Russian and Ukrainian Jews.

What Do Russian and Ukrainian Jews Think Being Jewish Is and Is Not?

To answer this question, I use the same survey data that my friends and colleagues Valeriy Chervyakov and Vladimir Shapiro have used in another chapter in this book. In contrast to American Jews, 47 percent of whom said in the 1990 National Jewish Population Survey that Jews are a religious group, Jews in the former Soviet Union (FSU) do *not* strongly connect the Jewish religion with being Jewish. Offered nine criteria for defining Jewishness, only 3 percent of our respondents in Ukraine and Russia say that practicing Judaism defines "being a Jew." In 1992–93 and 1997–98, we presented respondents with a list of eighteen items and asked them which are "necessary," "desirable," or "not important" in order for a person to consider himself or herself a Jew. Then we asked them to name the most important criterion for being a Jew. Table 1 shows that most answers to the latter question are focused on a sense of pride and belonging, on emotions rather than knowledge, and on the idea that beliefs and knowledge are not considered important to being a Jew. Thus, about half the respondents choose such items as "being proud of," not hiding, "defending" one's Jewishness, and remembering the Holocaust. Almost none believe that observance of religious mandates—such as keeping the Sabbath or the dietary laws, attending synagogue, or circumcising male sons—is an integral part of being Jewish. Fewer than 2 percent see marrying a Jew and less than 5 percent consider belief in God as vital components of Jewish identity.[4] Yet there is a strong consensus that Judaism has preserved the Jews as a nation, even among those who are not religious.

In America, Jewish identity is expressed, in part, publicly through affiliation and philanthropy. A "good Jew" is popularly conceived of as one who belongs to Jewish organizations, including synagogues or temples, and contributes to Jewish causes. These, however, are unknown behaviors among Jews in the FSU. Instead, our interviews reveal that the basis of Jewish identity in the FSU is a deeply internalized and not necessarily publicly expressed sense of kinship with other Jews and of connection with earlier generations.

What might alarm some Jews outside the FSU is that while 18–23 percent of our Russian respondents and 24–31 percent of the Ukrainian respondents say they believe in God—and another 24–25 percent of those in Russia and 24–30 percent in Ukraine are "inclined to such belief"—only

Thinking about Being Jewish in Russia and Ukraine

Table 3.1.

*What Is the Most Important Thing Required of a Person in Order
to Be Considered a Genuine Jew? (percentages)*

	Russia '92	Russia '97	Ukraine '92	Ukraine '97
Be proud of one's nationality	33.3	22.9	29.4	31.4
Defend Jewish honor and dignity	27.1	17.3	21.4	19.7
Not hide one's Jewishness	0.5	20.8	0.7	13.6
Remember the Holocaust	7.3	15.1	15.5	21.5
Know Jewish history	5.0	2.8	3.0	2.1
Marry a Jew	1.8	1.1	1.1	0.8
Know Jewish traditions	3.2	1.4	0.2	1.4
Help other Jews	7.1	4.3	6.6	6.4
Feel a tie to Israel	4.2	4.3	5.7	2.8
Believe in God	2.7	4.2	3.9	5.4
Know the basics of Judaism	1.0	0.7	0.2	0.3
Circumcise one's son	0.2	0.1	0.2	0.1
Observe *kashrut*	0.0	0.0	0.0	0.1
Observe the Sabbath	0.0	0.3	0.3	0.4
Attend synagogue	0.0	0.1	0.2	0.1
Know a Jewish language	2.2	1.2	1.6	0.4
Share Zionist ideals	0.2	0.2	0.3	0.2
Give children Jewish education	1.2	0.8	2.0	1.3
Don't know, no answer	3.1	2.4	0.7	0.4

about a third see Judaism as the most attractive religion, and over 10 percent see Christianity as most attractive.

The proportion of believers or those inclined to belief seems strikingly high in light of Soviet restrictions on religion and the militant campaign against it over seventy years. However, when all respondents, believers or not, were asked which religion they found most attractive, about a third as many as chose Judaism chose Christianity.

As we can see, for many Judaism no longer defines the content or boundary of Jewish identity. This is quite logical: if Jewishness is ethnicity only, then one should be able to practice whatever religion one wishes without affecting one's ethnicity. However, until very recently the two strongest barriers defining the Jews were set up against practicing a faith other than Judaism and against marrying a non-Jew. But in Russia and Ukraine, in both years of the survey, only 30–39 percent are prepared to condemn Jews

ZVI GITELMAN

Table 3.2.
Belief in God, Russian and Ukrainian Jews, 1992/93 and 1997/98

	Russia '92	Russia '97	Ukraine '92	Ukraine '97
Yes, believe	18.3	22.8	24.2	31.0
Inclined to such belief	23.9	25.3	29.7	24.4
Inclined not to believe	19.1	17.2	18.3	17.1
Do not believe	31.1	28.3	23.2	22.1
Don't know, no answer	6.4	7.6	4.8	5.5

Table 3.3.
Which Religious Faith Is Most Attractive to You?

	Russia '92	Russia '97	Ukraine '92	Ukraine '97
None	36.3	44.1	38.5	36.6
Christianity	13.2	13.7	10.7	15.5
Islam	0.0	0.0	0.1	0.1
Judaism	33.2	26.7	37.6	32.4
Other	4.4	5.4	0.0	2.9
Don't know, no answer	13.0	10.2	9.6	12.6

who "convert to Christianity." While only 4 percent condone this, 60 percent say they would neither condone nor condemn Jews who become Christians. As one St. Petersburg member of Betar, a Zionist organization, put it, "A Jew who practices a religion other than Judaism is not a bad Jew—it's his choice. . . . If you want to believe in Jesus Christ, believe, please, who forbids you to do so?" But a Kievan who accepts the idea that one does not have to be religious to be Jewish—"You can be a good Jew without being religious"—nevertheless maintains that if a Jew adopts another religion "he ceases to be a Jew because, even if one is not religious Jewishly, one must respect the traditions." Zhanna P., born in Moscow in 1956 and now living in Israel, says: "A Jew who is an atheist—this is normal. But to convert to another religion—this is betrayal of your people."

The other side of the coin of the separation of Judaism from Jewishness is represented by a woman who defines ethnicity so independently of religion that for her, practicing *Judaism* does not make one a Jew (contrary to Jewish tradition which admits any practitioner of Judaism—born a Jew or converted to Judaism— to the Jewish people).[5] "I can be a French person and practice Judaism, but that does not make me a Jew," she maintains.

Even among religious believers who prefer Judaism to other faiths, ritual observance is considerably more lax than among religious Jews elsewhere. Most of those who define themselves as religious do not think they are obligated to keep the Sabbath and *kashrut.* Perhaps this is because more respondents say they prefer Reform Judaism, a movement not native to the area but that has organized several congregations in the post-Soviet period, to any other variety, though only a third of the sample do so. Still, it is remarkable that in the year preceding the interview, only half the *religious* people fasted on Yom Kippur or participated in a Passover *Seder,* rituals generally observed by Reform Jews. In all, only half of those affirming Judaism observe the religious laws about which we inquired and a quarter do not observe them at all. Clearly, these "religious Jews" do not adhere to traditional behavioral norms.

There are thus at least two ways in which notions of Jewishness in Russia and Ukraine differ from those in much of the Diaspora and in Israel. The boundaries of Jewishness, fixed at crossing the line into other faiths for most Jews, are not as firmly established in Russia and Ukraine. Even in the United States, where over half the Jews marry non-Jews, "moderately affiliated" Jews, like our respondents, feel that the degree of belief is irrelevant to one's Jewishness, but believe, according to a recent study, that "The only way to cease being a Jew is to convert to another religion."[6] As we see, this view is less widely shared in the FSU. Secondly, in the FSU adherence to Judaism seems to imply much less practice and ritual than in Israel or among Jews elsewhere.

Of course, it is possible to use rituals and customs whose origins are in religion as the basis for a secular "ethnic" culture. A study among members of the United Synagogue (the umbrella Orthodox organization in the U.K.) in London—in which only 10 percent defined themselves as Orthodox and two-thirds labeled themselves "traditional"—found that outside the "Orthodox fringe," belief and traditional observance "seem to be virtually independent of each other."[7] But in the USSR, Jewish practices were discouraged or forbidden and the pull of acculturation and even assimilation was strong, so most rituals and customs fell into disuse. As in other countries, the Passover *Seder* was the ritual most commonly observed both in the respondents' childhood homes as well as in their present households. Yet only 26 percent of Jews in Russia and 30 percent in Ukraine participated in a *Seder* in 1997 (though 54 percent in Russia and 68 percent in Ukraine claimed they "observed" the holiday—perhaps by eating some matzoh!).[8] Thus, we do not discern an ethnicized culture with origins in religion emerging on a large scale in the FSU, though in future analyses we will examine holiday observances more closely.

Language, the nexus of ethnicity for groups such as French Canadians, Belgians, Basques, and Catalans, does not play that role among contemporary Jews. In 1897, 97 percent of Jews in the Russian Empire gave a Jewish language as their mother tongue and 73 percent still did so in 1926. By 1989, only 11 percent did so. In our surveys, fewer than 3 percent say knowing a Jewish language is important for being a "genuine Jew." Nor are organizational affiliations and activities measures of ethnic belonging and expression since it has been less than a decade since such pursuits have been permitted. About one in ten Russian Jews and one in seven Ukrainian Jews can be considered activists, and about a third participate passively (as an audience) in some Jewish events. What, then, does being Jewish mean to Russian and Ukrainian Jews?

If being Jewish is not fundamentally about Judaism, traditional customs, Jewish languages, or communal participation and activity, what *is* it about? Most Jews in Russia and Ukraine conceive of their Jewishness as, first, a matter of descent; second, as belonging to a "nationality" (ethnic group); and, third, as the subjective feeling of belonging to a group. The most fundamental basis of Jewish identity, in their view, is being born of Jewish parents. Some say that one must be born of a Jewish mother or that "One must be of Jewish origin according to *Halacha*" [Jewish law], but more say that descent from either a Jewish mother or father is sufficient for one to qualify as Jewish.

Second, Jewish identity is understood in the way the Soviet state defined it, that is, as membership in an ethnic group ("nationality"). Yet this membership goes beyond official designation. The sense of belonging to a distinct group is quite powerful for most respondents. Two-thirds of Russian respondents in 1992 said that "to feel oneself a part of the Jewish people" is what being Jewish is all about, and nearly as many say that "to be proud of the Jewish people" is the essence. The most popular way of expressing these sentiments among the Ukrainian respondents in 1997 was "to feel yourself part of the Jewish people [*narod*]" or "to feel an inner kinship with Jews, to feel we're one family." One respondent put it strongly: "When everything relating to Jews and Jewish life in the world, their culture and the Yiddish and Hebrew languages, that which relates to Israel touches my soul—that's what it is to be a Jew." As a British sociologist observes, "If there is one necessary and sufficient condition for membership of an ethnic group, it is surely a subjective feeling of belonging, of kinship, of a desire for group continuity and a sense of corporate identity."[9] For quite a few, the only necessary and sufficient condition for being Jewish is to *feel* oneself a Jew. As one says in a classic primordial statement: "I feel that way and I don't need any additional reasons for it." Even starker is the statement by an elderly lady in Ukraine: "*Kto Evrei, to znaet chto on Evrei, i vsë.*" [Whoever is a Jew knows that he or she is a Jew, and that's that]. In sum, two-thirds of the respondents chose descent and the feeling of being part of the Jewish people from among nine criteria offered them for establishing Jewish identity.

Many in Russia and Ukraine add a sense of pride to the feeling of belonging. To be a Jew, it is often remarked, is "to be proud of your nationality." A few connect pride with suffering and say that to be a Jew is "to proudly bear your cross" [*sic*]. Others see Jewishness as a burden and a curse with no redeeming features. "In Ukraine," say several, "to be a Jew is to be an outcast" [*izgoem*]. One put the same idea in a quintessentially Jewish way. He said simply, "to be a Jew? *az okh un vay*" [alas and alack]. Every sixth respondent in 1992/93 and every fourth in the later survey defined Jewishness largely in negative terms but these terms ranked seventh and sixth among the nine criteria offered. It is important to note that among the 16–29-year-olds, in 1997/98 only 7 percent mentioned antisemitism as the defining factor in Jewishness, and it is the factor least often mentioned by this group in both years of the survey.

On the spectrum of affect toward Jewish identity, the next position is that to be a Jew is to be defined as such by others, usually pejoratively. The spectrum of Jewish feelings moves from the holding of negative feelings, to indifference, and even to the rejection of the idea of having a Jewish—and perhaps any—nationality. "To be a Jew means nothing. You should be a human being [*chelovek*]." "The most important thing is to be a human being, and who you are by nationality is of no importance." A more positive understanding is the equation of Jewishness with decency. Quite a few respondents opine that to be Jewish is to "be a normal, decent [*poriadochnyi*] person." This is not the negation of Jewishness but its universalization.

Finally, the most radical, minority position in the Russian–Ukrainian context is the traditional religious one. "To be a Jew is to be a follower of Abraham, a wanderer and alien in this world, but to go in the direction that God commands people, to carry out his commands and to be blessed."

In sum, for most Russian and Ukrainian Jews sentiment and biology have largely replaced faith, Jewish law and lore, and Jewish customs as the foundations of Jewishness.

🕎 *Boundaries*

Boundaries may be more effective than content in defining Jews in the FSU. After religion, language, territorial concentration, and ethnically defined lifestyle were taken away, what might remain is state-imposed identity (no longer required in either Russia or Ukraine), social apartness (imposed in its most extreme form by antisemitism), lifestyle differences, and an awareness of being different. The sense of being different and apart prevailed even among some younger people living in cosmopolitan Moscow, though they apparently had no connection to Jewishness other than feeling themselves not-Russian. In the 1970s a prominent dissident, Larisa Bogoraz, expressed this feeling eloquently:

> Who am I now? Who do I feel myself to be? Unfortunately, I do not feel like a Jew. I understand that I have an unquestionable genetic tie with Jewry. I also assume that this is reflected in my mentality, in my mode of thinking, and in my behavior. But . . . a more profound, or more general, common bond is lacking, such as community of language, culture, history, tradition. . . . And, nevertheless, no I am not Russian, I am a stranger today in this land.[10]

Most of our respondents describe their national self-consciousness and lifestyles as a mixture of Jewish and Russian (rarely Ukrainian) elements, with the Russian prevailing in most instances. Yet their closest friends are mostly Jews. Of course, the overwhelming majority reject the *idea* that one should choose friends of one's own nationality, but in practice they seem to do just that. However, in Ukraine and, especially, Russia we find rather weak identification with Jews not only in the rest of the world but even in non-European parts of the FSU. Only 41 percent of those queried in Russia and 51 percent in Ukraine agree with the statement, "Jews all over the world constitute a single people." In Russia, two-thirds of those interviewed in 1992/93 said they feel "spiritually and culturally" closer to the Russians of their city than to Georgian, Bukharan, or Mountain Jews, and 46 percent said they feel closer to local Russians than to Jews in Belarus or Ukraine (whence most Russian Jews originate). The distance from Jews elsewhere increases somewhat in 1997/98, either because the most conscious Jews have emigrated or because the breakup of the USSR has also increased the psychological distance among Jews (and others) in its now independent parts. In contrast to Russian Jews, more Ukrainian Jews feel affinity for Russian Jews than they do for Russians living in Ukraine, and they feel greater affinity for local Russians than for Ukrainians. Like Russian Jews, they are distant from non-Ashkenazic Jews, though less so than Russian Jews. Other measures also indicate that Jews in Ukraine have a more powerful sense of Jewish kinship and affinity than Jews in Russia.

The traditional ban on marriage to non-Jews, which goes back centuries, is, perhaps along with the dietary laws, the most explicit expression of the Jewish sense of apartness.[11] Today the taboo of intermarriage is weakening in most Diaspora countries. While nearly everyone in a sample of

United Synagogue members in London agreed with the proposition that "A Jew should marry someone who is Jewish,"[12] among our respondents in the FSU only 37–43 percent agreed in 1997 that a Jew should choose a spouse of the same nationality, a decline from 1992.[13] Robert Brym's and Rozalia Ryvkina's 1993 survey of a thousand Jews in Moscow, Kiev, and Minsk found that "only 26 percent said that it was important for Jews to marry other Jews."[14] In the United States, the 1990 National Jewish Population Survey found that 52 percent of Jews who had married since 1985 had married non-Jews. In the FSU, intermarriage, high mortality, and low fertility are undermining the biological base of Jewishness. In 1988, 48 percent of Soviet Jewish women and 58 percent of Jewish men who married, married non-Jews.[15] In the Russian republic, with the largest Jewish population, the figures were 73 percent for men and 63 percent for women. One of every five of our respondents has a spouse who has no Jewish ancestry at all and another 2 percent are in marriages where both spouses are of partially non-Jewish descent. Moreover, a third of those advocating marriage only to Jews claim they would *not* be upset were their children to marry non-Jews. A September 2000 survey of American Jews shows that 56 percent of a purportedly national sample are either neutral about marriage between Jews and non-Jews or have positive attitudes about it.[16] Thus, the historic boundary setting Jews off from others is rapidly blurring.

Obviously, what has set Jews apart from others in the FSU more than anything else is antisemitism. Indeed, over half our respondents in both waves of interviews say their Jewish consciousness was first established and even basically formed by negative experiences, though this is less true among the oldest (over 70) and youngest groups. When asked to name the single greatest influence on the formation of their national consciousness, over half cite antisemitism.[17] And over half point to an antisemitic encounter as the one that first made them conscious of their Jewishness, though this is remarkably not the case among the young. Between 43 percent (Russia and Ukraine, 1997/98) and 52 percent (Ukraine, 1992/93) said that people could usually tell at first glance whether they were Jewish.[18] Only a fifth say that people usually cannot tell that they are Jewish. We shall be exploring how others' perceptions relate to one's sense of Jewishness and how having "a Jewish appearance" shapes Jewish identity and affect toward it.

🕎 *Conclusion*

The Jewish identity of Russian and Ukrainian Jews is stronger than many would suppose but is problematic in several ways. First, the identification may be uniquely the product of a Soviet environment that no longer exists. Ethnic identities are often reformulated and "Jewish identities in general are to be understood as constructs in response to the circumstances."[19] In the USSR, state-imposed identity and governmental antisemitism combined with grassroots antisemitism to maintain boundaries between Jews and others long after Jewish content had largely disappeared from Jewish ethnicity. Russia and Ukraine no longer impose official ethnic identity and none of the successor states to the USSR pursues an antisemitic policy. Popular antisemitism, which may wax and wane, may be the last barrier to assimilation. Some of the ingredients of Soviet Jewish identity have therefore been changed, though, of course, descent and feelings of kinship remain. The historically unique Jewish identity created in the USSR may not survive the demise of the conditions that created it.

Second, the conceptions of being Jewish held by the great majority of Russian and Ukrainian Jews are so different from those prevailing in most of the rest of the Diaspora and in Israel that sensitive questions of mutual recognition inevitably arise. The criteria for admission to the "Jewish club" that are set in the Jewish world, though by no means uniform, are not shared by a significant portion of post-Soviet Jewry.

Third, and most generally, the challenge of developing a viable Jewish identity in Russia and Ukraine is formidable because it involves constructing a secular Jewish identity. One must assume that for the foreseeable future most Jewish identities in the European FSU will be secular. Secular Jews have long struggled with the problem of maintaining ethnicity divorced from religion and its symbols. A secular Yiddish educator observed that when the "secular ship" floats on the "Jewish sea," one permeated by religion, "it turns out that one floats empty, with no ballast. And a terrible similarity appears between secularism and simple assimilation."[20] As Henry Feingold has written, "The survival dilemma posed by secular modernity is whether the corporate communal character at the heart of Judaism can accommodate the individuation that is the quintessence of modern secular life. It is whether Jewishness can become again a living culture without its primary religious ingredient, Judaism, from which it has become separated."[21] Secular Jewishness as it emerged just a century ago was based on a common language (Yiddish), territorial concentration of Jews (the Pale, ethnic neighborhoods), a high degree of concentration in certain professions (needle trades, artisans, commerce and trade), and a strong sense of being part of a distinct Jewish entity. Jews were kept distinct both by antisemitism or—for immigrants—by their cultural apartness, and by their sense of cultural superiority in many countries (Lithuania, Russia, Romania), though in others they tried to adopt the "higher culture" as they perceived it (France, England, Germany, the United States). Today, these conditions no longer exist. Without them, can there be a viable, transferable secular Jewish life? If the classical definition of Jewish identity is discarded, as Jonathan Webber notes, "there would appear to be no simple, self-evident, and adequate formula to replace it with."[22] For some this might not be problematic, but when the decision of who and what Jews are is left to others, this not only cedes the sovereignty of a people to outsiders but, as Jews have learned, the results may be catastrophic.

NOTES

1. Stephen Cornell, "The Variable Ties that Bind: Content and Circumstance in Ethnic Processes," *Ethnic and Racial Studies* 19, no. 2 (April 1996): 271.

2. For an elaboration of this argument, see Zvi Gitelman, "The Decline of the Diaspora Jewish Nation: Boundaries, Content and Jewish Identity," *Jewish Social Studies* 4, no. 2 (Winter 1998): 112–32.

3. The seminal work on boundaries is Frederik Barth, *Ethnic Groups and Boundaries: The Social Organization of Cultural Difference* (Boston: Little, Brown, 1964). One analyst points out that boundaries may be set by ethnic group awareness, with "the recognition that common ascriptive characteristics are shared among a set of individuals, without any salience necessarily being placed on these commonalities"; by ethnic solidarity, which "indicates that social resources of some type (affectual, cultural, organisational) are shared among a set of individuals with common ascriptive characteristics"; or by "the ascriptive criteria that determine membership in particular groups organised for collective action." Sun-ki Chai, "A Theory of Ethnic Group Boundaries," *Nations and Nationalism* 2, no. 2 (July 1996): 282.

4. Very similar results were obtained in surveys of Jewish identity in the Volga region and in St. Petersburg. See Solomon Krapivensky, "Jewish Identity of Russian Jews in the Volga Region: A Sociological Survey," *Jews in Eastern Europe* 2(27) (Fall 1995), and Marina Kogan, "The Identity of St. Petersburg Jews in the Early 1990s, a Time of Mass Emigration," *Jews in Eastern Europe* 3(28) (Winter 1995). See also Rozalina Ryvkina, *Evrei v postsovetskoi Rossii—Kto oni?* (Moscow: URSS, 1996).

5. See Zvi Zohar and Avraham Sagi, *Giyur vezehut Yehudit* (Jerusalem: Mosad Bialik and Machon Hartman, 1994).

6. Steven Cohen and Arnold Eisen, *The Jew Within: Self, Community, and Commitment among the Variety of Moderately Affiliated* (Boston–Los Angeles: Wilstein Institute of Jewish Policy Studies, 1998), 20.

7. Stephen Miller, "Religious Practice and Jewish Identity in a Sample of London Jews," in Jonathan Webber, ed., *Jewish Identities in the New Europe* (London: Littman Library, 1994), 198. The "Orthodox fringe" seems to be the 10 percent among United Synagogue members who said they observed the Sabbath. Though the United Synagogue is an organization of Orthodox synagogues, two-thirds of the sample defined themselves as "tra-

ditional (not strictly Orthodox)," 4 percent said they were secular, 16 percent said they were "just Jewish," and 3 percent said they were Progressive or Reform (pp. 194–95).

8. A survey of a thousand Jews in Minsk, Kiev, and Moscow in 1993 found that 42 percent claim to have observed Passover. Robert Brym with the assistance of Rozalia Ryvkina, *The Jews of Moscow, Kiev and Minsk* (London: Macmillan, 1994), 25.

9. Miller, 199.

10. Larisa Bogoraz, "Do I Feel I Belong to the Jewish People?" in Aleksandr Voronel, Viktor Yakhot, and Moshe Decter, eds., *I am a Jew: Essays on Jewish Identity in the Soviet Union* (New York: Academic Committee on Soviet Jewry and the Anti-Defamation League of B'nai Brith, 1973), 63–64.

11. See Genesis 24 and 27, Numbers 25, for the prohibitions on marrying Moabites and Ammonites (Deuteronomy 23), and see the condemnation of King Solomon for having taken non-Jewish wives. Of course, the Bible recounts many instances of marriage between Jews and non-Jews. My colleague Todd Endelman suggests that prohibitions on intermarriage in antiquity probably reflect greater contact between Jews and their neighbors and that when Jews were ghettoized it was less necessary to make such prohibitions explicit. Intermarriage became a serious issue again when Jews were emancipated and could mix with non-Jews.

12. Miller, 199.

13. In 1992, 53–55 percent agreed that one should marry a Jew. The decline over five years reflects the increase in intermarriage and the greater proportion of endogamous marriages among émigrés.

14. Brym and Ryvkina, 26. Only 69 percent of the sample said they were registered as Jews in their passports (pp. 22–23). One can reasonably assume that if a higher proportion of registered Jews had been interviewed, the proportion opposed to intermarriage would have been higher.

15. Mark Tolts, "Jewish Marriages in the USSR: A Demographic Analysis," *East European Jewish Affairs* 22, no. 2 (1992): 8.

16. American Jewish Committee, "2000 Annual Survey of American Jewish Opinion" (New York, 2001), 3.

17. Brym and Ryvkina found that five factors "explain a very respectable 42 percent of the variation in Jewishness among the respondents" but that antisemitism ranked only fourth among them (p. 34).

18. In Russia in 1992, 49 percent said people could tell they were Jewish at first glance.

19. Webber, "Modern Jewish Identities," in *Jewish Identities in the New Europe,* 82.

20. Yudl Mark, "Yidishkayt un veltlikhkayt in un arum undzere shuln," in Shloime Bercovich et al., eds., *Shul-Pinkes* (Chicago: Sholem Aleichem Folk Institute, 1948), 14.

21. Henry Feingold, *Lest Memory Cease* (Syracuse: Syracuse Univ. Press, 1996), 8.

22. Webber, 8.

FOUR

❦

Valeriy Chervyakov, Zvi Gitelman, and Vladimir Shapiro

E Pluribus Unum? *Post-Soviet Jewish Identities and Their Implications for Communal Reconstruction*

The problems inherent in reviving Jewish community life in the Former Soviet Union (FSU) are challenging not only because there are different approaches to the process, but also because even the desirability of such reconstruction itself is open to discussion. For example, Israeli politician (and now Prime Minister) Ariel Sharon, who visited Russia in early 1999, called on all Russian Jews to emigrate to Israel. But this point of view is not universally agreed upon in both countries, and not only among Jews. The issue of reconstructing Jewish community life in the former Soviet Union will be on the agenda of FSU Jews and their co-ethnics abroad for the foreseeable future. This makes it all the more important to understand who Russian and other FSU Jews are, because Jewish self-awareness is not universal but is quite different in different countries. As we have discovered, Russian Jews differ in their self-conceptions and ways of thinking not only from American or Israeli Jews, but also from Ukrainian Jews. Therefore, this chapter focuses on two problems: what are the peculiarities of the national consciousness of Russian Jews, and how should these peculiarities be taken into account when we deal with the issues of reconstructing Jewish national life in Russia?

Our empirical study leads us to conclude that conceptions of Jewishness held by Russian and Ukrainian Jews are radically different from both historical understandings and contemporary notions held by most Jews in the Diaspora and Israel. For FSU Jews, the Jewish religion is hardly a factor in Jewishness. Russian and Ukrainian Jews consider belief in God, observance of the Sabbath, the dietary laws (*kashrut*), and circumcision as quite irrelevant to being a "good Jew." What makes a good Jew is knowledge of history and culture and, especially, feeling—pride in one's Jewishness and a duty to remember the *Shoah,* or Holocaust. We also find that the great majority of Jews in Russia and Ukraine feel themselves culturally and in other ways Russian (rarely Ukrainian) as well as Jewish. Over time, they seem to be less closely tied to the other Jews of the Diaspora, though family and friends in Israel insure an ongoing and close connection to that country. For the young, the family seems to decline as an agent of Jewish socialization; instead, the efforts of "ethnic entrepreneurs" seem to be having some effect. However, we note an overall decline in the period of five years between our surveys in the number of people interested in Jewish matters. On the other hand, those who express interest seem to attend more Jewish events and observe more Jewish holidays in some fashion than they had five years earlier. Thus, there is no clear and unidirectional answer to the question of whether Jews are becoming more or less communally active and engaged. Our respondents are in favor of Jewish schooling for their children but they prefer secular schools, though it seems that most private Jewish schools have a religious character. In sum, we see a community in transition, with marked differences in behavior and attitudes between the youngest generation and its elders. If a self-identifying Jewish public survives the demographic erosion it is experiencing, it is likely to resemble other Jewish communities in Europe in its activities and organization, but it will be distinctly more secular, raising the question of how a meaningful Jewishness divorced from religion and not imposed by the state can ultimately be evolved and sustained.

The conclusions of this chapter, like those of Gitelman in his chapter, are based on the results of two surveys of Russian and Ukrainian Jews, undertaken by the Jewish Research Center associated with the Russian Academy of Sciences.[1] The survey involved face-to-face interviews conducted in respondents' homes by interviewers of Jewish origin who were trained specifically for this project. Interviews generally lasted between one and one-and-a-half hours. The 1992/93 survey was replicated in expanded form during 1997/98 in the same three Russian cities and five Ukrainian cities. The same kind of sample was constructed in each of the survey years, and the majority of questions were phrased in exactly the same way in both "waves" of the survey, assuring a high degree of comparability. We surveyed subjects in Moscow and St. Petersburg (Leningrad) because these cities have the largest concentrations of Russian Jews, and in Ekaterinburg, an industrial city in the Urals with a population of about 10,000 Jews, the fifth largest in Russia, which we regard as a fairly typical provincial Russian-Jewish community. Our Ukrainian research sites were Kiev, the capital and home to the largest Ukrainian Jewish population; Odessa, a historically "Jewish" city with a distinct character; Kharkov, an industrial city in East Ukraine where Russians are concentrated and where Russian culture prevails, even among ethnic Ukrainians; Lviv (Lvov, Lwow, Lemberg) in West Ukraine, the center of Ukrainian nationalism where Ukrainian culture dominates; and Chernivtsi (Chernovtsy, Czernowitz), which, like Lviv, was annexed to the USSR only in 1939–40. We interviewed 1,300 people in Russia[2]—500 each in Moscow and St. Petersburg and 300 in Ekaterinburg—and 2,000 in Ukraine—500 each in Kiev and Kharkov, 400 in Odessa, and 300 each in Chernivtsi and Lviv. Respondents had to be at least sixteen years old but no upper age limit was established.

In 1992/93, our sample replicated very closely the gender and age distribution of the Jewish population over age sixteen in each city. Because of a lack of updated information, in the second wave we structured the local samples according to the 1989 age–gender distributions. The only important change from 1989 was seen in the dramatic aging of the Jewish population, a result of the very unfavorable birth:death ratio and the emigration of younger people.

Because there were no lists of Jewish residents of each city, we created the sample by a "snowball" technique. In each city we created a group or "panel" of several dozen Jewish men and women of different ages and social-economic status. We did not interview them but asked them to name several relatives, friends, and acquaintances whom they considered Jewish and who would tentatively agree to be interviewed. Then we asked these friends and relatives to agree to be interviewed. In turn, we asked them to identify *their* friends and relatives who would tentatively agree to be interviewed. Only one member of each family could be interviewed. The "panels" informed us of the gender, age, type of employment, and professional background of potential respondents. This allowed us to adjust the sample structure constantly in order to conform to the parameters of the overall Jewish population over age sixteen in each city. The age and gender structure of the Russian and Ukrainian samples conforms very closely to the profile of the Jewish population in general.

🕎 *Ethnicity and Consciousness*

In the 1992/93 Russian sample, 86.2 percent asserted that both their parents were Jews. Another 12.2 percent said they were half- or quarter-Jewish. The others had more remote Jewish roots. In the 1997 sample, the parallel figures were 80.3; 17.5; and 2.2 percent. Of the 1992/93 Ukrainian sample, 89.7 percent said both parents were Jews; half- or quarter-Jews comprised 9.1 percent; and the Jewish connections of the others were more distant. Interestingly, the proportion of those with two Jewish parents fell even more drastically in Ukraine than in Russia in 1997 (to 75.4 percent). The proportion of half- and quarter-Jews rose to 20.5 percent and that of remotely connected Jews to 4.1 percent. No doubt, in most places in Russia and Ukraine in the years between our surveys, those with stronger Jewish roots had either passed away or emigrated.

The tendency toward a decline in the proportion of Jews with two Jewish parents is especially strong in Lviv. There, the proportion of fully Jewish respondents (*"chistokrovnye,"* or "full-blooded" in Russian) fell by a quarter, from 86.3 to 61.7 percent. A possible explanation for this phenomenon is that Jews in Lviv, the center of Ukrainian nationalism where Russian speakers (which the great majority of Jews are) often feel unwelcome, are more likely to emigrate than those in other cities. They are less likely to have local non-Jewish relatives in Lviv who would serve as a brake on emigration, and they may be more fearful than residents of other cities that the ongoing economic crisis in Ukraine will provoke antisemitism, already visible in Lviv, in the form of scapegoating. Those who remain have a more tenuous connection to Jewish identity.

The decline in respondents of purely Jewish origins over our five-year interval is explained, of course, by the steady increase in interethnic or "mixed" marriages. One can observe that among 30–39-year-old people of purely Jewish origin the proportion of those married to spouses who have no Jewish antecedents is twice as great as among the oldest groups, 47.5 percent *vs.* 23.2 percent (see Table 4.1).

Table 4.1.
Ethnicity of Spouses of "Pure Jews" in Relation to Age, Russia 1997–98

	16–29	30–39	40–49	50–59	60–69	70+
Jewish	42.9	39.3	42.2	56.0	58.0	70.5
Partly Jewish	14.3	13.1	17.6	12.0	10.7	6.3
No Jewish roots	42.9	47.5	40.2	32.0	31.3	23.2

The differences between the generations are clear. Some of the older generation received pre-revolutionary Jewish education, and most were exposed to Jewish traditions observed by parents or grandparents. The younger cohorts, by contrast, grew up under Stalinism and thereafter. In turn, the generations growing up after World War II lived in environments even more conducive to interethnic marriage; there is reason to believe this has not changed much in the post-Soviet era.

One important finding indicates that whether one is of wholly or partly Jewish origin makes a major difference in determining one's behavior and the Jewishness of future generations. Among part-Jews, there is an exponential tendency over time to marry non-Jews. Our research reveals that the 80 percent of our 1997 Russian sample who are purely Jewish are significantly less inclined to choose a non-Jewish spouse than those who are partly Jewish. Purely Jewish respondents are twice as likely to marry purely Jewish people than are partly Jewish respondents. Of course, the ethnic origins of our respondents do not interest us from a genetic perspective but as a means of determining whether they make a difference for the national or ethnic consciousness of different groups of Jews. People who identify as Jews but who are not fully Jewish in a genetic sense increase in number each year. Since we find that socialization and acquisition of Jewish traditions and culture go on quite differently in purely Jewish than in mixed families, it seems likely that Jewish traditions and culture will weaken over time. On the one hand, this is explained by purely ethno-cultural factors (ethnic factors are relegated to a secondary position in the daily lives of mixed families). On the other hand, there are purely historical changes and generational effects at work here. After all, when speaking of respondents of only partly Jewish origin, we are dealing mostly with younger generations educated in different historical circumstances than their elders. The average age of this group is fifteen years younger than the average age of the "pure Jews" in Russia (43 years old, compared to 58 among "pure Jews") as well as in Ukraine (41 years old, compared to 56).

In theory, a person whose parents were of different nationalities (ethnic groups) could choose to identify as one while ignoring the other part of his or her ethnic background. This situation would quite likely have occurred under Soviet conditions where one was forced to choose between the different nationalities of one's parents when registering for an internal passport at age sixteen. However, as it turns out, most of our respondents have two or more identities in their national consciousness, usually Russian and Jewish. Those of only partly Jewish parentage tend not to identify wholly as Jews and choose the response, "I do not belong to a particular nationality" or sponta-

VALERIY CHERVYAKOV, ZVI GITELMAN, AND VLADIMIR SHAPIRO

neously categorize themselves as "citizen of the world" or "Russian Jew" or "Jew and Russian simultaneously." In sum, whereas 94 percent of both Russian and Ukrainian Jews unequivocally identify themselves as Jews, among part-Jews in Russia only three-quarters of the respondents do so and in Ukraine just over half (53 percent) identify themselves simply as Jews.

The number of "passport" Jews—those officially registered as Jews on their Soviet-era identity documents—diminishes from one generation to the next. This trend is likely to be accelerated because a law passed by the Russian Duma states that as of October 1, 1997 nationality no longer is registered on one's internal passport. We know that identification with Jews was transformed from being just an entry on a passport to becoming part of one's consciousness because previously one was reminded of one's official status every time the passport was shown and also because passport registration became a means of ethnic discrimination. Because of the latter policy, many respondents now disapprove of having nationality entered into the passport. Only 43 percent of respondents in Russia say they would voluntarily enter "Jew" into their passports were they to have a choice. Most would prefer to have no nationality registration at all, and would leave the relevant paragraph blank (13.6 percent) or would register simply as "citizen of Russia" (39.1 percent). Those of purely Jewish descent are somewhat more inclined to be registered as Jews, but this preference is strongest among those 70 years old and older, among whom half say they would prefer to be identified explicitly as Jews. By contrast, fewer than 40 percent of those under 30 prefer this option and 20 percent would leave the "nationality" entry blank.

Table 4.2.

Nationality Registration of Russian Federation Respondents, by Age, Russia 1997–98

	16–29	30–39	40–49	50–59	60–69	70+
Registered as a Jew	57.6	76.3	79.2	86.0	88.4	96.1
Registered as Russians	39.6	21.2	18.3	11.3	10.8	2.3
Registered as Ukrainians or Others	2.8	2.5	2.5	2.7	0.8	1.6

Those of mixed parentage differ from those with two Jewish parents in another respect: they become conscious of their nationality later in their lives. Half the "pure Jews" in Russia and Ukraine declared that they became aware of their Jewishness before they had reached the age of nine. Only a quarter of those of mixed background claimed such an early awareness of Jewish identity. About a fifth of those of mixed parentage became

E Pluribus Unum?

aware of a Jewish identity only in adulthood, whereas among those of exclusively Jewish parentage this late an awareness occurred in only one of ten cases.

Not surprisingly, those of mixed background have less of an emotional tie to their ethnicity. In their answers to "In the course of your life, did you have more occasion to be proud or ashamed of the fact that you are Jewish," more than a third of those of mixed background said that there were no occasions to be proud or ashamed, whereas only a fourth of the fully Jewish respondents answered this way. No doubt, the difference lies in that those of fully Jewish parentage were exposed to Jewish culture and traditions in their childhood more often, whereas the part-Jews were influenced more by secondary factors of socialization such as the influence of spouses and colleagues (Table 4.3).

Table 4.3.
"Who Most Influenced the Formation of Your National Consciousness?" Responses of Jews with Two Jewish Parents and with One Jewish Parent, Russia and Ukraine

| | Russia, '97–98 | | Ukraine, '97–98 | |
| | | Have Some | | Have Some |
	Pure Jews	Jewish Roots	Pure Jews	Jewish Roots
Grandfather, grandmother	25.6	27.3	32.6	32.7
Mother	49.4	32.3	51.9	33.5
Father	41.7	25.8	43.5	26.0
Spouse	4.9	8.1	5.8	6.3
Daughter, son	4.0	3.8	4.6	2.6
Other relatives	13.0	11.2	9.0	11.4
Friends, schoolmates, co-workers	19.8	30.4	18.7	30.9
Others	12.0	16.9	8.1	9.3

Apparently, antisemitism plays a somewhat greater role among "pure Jews" than among part-Jews in bringing one to a sense of belonging to the Jewish people. We posit that among pure Jews, expressing one's pride in Jewishness serves more often as a psychological reaction to xenophobia and as a defense against it. The fully Jewish respondents mentioned "pride in one's nationality" twice as often than the others when asked, "What does being a Jew mean?" On the other hand, part-Jews were four times as inclined as pure Jews to mention "to feel oneself different from people of other nationalities." It seems that those who have two Jewish parents are more likely to come to Jewish awareness through experiences, whereas the others are more

VALERIY CHERVYAKOV, ZVI GITELMAN, AND VLADIMIR SHAPIRO

Table 4.4.

"What Most Influenced the Formation of your National Consciousness?"
Responses of Jews with Two Jewish Parents and with One Jewish Parent, Russia and Ukraine
{Multiple Answers Possible}

	Russia, '97–98		Ukraine, '97–98	
	Pure Jews	Have Some Jewish Roots	Pure Jews	Have Some Jewish Roots
Antisemitism	56.3	48.5	42.2	34.8
Books, literature	47.1	51.2	43.6	46.5
Music	39.1	35.8	37.7	37.0
Holiday observance, observance of important days	29.8	18.8	34.1	20.1
Ethnic cuisine	26.3	16.5	26.9	19.7
Family archive, photographs, letters	24.5	26.9	27.5	29.9
Observance of religious customs	8.6	5.4	10.5	5.5
Other	9.1	10.8	7.4	9.8
Could not answer	4.2	3.5	4.2	6.9

likely to do so through cognitive processes. Antisemitism is the single most powerful factor in the formation of Jewish consciousness among Jews over fifty years old, as it is among pure Jews irrespective of age. However, among part-Jews, it takes second place by a very small margin to written materials.

Note that among pure Jews the influence of Jewish foods and holiday observances plays a greater role in the formation of ethnic consciousness than it does among part-Jews, among whom something they *read* plays a greater role. In other words, Jews who grow up in a home with two Jewish parents are more likely to be exposed to early, personal, and direct experiences of expressions of Jewishness, whereas those with one non-Jewish parent are more likely to come to Jewish consciousness later and through more abstract means and cognitive processes.

The majority of all respondents (52.5 percent) connect the realization that they are Jewish to emotionally negative experiences. Among the oldest cohort (those over seventy), nearly 40 percent associate their first consciousness of being Jewish with warmly remembered events, but already in the next younger group, the 60–69-year-olds, the proportion of those experiencing their Jewishness positively declines by half—two-thirds of them mention insults or tactless remarks as that which first aroused their self-awareness as Jews. This tendency, with slight variations, accelerated over the duration of the Soviet period. Only among the youngest people, those under thirty, do we observe again coming to Jewish consciousness in a positive emotional context (34 percent) to a slightly higher degree than in a negative (32 percent). Perhaps this is because the youngest people have spent a good part of their lives in a post-Soviet environment where official antisemitism has disappeared, though grassroots antisemitism is widely evident and sometimes very virulent. Either the absence of official antisemitism has shielded them largely from discrimination in education, employment, housing, and other encounters with the state, or they are too young to have had many of the daily life (*"bytovye"*) experiences of their elders.

On the other hand, fewer than a fifth of this youngest generation claims to have grown up in intensely Jewish households and more than a third say there was no Jewish ambience at all. Those over seventy can recall Jewish holiday celebrations in parental and grandparental homes—only 13 percent of these people say there was no Jewish atmosphere or national spirit in their childhood home. Their children and grandchildren had few such experiences since they grew up in the late 1930s or later when all Jewish institutions had been closed, religious practices had withered, and all that was left of their Jewish consciousness was to see themselves as "invalids of the fifth category" (a play on the fact that nationality was registered on the fifth line of one's passport). About half of the oldest respondents (over seventy years old) in Ukraine and even Russia recall Rosh Hashana being observed every year when they grew up, whereas less than a fifth of Ukrainian respondents under thirty and only 7 percent of Russian respondents of this age make the same claim. More than half of the older Russian and Ukrainian Jews recall Yiddish as the language of their childhood households, but few of the youngest people grew up in such homes. The one Jewish experience common to both widely separated generations and in both republics is the practice of reading books with Jewish themes. Over 60 percent in Ukraine and nearly that proportion in Russia have shared this experience, which they regard as a family tradition.

🏵 Ethnic Self-Definition

As noted, the great majority of our respondents—84 percent in Ukraine and 91 percent in Russia—consider themselves Jews. The proportion of those who do not identify with any particular nationality rose between the 1992/93 and the 1997/98 survey, especially among those under thirty (from 2.8 percent to 8.6 percent). However, respondents in both republics consider themselves products of both Jewish and Russian cultures. This identification engenders among them a dual consciousness.

VALERIY CHERVYAKOV, ZVI GITELMAN, AND VLADIMIR SHAPIRO

Table 4.5.
"How Would You Describe Your National Consciousness?" (Russia 1997–98)

Mostly Jewish	24.3
Jewish and Non-Jewish at the same time	60.5
Mostly Non-Jewish	8.5
Neither	4.2
Other	2.5

The sense of dual national consciousness grows somewhat between the first wave, when 55 percent of the respondents in Russia characterized their consciousness as both Russian and Jewish, and the second wave, when 61 percent do so. Contrary to what one might expect, it is among the young that one finds the largest proportion—nearly a third—who consider their national consciousness primarily Jewish. At this point, we can only speculate why this is so: perhaps it is a largely subjective expression, connected more to the diminution of negative feelings about being Jewish than to the objective fact that their direct experience of Jewish traditions is less than that of the oldest generation, though those under thirty are more likely to have been exposed to the revival of Jewish religious and cultural activity in the FSU.

Having been deprived of access to Jewish culture and tradition, and simultaneously powerfully attracted to Russian culture, most of the respondents in Russia understandably choose to define themselves not exclusively as "Jews" (18.4 percent) but either as "Russian Jews" (41.3 percent) or as *"Rossiianie"* (21.6 percent). The latter means residents and citizens of Russia, a civic concept, rather than *Russkie,* ethnic Russians. Those of purely Jewish ancestry are more inclined to identify themselves as "Russian Jews" (44.4 percent) or "Jews" (21.4 percent), whereas nearly a third of those of mixed ancestry lean toward the term *"Rossiianin,"* and nearly a quarter of them describe themselves as "cosmopolitans" or "citizens of the world," terms infrequently used by pure Jews.

The ethnic self-definition of Ukrainian Jews is more complex. Though they are citizens of Ukraine, they are more influenced by Russian than by Ukrainian culture, as has historically been the case,[3] and feel themselves closer to the Russian-speaking residents of their cities than to the Ukrainian speakers. More define themselves as "Russian Jews" (24.2 percent) than as "Ukrainian Jews" (19.3 percent), which indicates that culture is somewhat more salient than geography for them.

The profile of our respondents' ethnic consciousness is made quite clear by responses to the question, "What, in your opinion, is required in order for a person to be considered a genuine Jew?" (see Table 4.6).

E Pluribus Unum?

Table 4.6.

*"What Is the Most Important Thing Required of a Person in Order to Be
Considered a Genuine Jew?" (percentages)*

	Russia '92	Russia '97	Ukraine '92	Ukraine '97
Be proud of one's nationality	33.3	22.9	29.4	31.4
Defend Jewish honor and dignity	27.1	17.3	21.4	19.7
Not hide one's Jewishness	0.5	20.8	0.7	13.6
Remember the Holocaust	7.3	15.1	15.5	21.5
Know Jewish history	5.0	2.8	3.0	2.1
Marry a Jew	1.8	1.1	1.1	0.8
Know Jewish traditions	3.2	1.4	0.2	1.4
Help other Jews	7.1	4.3	6.6	6.4
Feel a tie to Israel	4.2	4.3	5.7	2.8
Believe in God	2.7	4.2	3.9	5.4
Know the basics of Judaism	1.0	0.7	0.2	0.3
Circumcise one's son	0.2	0.1	0.2	0.1
Observe *kashrut*	0.0	0.0	0.0	0.1
Observe the Sabbath	0.0	0.3	0.3	0.4
Attend synagogue	0.0	0.1	0.2	0.1
Know a Jewish language	2.2	1.2	1.6	0.4
Share Zionist ideals	0.2	0.2	0.3	0.2
Give children Jewish education	1.2	0.8	2.0	1.3
Don't know, no answer	3.1	2.4	0.7	0.4

This table dramatically illustrates how conceptions of Jewishness held
by Russian and Ukrainian Jews are radically different from both historical
and contemporary understandings of most Jews in the Diaspora and Israel.
Judaism is largely irrelevant to Jewishness. Belief in God, observance of
Shabbat and *kashrut,* and circumcision are all rated as quite irrelevant to
being a "good Jew." What makes a good Jew is knowledge of history and
culture and, especially, feeling—pride in one's Jewishness and remembering
the *Shoah.* To many non-FSU Jews this sounds anachronistic. Many will recall the emphasis placed in rabbinic sermons and popular Jewish literature
in the early twentieth century on the achievements of Jewish scientists, musicians, artists, captains of industry, and even athletes; their accomplishments were pointed out not only as examples of the "Jewish contribution to
civilization" but also as reasons to remain Jewish and be proud of it. Jewish
heroes were no longer rabbinic sages, Judaic scholars, or the patriarchs, ma-
triarchs, and kings of Israel, but had the names of Albert Einstein, Sigmund
Freud, Jascha Heifetz, Levi Strauss, and even, in America, Hank Greenberg.
As Jews have become more secure and less defensive, the need to "prove"

that Jews are "worthy" of living among the nations has declined. More recently, the rationale for remaining Jewish has had more to do with Israel, the *Shoah,* and some form of religious commitment. Since the Soviet Union was generally hostile to Israel, downplayed the *Shoah,* and was militantly opposed to Judaism (and after 1930 discouraged even secular Yiddishism), it is not surprising that many Jews in the FSU do not see these features as integral to Jewishness. Understandable though this may be, it raises many complex questions for those trying to promote a revival of Jewish life in the FSU. Issues of relevance, feasibility, and "cultural imperialism" (in the sense of the imposition of external agendas on people whose value hierarchy is different) are raised by the disparity our research has revealed between Western "normative" understandings of what makes a "good Jew" and those held by most Jews in Russia and Ukraine.

Conclusion

1. Comparison of surveys taken five years apart reveals an ongoing intensive process of the "erosion" of Jewish ethnicity. There are more people who consider themselves Jews and who have some other components of Jewish self-consciousness but are only partially Jewish by their ancestry. Most respondents define their self-awareness dualistically—as Jewish and Russian at the same time. The proportion of this category of respondents increased over the five years. This dual consciousness manifested itself explicitly in the most common self-definition of our respondents as "Russian Jew" or "Russian citizen," but not simply "Jew."

2. Among Russian Jews, the process of creating their own identities is accompanied by a distancing of themselves from other Diaspora Jews. While they have close personal ties to Israelis, they do not regard Israel as the only place for Jews to live. Nor do they express strong identification with Israel in general. More than half the respondents do not consider Jews who live in different parts of the world to be a single nation. Over the five years between the two stages of our survey, the proportion of those who feel kinship with Israeli Jews decreased from 38 to 21 percent.

3. Judaism and purely religious values do not play a significant role in the Jewish identities of most Russian and Ukrainian Jews. The main components of Jewish consciousness are connected to the historical memory of the people, national dignity, ethnic consolidation in the face of contemporary problems, and familiarization with the cultural heritage of the people. The proportion of those who practice Judaism in everyday life remains as small five years after the first survey as it was then.

4. Though the Jewish family retains the leading role in the formation of Jewish identity, extrafamilial factors acquire an increasingly significant role in ethnic socialization. For Jewish young people, friends and Jewish educational institutions mean nearly the same thing as family upbringing.

5. One can observe the growth of the specific weight of intermarriages as well as in marriages of Jews to part-Jews. At the same time, the proportion increases of those who do not consider endogamous Jewish marriages a must, or are tolerant of the "mixed" marriage of a son or daughter. This, along with the shrinking "marriage market" caused by continuing emigration and a low birth rate, is the basis for our forecast of increasing assimilatory tendencies among a certain part of Jewish young people.

6. Over the five-year interval between the first and the second "waves" of our survey, there was a general decrease in Jewish educational activity by the Jewish population. We observe this when analyzing data on the respondents' attendance at lectures and seminars on Jewish history, religion, and traditions, and listening to Jewish radio programs. However, in the same time period the proportion of those who attend such meetings *regularly* has not decreased but has even increased. The same applies to those who read Jewish press regularly. These and other indicators bring us to the conclusion that the more widespread interest in Jewish culture of the early 1990s has been replaced to some extent by less general but deeper interest.

7. Approximately one-fourth of parents who have children of school age would prefer to send them to Jewish schools, though at the time they were surveyed only half of those who express such a preference actually sent their children to such schools. Our respondents are almost unanimous in favoring Jewish secular, but not religious, education for the young. This applies to high schools as well as to higher education.

8. The survey shows very clearly that for a significant part of the respondents it is important that Jewish social and cultural institutions be located close to their places of residence. Expectations of such institutions and of the Jewish community vary significantly and include, first of all, social assistance to the old and disabled, help in getting acquainted with the Jewish heritage, the organization of leisure time in a Jewish environment, and protection against antisemitism. Not surprisingly, these and other expectations are not fully satisfied by the Jewish organizations in the eight cities in which the surveys were taken. It is foreign, rather than domestic, organizations that are seen as playing a more significant role in the provision of Jewish cultural (and other) services.

9. Prejudices against Jews and antisemitism now play less significant

roles in the formation of Jewish consciousness than five years ago. This pertains above all to the youngest respondents, whose ethnic socialization is taking place under new circumstances that include the revival and openness of Jewish life, easier transmission of ethnic values, and the lessening of the psychologically destructive feeling of social encirclement. Yet feelings of pride in one's own people, including the desire to protect its honor and dignity as natural reactions to anti-Jewish attacks, are still considered by the majority of respondents requisite components of Jewish identity.

10. In 1997/98, the proportion of those offering a positive forecast of unfettered national Jewish development in Russia doubled as compared to the survey of 1992–93; this attitude was common to nearly two-thirds of the sample. At the same time, the emigration potential of Russian Jews declined as the proportion of those who do not want to leave Russia in any circumstances increased by two-thirds.

Thus, we observe continued demographic erosion, as Mark Tolts's chapter makes dramatically clear, and a weakening of exclusively Jewish consciousness among post-Soviet Jews. Emigration has undoubtedly taken the most conscious Jews out of the country. Those who are left seem to have weaker emotional ties to the rest of world Jewry. Families are becoming less important as agencies of Jewish socialization; peer groups and Jewish institutions, especially those with foreign connections, are becoming more important. A group of Russian and Ukrainian Jews are deeply interested in Jewish culture, but their preference is for secular culture and easily accessible institutions. In some respects they resemble Jews outside the FSU, but their conceptions of Jewish identity and culture differ significantly from many of those held in Israel and the rest of the Diaspora, presenting potential problems of mutual recognition and understanding.

NOTES

1. The first stage of the project on Jewish identities in Russia and Ukraine was supported by the National Council for Soviet and East European Research, the Wilstein Institute of Jewish Policy Studies, IREX, and Dr. David Egger (Princeton, N.J.). The 1997–98 follow-up survey was made possible by grants from the American Jewish Joint Distribution Committee, Samuel Frankel, Irwin Green, the Jewish Community Development Foundation, Memorial Foundation for Jewish Culture, the Russian Jewish Congress (Moscow), the Charles and Lynn Schusterman Family Foundation, and the Jean and Samuel Frankel Center for Judaic Studies at the University of Michigan.

2. Actually, there are 1,317 people in the Russian sample, but this did not affect the structure of the sample.

3. See Zvi Gitelman, "Native Land, Promised Land, New Land: Jewish Emigration from Russia and Ukraine," in Zvi Gitelman, Lubomyr Hajda, John-Paul Himka, and Roman Solchanyk, eds., *Cultures and Nations of Central and Eastern Europe* (Cambridge, Mass.: Harvard Ukrainian Research Institute, 2000), 137–64.

FIVE

MARSHALL I. GOLDMAN

Russian Jews in Business

An overstatement perhaps, but Russians seem to be manic-depressive in their treatment of Jews, especially toward Jews holding positions of economic and political power. At times it has seemed that there are no bounds to the positions or authority Jews in Russia might hold. Unfortunately, more often than not, those brief interludes were followed by a lengthy period of quotas and restrictions, and even repression. On occasion this has brought with it pogroms, expulsion, and even death. Then, when it seems there is no hope that the situation will ever change, it sometimes does and once again Jews rise to positions of power and responsibility. What explains these cycles of extremes, and why do Jews, including those Russian Jews who most recently rose to positions of economic and political power, stay on (only to be demoted or removed again), when they must be aware of what happened in the past?

The Historic Setting

There is no simple explanation for the up-and-down treatment of Russian Jews. It seems, however, that Jews do best in the immediate aftermath of a major upheaval in Russian economic, political, and social life. This is in part because a disproportionate number of Jews end up as participants in preparing and facilitating that upheaval or in taking advantage of new opportunities made possible in its aftermath. Then, because they have played such a prominent role, when the political and economic situations deteriorate (and in Russia sooner or later they almost always seems to) many of the more prominent Jews are blamed for the problem. In some cases such criticism of individuals is deserved. Unfortunately, however, the blame is usually assigned collectively; a "Masonic-Jewish conspiracy" is how it is usually described. There follows a lengthy period of exclusion and repression during which, with few exceptions, Jews are excluded from all positions of power and authority both in the government and in business affairs.

After several decades, they begin to reawaken and in reaction to their exclusion and persecution, they begin to agitate for change. Some begin to plot and organize with other oppressed groups and critics of the regime so that when the upheaval finally occurs, many of the rebels now find themselves on the other side of the badge of authority and in positions of power. In much the same way, business activities that once were illegal and could only be conducted underground suddenly become legitimized. Thus, those who were treated as outside the law are now very much inside it. In the switch to the market, for example, this means that those who were once vilified as social parasites are now lionized as entrepreneurs or "oligarchs," the type of business leaders that a market economy must have.

Ethnic Russians in their midst, however, who had once occupied positions of power now sometimes find that their own posts have been abolished. Suddenly they find themselves at a disadvantage. The most talented among these Russians aspired to the traditional posts of power and prestige within the government, the type of positions denied to Jews and others who were not members of the dominant ethnic group. Therefore, when the political and economic paradigm changes, the dominant Russian ethnic group finds itself disadvantaged, a situation that in the long run is seldom viable. This is at least a partial explanation for the transition that occurred at the time of the Bolshevik revolution of 1917 as well as at the break-up of the Communist Party and Soviet Union in the late 1980s and early 1990s.

Consider the status of Jews in Russia before World War I. Most Jews at the time were confined physically to the Pale, an area limited mainly to what is today Lithuania, Belarus, and Ukraine. Relatively few were able to work their way into such large cities as St. Petersburg or Moscow. Occupations were similarly restricted for Jews. They were excluded from the ranks of government service, especially the officer corps, elected office, teaching, the foreign service, and even the civil service. Officially, Jews were also excluded from leadership positions in shipping, railroad, insurance, and mining corporations.[1] Occasionally some of the tsar's ministers, especially late in the nineteenth century as well as between 1905 and 1906, relaxed some of these restrictions.[2] On the books at least, the laws of 1864, 1865, 1903, and 1912 barred Jews (as well as Poles) from acquiring or even managing rural land in the provinces of Vilna, Kiev, Kovno, Grodno, Minsk, Mogilev, Vitebsk, Podolia, and Volhynia.[3] Of necessity, that limited Jews primarily to service-type activities such as trade, banking, and timber processing. There were also instances in which corporations owning land or engaging in manufacturing that were officially dominated by Russian corporate officers were in fact effectively run behind the scenes by Jews.[4]

For centuries the Jews suffered such restriction in relative silence. By the late nineteenth century, however, some became emboldened and decided to work to end such discrimination and at the same time to reshape the nature of the whole society. Those so motivated eagerly joined in movements, some revolutionary and violent, to overturn the regime. Moreover, unlike the barriers erected against Jews seeking positions in the established state and social sector, the door to revolutionary activity was wide open. After all, revolutionaries are usually drawn from the oppressed and déclassé and usually are not too fussy about who joins their ranks. For good reason, then, Jews played a prominent role in the whole spectrum of anti-regime opposition.

Having played a prominent role in the revolution, it was only natural that the Jewish revolutionaries would join other revolutionaries in running their new state. What would have been unthinkable under the tsar became possible in the new atmosphere of equal opportunity, and Jews were appointed to some of the country's most sensitive and prominent positions. Of course they had little to do at this point with the traditional Jewish community. For that matter, in the 1920s the Soviet state embarked on an active program of closing and destroying not only churches but also synagogues. Nonetheless, over the next few years, Jews were involved in almost all aspects of the revolutionary regime. Examples include Leon Trotsky (Bronshtein), who served as the equivalent of the Minister of Defense; Maxim Litvinov (Isser Meir Wallach), as the equivalent of the Minister of Foreign Affairs; and, sad to say, Genrikh Yagoda, the head of the secret police. All three sensitive positions had almost never been held by Jews in even the most enlightened countries. Other prominent Jews in the pre–World War II era included Lazar Kaganovich and Yakov Sverdlov. Even Lenin might have had a Jewish grandparent.

By contrast, after World War II, with the exception of Kaganovich, Jews were purged not only from the senior positions in their agencies, but more often than not from the lower administrative ranks as well. (There were, of course, a few Jews among the higher Soviet military ranks.) Jews were in the universities (limited by quotas) and arts, especially in music, but relatively few served in industrial ministries or as directors of factories.

The disappearance of Jews from positions of prominence is more difficult to explain than their sudden inclusion. They were included because they were among the dispossessed, the disenfranchised, the discontent, the abused, and the challengers to the system—who suddenly found themselves empowered. With the removal of the existing elite, there were vacancies to fill, patronage to bestow, and rewards to claim. But why and how did they wear out their welcome? In part they were singled out as scapegoats for policies gone wrong. Some of the decisions they made were taken with the public good and well-being in mind, but were, nonetheless, unrealistic and sometimes counter to what the people may have wanted. In other cases, some policies adopted by Jews in authority were mean-spirited, a sort of revenge and a settling of scores for centuries of discrimination and persecution. Among those targeted were the Cossacks, the peasants, and reactionary groups like the Black Hundreds. Of course, Jews were not alone in seeking to diminish the influence of such rightist forces, but at the popular level, retaliation and repression of this sort often came to be associated not just with individuals but with Jews involved in a coordinated and unified conspiracy.

It was no surprise that many of the actions ascribed to Jews ultimately provoked a backlash, especially those policies that seemed to be an attack on the Russian Orthodox Church or the peasants. Jews were also associated with the destruction of churches. After a time, a sense of nationalism began to resurface, leading to calls once again for the russification of policies and personnel. Reactions of this sort have also occurred in recent times in places like Malaysia and Indonesia. As in Russia, indigenous people seek to reduce the influence and status of those whom they see as outside groups, in those two instances not the Jews but the Chinese. When so many members of a particular minority group suddenly become dominant, the majority often fantasize that these minority groups are tightly coordinated and unified in their efforts to damage the state and promote their own interests at the expense of the majority. That no such coordination can be demonstrated is generally beside the point. When all else fails, proof can be found in fabricated evidence such as the *Protocols of the Elders of Zion.* For those who want to believe the scheme, this forgery is clear proof of a Jewish conspiracy. How the Masons of the "Masonic-Jewish conspiracy" fit in with the *Protocols of the Elders of Zion* is more of a mystery.

Stalin also seems to have been influenced by Hitler and the Nazi emphasis on antisemitism. His feelings first surfaced in the prelude to the Nazi–Soviet pact when Maxim Litvinov was fired, probably because he was Jewish, hardly the person to sign pacts with Nazis. Antisemitism was reawakened among many peasants, who initially welcomed German troops, seeing them as liberators from the Jewish Bolshevik commissars who had led the battle to collectivize peasant land. But the need for a broad-based coalition in the darkest days of World War II resulted in a muting of antisemitism. Russian Jews rallied support for the Soviet Union among fellow Jews in other allied countries, especially in the United States. However, once the war was won, latent antisemitism became official policy, especially after Soviet Jews defied Stalin's policy of isolationism and openly demonstrated in front of the newly opened Israeli embassy just after the achievement of Israeli independence. These links to Israel confirmed the worst of Stalin's paranoia. As he saw it, there was indeed a conspiracy; Jews in positions of authority in the Soviet government would be controlled not by Moscow but by Tel Aviv.

The Incubators of the Jewish "Oligarchy"

Eight decades after the Revolution, there was again an opening of the gates. Two of Russia's prime ministers in the 1990s, Sergei Kiriyenko and Evgeny Primakov, had at least one Jewish parent. Kiriyenko "even" acknowledges being partly Jewish. How many other countries of the world have had even *one* Jewish prime minister? In addition, at least two of the country's first deputy prime ministers during the 1990s when Boris Yeltsin was president (Anatoly Chubais and Boris Nemtsov), along with several of the deputy prime ministers, also had at least one Jewish parent (both of Chubais's parents were Jewish). What we will focus on, however, is the unusually large number of Jews who became business leaders, bankers, or "oligarchs," as they are generally characterized.

The exclusion of Jews from traditional positions of power in the post–World War II years helps explain why they appeared to emerge so prominently during the Gorbachev–Yeltsin eras. The pattern is highly reminiscent of the Jewish condition in tsarist times, which was followed by the increased prominence of Jews after the revolution. The model introduced at the beginning of this paper fits perfectly. In contrast to their position in the early days of Communism, talented and energetic Jews after World War II found vast areas of government and economic life closed to them. Just as in the last days of the tsar, there was little in the larger society to absorb their energies and ideas. Not surprisingly, they sought outlets elsewhere. This time, however, they did so not as revolutionaries but as advocates in academic circles of economic and political reform and as underground wheelers and dealers in the economic sphere. Of course, the great majority turned to science and technology, areas relatively not politicized and where there was an ongoing need for well-educated and well-trained "cadres." Israelis and Westerners are often struck by the high proportion of "engineers" among Soviet and post-Soviet Jewish émigrés. Much of the explanation behind this career choice lies in the fact that it was the channel most open to Jews in Soviet society. An important minority became active reformers, especially in economic areas. Economic analysts such as Anatoly Chubais, and political and environmental reformers like Boris Nemtsov often evolved into politicians, sometimes at the most senior level. We will concentrate here on what was often the seamier though more lucrative side—what eventually came to be *business*.

Despite—or maybe because of—the state monopoly and its central planning format, the Soviet economy provided an unintended training ground for many of those who ultimately emerged as the country's leading business oligarchs. In the Soviet era, private trade and manufacturing were officially prohibited. Stalin allowed the peasants to have private plots and sell their harvests in special collective farm (*kolhkoz*) markets. Individuals could also sell their homemade handicrafts. But it was an "economic crime" to hire ("exploit") employees to manufacture goods or sell something produced by another person. As a measure of the State's determination to eliminate such actions, "economic crimes" were punishable by death, and there were many such sentences, especially during the Stalin and Khrushchev eras. That undoubtedly discouraged many. But we know that private trade and manufacturing flourished widely underground, despite such severe decrees, even under Stalin.

In many ways, central planning made private and illegal business activity inevitable and irresistible. In a perfect world, central planning would anticipate everyone's business and personal needs. But it was not a perfect world and central planning was anything but a perfect science. Thus, there were always imbalances and disequilibria in the economy that bureaucrats and an excessively cumbersome state apparatus could not remedy. The system had a difficult enough time responding to long-term needs—and short-term flexibility in central planning was a contradiction in terms. Compounding the problem was the regime's emphasis on heavy industry. The drive to industrialize and overtake the West meant that priority would always be given to fulfilling the needs of the machinery manufacturers and to building an industrial infrastructure. If something had to be sacrificed, it was the production of consumer goods.

Consumers unwilling or unable to go without a particular item would almost always be willing to pay a little extra on the side, "*na levo,*" to a "middleman" who would dig up what was missing on shop counters. Middlemen could also provide hard-to-get, state-supplied services such as plumbing, carpentry, and automobile repairs. Those who specialized in unearthing and supplying foreign-made products were called *fartsovshchiki;* those speculating in foreign currency were *valiutchiki,* and those who provided services were called *deltsy.* They were not only daring but an imaginative and entrepreneurial lot. Because of the illegal nature of what they were doing, these suppliers could not be found through the typical guides that we are accustomed to searching. Hard as it might be for those in the West to believe, the Soviet system did not even supply phone books, much less "Yellow Pages." This means *fartsovshchiki* and their comrades had to operate with a level of ingenuity that was at least on a par with, if not superior to, that of dealmakers in the West. This also meant that, as unlikely as it may have sounded, if the day ever came when private business in the Soviet Union might be legalized, such operators would move quickly from the rear ranks of the dregs of society to the front ranks to become merchant princes, captains of commerce, or, as the Russians would come to describe them, the "oligarchs." Their secret operations would be perfect preparation for a transition to the market economy.

The transactions of the *fartsovshchiki* and others like them were not always illegal. In many cases, the items and services were provided as barter for other goods and services already provided or delivered. Once, while visiting the apartment of a director of a Moscow hospital, I was stunned by the array of delicacies set out solely for my visit. I was impressed with exotic goods that I had never seen in Moscow's markets or shops. When I noted that my host must have spent a fortune in money and hours in time searching for such items, he protested that, on the contrary, he had spent neither time nor money on any of it. "These were all given to me by patients and prospective patients seeking favors or admittance to my hospital."

It was not just individual consumers who found it difficult to live within the boundaries of five- and one-year plans. Enterprise directors were generally even more dependent on extra-planning practices. Since their success as enterprise directors was determined by whether or not they were able to fulfill their planned targets, they were under enormous pressure to have access to supplies needed for production. If because of bad weather, a disruption of shipping, a breakdown in production, or inadequate foresight the plan could not be fulfilled, most enterprise managers had no compunction in cutting a corner or two. Most of them, in fact, had recourse to what was referred to as a *tolkatch,* a "pusher" or broker. These brokers operated much like the *fartsovshchiki* but on a much grander scale and without quite so descriptive a title. The *tolkatch* phenomenon was not unique to the USSR. For example, when supplies are disrupted in the West, a so-called gray market is formed, enabling Western businesspeople frequently to call on expediters to replace curtailed supplies.

By no means were Jews the only ones who became *fartsovshchiki* or *tolkatchi.* There were Russians as well, but since such activities were generally regarded as anti-social if not illegal, those Russians who had the talent required for these operations usually had hosts of other opportunities open to them and did not need to attempt something considered socially unacceptable. Jews after World War II were much more constrained in their choices. Besides, Jews historically, in tsarist times as well as outside of Russia, have long come to deal with the fact that they must settle for activities several steps below what was socially desirable or even acceptable. In the extreme case, they were the Soviet Union's "untouchables."

✡ *Perestroika and the Transition to a Market Economy*

When the Soviet Union began to turn its back on central planning and open its doors to the market and private business, much of what had been disreputable in the Soviet era suddenly became admirable, as unlikely as it may seem. Talents and skills that were of no use, at least officially, in the plan era, suddenly became desirable and sought after. This also meant that many of the Russians who had held power in the official Soviet hierarchy now found themselves disadvantaged because they had no experience in the techniques required for trading or finance. By contrast, those who had dealt in the black market or in procurement, who before were tolerated as undesirable but necessary nuisances, now found a great demand for their talents. Just as in tsarist times, when the Russian landlords would call in Germans as managers and supervisors, so in the late Gorbachev and Yeltsin eras, there were some who found it expedient to bring in Jews.

In many other instances, no one had specifically to call in the Jews—individual Jews simply took advantage of the void that suddenly opened up when the planning infrastructure that had dominated the Soviet Union for sixty years was destroyed. The planning and supply agencies, *Gosplan* and *Gossnab,* as well as the ministries, were effectively abolished. That meant there was no longer anyone to decree who would be purchasers of inputs, who would be producers, or who would be shippers of output. On top of that, the authorities decided to privatize most of what had been state-owned property. Suddenly, billions of dollars of assets were being thrown up for grabs. This was a moment unique not just in Russian but in world history. Who better to take advantage of such opportunities than those who all along had been wheeling and dealing? Those who had spent their entire lives in the corridors of state power certainly had connections and influence with their counterparts throughout the system. But under the new circumstances, many of these contacts were no longer of use since they no longer had control over the assets or the administrative authority. It was a brand new playing field.

An early sign of things to come followed Mikhail Gorbachev's decision in 1987 to allow the opening of cooperatives and private business. Gorbachev had been speaking for some time of a new era in the Soviet economy, which he called *perestroika*. Yet he himself seemed uncertain about exactly what this meant. He called for intensification and acceleration. But in 1986 he launched a crackdown on all private trade unless sellers could prove that what they were selling had been produced or grown by themselves. This hardly seemed to signal something new. But after what had seemed to be this step backward, Gorbachev's subsequent decision in 1987 to allow cooperatives and private trade—something unseen since the New Economic Policy (NEP) of the 1920s—was initially treated with some skepticism. This caused some hesitation among those who feared Gorbachev might reverse himself yet again and then punish those who had adopted capitalist ways in the interim, something that had happened at the end of the NEP period and after World War II.

Gradually it began to look like Gorbachev would hold to the path of reform and adopt even more forthcoming liberalization, including the legalization of joint ventures with foreigners. For some *fartsovshchiki* it didn't matter. They were determined to take advantage of the new opportunity by setting up legal cooperatives. In so doing, they could not only act within the law but could also take advantage of the public's pent-up hunger for more consumer goods and services. Not incidentally, this also presented opportunities for them to launder the money they had been forced for decades to hide.

After a ban of sixty years on private and cooperative activity, the transition, as might be expected, proved to be anything but simple. To prevent what he feared might be the wholesale defection of masses of Russians from their jobs at state enterprises, Gorbachev initially limited who could open such businesses to pensioners and students. Other able-bodied workers could operate privately only during off hours or weekends. The new rules tended to complicate life for the police and other regulatory authorities. Prior to 1987, and especially before 1986, anyone found selling or manufacturing on their own was *prima facie* guilty of an "economic crime." Control was easy. After the 1987 decree, it became much more difficult. Moreover, those who had been regularly harassed by the police for such activities could now thumb their noses. Few were so brave, though, since the police soon discovered that they could continue to harass by inspecting for licenses and demanding adherence to other forms of state control that more often than not was simply a form of extortion. But harassment and extortion, whether by the state authorities or by the rapidly expanding Mafia that also began to emerge from closed doors, simply became a cost of doing business. Given the enormous profits to be made during that era of transition, these were a small price to pay and a minor deterrent to those who quickly rose to the ranks of some of the wealthiest individuals of the world.

Creating cooperatives, as small as they may have been, provided an excellent launching pad for those who were willing to take the risk. It became a legal way to build up capital. Others would find money by appropriating what had been state or party assets for their personal use or taking the assets of several state enterprises and using them to fund private activities. This was how many of the private commercial banks were initially capitalized.

As indicated earlier, the Jews who ended up as oligarchs almost all started out through the cooperative route, most building on their hard knocks as *fartsovshchiki,* but at least one gaining access to state and party assets. At the high point, before the collapse of the economy on August 17, 1998, Jews created and dominated five of the seven largest newly created private commercial banks, all of which had been established over a ten-year period. How they did it fits our prototypical pattern.

Alexander P. Smolensky, born in 1954, is probably one of the best examples of a Jewish outsider who in the market environment became an enormously influential insider. After entering the labor force, Smolensky moonlighted at a second job in a bakery, for which he lacked a permit. He then helped typeset and publish a Bible, using government presses and ink to do so. For this he was arrested by the KGB in 1981 as a *fartsovshchik,* and was charged with economic crimes. Today such initiatives would be applauded, but then he was sentenced to two years at hard labor (though he only served one day).[5] Smolensky graduated from the Dzhambulskii Geological Technical Institute in Kazakstan,[6] where he met his wife.[7] Forsaking his training as an economist, he became a typesetter (whence his work on the Bible). After his brush with the KGB in the mid-1980s, Smolensky began to do construction work. Many people at that time were involved in working "on the side" in this way.

As a risk taker, Smolensky responded to Gorbachev's 1987 decree allowing the formation of cooperatives and private businesses. Smolensky founded the "Moscow No. 3 Construction Cooperative" which started as an industry that sawed up logs into timber and from there expanded to provide contractor services for home construction. This was at a time when there were no readily available supplies, including such simple things as nails and lumber, a situation made to order for someone with Smolensky's ingenuity. Using his trading experience, Smolensky was able to work the system and avail himself of seemingly unavailable supplies. Since this proved to be very profitable, he then began to search for a place to put his money. Rather than trust state banks that were not accustomed to dealing with large private accounts, he decided to create his own bank, the Stolichny Bank—which he did on February 14, 1989. In an interview with the *Washington Post* in 1997, Smolensky acknowledged that at that point he knew nothing about commercial banking. His main consideration was his determination "to evade the state banks and become as independent of state authorities as he could."[8]

While Smolensky was applauded for his charity as well as his business savvy, allegations about his past haunted him. The newspaper *Rossiiskaya gazeta* ran an investigative article on March 14, 1995, charging that he had participated in a forgery scheme to smuggle $25 million in cash out of Russia to Austria, the home of his grandfather and a country of which Smolensky is a citizen and where his wife has a home and office.

Unlike many of his fellow bankers, Alexander Smolensky has not actively sought to build up a large industrial empire. While his bank had some interest in the newspapers *Kommersant* and *Novaya gazeta* and he shared in the ownership of the Sibneft oil company and the television network ORT with Boris Berezovsky (whom we shall consider shortly), for the most part he focused instead on developing a large network of bank branches. In November 1996, he won a controversial bid for what had been the state-owned Agroprombank, which had some 1,250 branches in rural areas. Several critics have charged that Smolensky won the bid with the help of Anatoly Chubais, at the time a first deputy prime minister.[9]

Suspicions were heightened after it became known that when President Yeltsin fired Chubais a few months later in January 1996, Smolensky cushioned the fall by extending Chubais an interest-free $3 million loan that Smolensky has reportedly claimed was never repaid.[10] After acquiring Agroprombank, Smolensky changed the name of all of his banks to SBS/AGRO (which stands for Stolichny Bank Savings Agro). Until August 1998, his bank had the largest number of private branches in the country and was second only to the government's Sberbank in its number of branches. His was also among the first Russian banks to offer a credit card. However, having so many outlets also made SBS/AGRO vulnerable in a time of panic. Following Black Monday on August 17, 1998, when rumors that Russian banks had become illiquid began to spread, SBS/AGRO was forced to seek a $1 billion credit line from the Russian Central Bank to prevent a run on its deposits.[11] That was not enough to save the bank and the loan was never repaid. What assets remained were transferred to another bank, called Pervoie OVK. Officially, at least, Smolensky was replaced as director, although the suspicion is that he continues to play a role.[12]

Among the Jewish oligarchs, Vladimir A. Gusinsky has one of the most unusual backgrounds. Born in 1953, he attended not only the Gubkin Institute of Petrochemicals and Natural Gas (he says for four years—the Institute says for one) but also was on the directors' faculty of GITIS, the State Theater Institute.[13] After a stint as a theatrical producer in the provinces, including Tula, and a two-year term in the army, he returned to Moscow where he drove a cab on the side to earn money. Some say that he also became involved with under-the-counter street trading.[14] One newspaper, *Rossiiskaya gazeta,* reports that he had been charged with embezzlement and had engaged in other questionable activities.[15] Gusinsky denies such accusations and has successfully sued several of his accusers. He also continued with his theatrical work and, at one point, apparently, attended the University of Virginia, where he studied financial management. His work in the theater enabled him to make some important connections. He began to work with the Komsomol in Moscow, helping them organize "mass events." Reportedly he did some work for Ted Turner's Good Will Games as well as the International Youth Festival in 1986.[16] (In a private conversation, Gusinsky denied ever having worked with Turner.)

He opened his first cooperative in 1988 and claims to have made his first $1 million by stripping transformers of their copper wire and converting them into bracelets. In 1989, Gusinsky formed MOST, a consulting firm. According to Gusinsky, the name MOST, which means "bridge" in Russian, was inspired by an ATM machine that he saw while visiting the United States. MOST initially was a fifty–fifty joint venture with APCO, an offshoot of Arnold and Porter, a prominent law firm in Washington, D.C. By 1992, Gusinsky had bought out APCO; MOST then became a wholly owned Russian company.

Gusinsky's cooperative branched out in several directions. While procuring office supplies for his consulting firm, he realized that if he could purchase items on a larger scale, he would not only obtain cheaper supplies for himself but could also act as a wholesaler for others.[17] From there he moved into renovation and construction, especially for apartment and office rentals for foreigners. Along the way he also began to purchase construction material factories that provided bricks and other building supplies. His construction work brought him into contact with Moscow's vice mayor in charge of construction, Yuri Luzhkov. When Luzhkov became mayor, he assigned prime properties to Gusinsky for renovation and management. Most important, in January 1993 Mayor Luzhkov also designated MOST Bank, the new banking affiliate of the MOST Group that was established in 1992, as one of the main depositories for Moscow's municipal funds.[18] In 1994, MOST Bank was given control over all the banking operations. MOST Bank could work with the funds on an interest-free basis to earn speculative profits on foreign exchange and could also use them to purchase federal state securities that yielded interest levels of 150–200 percent. This helped the bank grow rapidly. By 1994 it was one of the country's largest banks, even though in January 1993 it had not even qualified among the top hundred banks. Mayor Luzhkov ultimately decided that he and the city could use the cash flow; on January 6, 1995, he set up the Moscow Municipal Bank as the main depository for the city's funds.[19]

The diversion of Moscow city funds certainly meant a loss for MOST Bank, but by then the institution had attracted other depositors. The bank also provided the wherewithal for Gusinsky to expand into non-banking activities. But unlike the other oligarchs, Gusinsky had very few industrial holdings except for some construction and pharmaceutical companies. Most of the MOST Group properties, other than its financial and consulting interests, were media holdings. Gusinsky also differed from the other oligarchs in that much of what he controlled had been created anew. The wealth of the other oligarchs came largely from takeovers of existing state industrial properties.

At the height of his power, Gusinsky's ventures included his radio and television network ECHO and NTV (established in 1994) as well as his newspaper *Segodnia* (1992) and his magazines. Until President Vladimir Putin decided to punish him in 2001 for refusing to adhere to the official government line, Gusinsky was one of Russia's most influential media barons.

Weakened by the financial collapse of August 17, 1998, Gusinsky nonetheless continued to expand his media empire. But with a stricken economy and the resulting slump in advertising revenue, he needed to borrow substantial sums of money (perhaps $1 billion) either provided by or guaranteed by Gazprom, Russia's natural gas producer. This worked well as long as Boris Yeltsin was president, as Yeltsin was willing to acquiesce to such loans. But when Putin became acting president and Gusinsky supported the opposition candidates, Putin ordered Gazprom to call in its loans, pushing Gusinsky out of NTV and its holdings in MEDIA-MOST. (Putin could do this because the state held 38.4 percent of Gazprom's stock and was thus the company's largest stockholder.) To accelerate the process, the government sent masked police to raid MEDIA-MOST's office and check its books. There were fifty such visits. During the investigation, Gusinsky was put into the Butyrskaia jail for three days. Upon his release he fled to Spain. While awaiting the Spanish Court decision as to whether or not to honor the Russian prosecutor general's request to extradite him, the Spanish authorities jailed him as well. Ultimately the Spanish judge decided that none of the charges had merit. Gusinsky was freed, but over the course of events, Gazprom seized NTV and creditors seized most of his other properties. Since then Gusinsky has been fighting criminal charges and has been living outside Russia. Clearly, his economic and political power has been broken.

Included in the June 22, 1998 *Forbes* magazine list of the world's richest millionaires, Boris Berezovsky was described in the December 30, 1996 issue of *Forbes* as the head of the Russian Mafia. Berezovsky took exception to this depiction and has been attempting to sue the publication for slander. Others have also raised questions about how Berezovsky went about accumulating his wealth. Born in 1946, he started out at the Moscow Institute of Timber Technology, an obscure but highly prestigious establishment, where he displayed talent as a mathematician. From 1967 to 1969, he worked at the Scientific Institute for Instruments and then the Soviet Hydrometeorology Center. In 1969, he transferred to the Research Institute of Control Sciences of the Soviet Academy of Sciences, where he earned a Ph.D. in Mathematics and Physics and ultimately moved into operations research. Sometime in the late 1970s, he spent about three weeks pursuing his research at the Harvard Business School. One of his subsequent projects involved designing a management system for the Soviet Union's largest automobile manufacturer Avtovaz, the manufacturer of the Zhiguli Lada.

With the break-up of the Soviet Union and the collapse of the state distribution system, most of the country's large manufacturers found themselves adrift and unable to figure out how to sustain or develop market and trade relations with their customers as well as their suppliers. Their only experience in dealing outside the planning and services of Gosplan had been with their *tolkatchi*. Building on that principle, many manufacturers established or facilitated the launching of local trading companies. These companies took on the task of finding buyers and suppliers for clients who, in growing numbers, did not want to be paid in rubles. These barter transactions were, after all, a specialty of the *tolkatch*. Moreover, many of the trading companies were in reality fronts for the senior staff of these enterprises. By prearrangement, the factory's products would be consigned to the trading company at a low ruble value. The trading company would then barter the product and split whatever profits were earned on the transaction with a few members of the senior management.

Calling on his contacts at Avtovaz, Berezovsky worked out a similar arrangement, in 1989 setting up Logovaz, a cooperative, to design and market management systems. Berezovsky then persuaded Avtovaz to consign the bulk of its automobile output at a sharp discount to Logovaz, which had been transformed by then into a trading company cooperative for this purpose. Logovaz then resold these cars at a much higher price. Not long after, he opened Fiat and Mercedes dealerships in Moscow and eventually came to control a substantial share of all the foreign and domestically produced automobiles sold in Moscow. Along the way, there were efforts to break up Berezovsky's near monopoly of the automobile business. The author Paul Klebnikov claims that to protect the franchise, Berezovsky worked with members of the Chechen Mafia to dissuade other Mafia groups from attempting to muscle in.[20] Attempts were made on his life, and some rivals and his driver were killed. In the process, however, Berezovsky built up a substantial fortune that he used to help finance several banks. In addition, Berezovsky went on to establish effective operating, but not ownership, control over Aeroflot, the oil company Sibneft, several newspapers and magazines, and ORT, the country's state-owned and largest television network.

In 1997, Yeltsin appointed Berezovsky deputy secretary of Russia's security council. This appointment was initially met with considerable criticism, in part because of suspicions of the sort reported in the 1996 *Forbes* magazine article and also because a few months earlier, when he had been worried about his physical safety, Berezovsky applied for and received Israeli citizenship. Eventually he was fired from his position as deputy secretary, and was then appointed and later fired as executive secretary of the Commonwealth of Independent States, the organization that attempts to coordinate activities of the former republics of the Soviet Union.

In a study focusing on the Jewish origins of the business oligarchs, Berezovsky's verbal attack on Boris Nemtsov in August 1997 is highly relevant. Formerly the governor of Nizhnii Novgorod, Nemtsov was brought to Moscow by President Yeltsin to serve as the first deputy prime minister in charge of the economy. Nemtsov moved quickly to reduce the power of the oligarchs and to increase tax collections. Initially, Yeltsin took Nemtsov under his wing and hinted broadly that Nemtsov would be his choice to become the next president. Angered by what he evidently regarded as Nemtsov's aggressiveness, Berezovsky attacked Nemtsov at a press conference on August 20, 1997. Nemtsov would never be president of Russia because, as Berezovsky put it, Nemtsov has a "purely genetic problem . . .

Nemtsov is a Boris Yefimovich; at times he is a Boris Abramovich; but he wants to be Boris Nikolayevich." By this he signaled that Nemtsov, whatever his aspirations, should remember his Jewish origins. Whether his father's name is Yefim (a common Russian-Jewish name, the equivalent of Chaim), or Abraham, he could never have a patronymic like Boris Nikolayevich Yeltsin. Incidentally, Berezovsky's own patronymic is Abramovich.[21]

At that time, Berezovsky regarded himself not only as a prominent operator in the world of business but also as a behind-the-scenes political kingmaker. He developed a close relationship with Yeltsin's presidential advisers, including Yeltsin's daughter Tatiana Dyachenko, and also claimed to have been the one who put forward Putin's name as a candidate to be prime minister. In a yet-to-be-explained parting of the ways, by 2001 Putin decided to sever his relationship with Berezovsky. Berezovsky, like Gusinsky, soon found himself in exile and in danger of arrest or at least interrogation were he to return to Moscow.

Mikhail Fridman, along with Peter Aven, founded the Alfa Group Consortium, a holding company that controls the Alfa Bank (opened in 1991), Alfa Capital, Tiumen Oil, and several construction material firms (producing cement, timber, glass) as well as food-processing businesses and a supermarket chain. They are also a major holder of plants that process tea and sugar. (Curiously, these are areas in which two Jews, Visotsky and Brodsky, made great fortunes before the revolution.) One of the youngest of the newly rich presented here, Fridman, was born in 1964. He is a graduate of the Moscow Institute of Steel and Alloys. From 1986 to 1988 he worked as an engineer in the *Elektrostal* factory.

Fridman began early to work as a private entrepreneur. While still a student, he washed windows on the side, a *deltsy* form of activity that was officially illegal. When it became legal to open cooperative and private concerns in 1987, Fridman was well prepared and in 1988 he set up his own photo cooperative, Alpha FOTO, and then ALFA/EKO and AlfaKapital. These establishments were the precursors of the Alfa Group Consortium. Anticipating that the Russian economy was heading toward a crisis, Fridman and Aven sold off most of their Russian government securities in August 1998. Unlike most of the other entrepreneurs considered here, Fridman emerged relatively unhurt from Black Monday, August 17, 1998.

Unlike some of the oligarchs like Alexander Smolensky and Mikhail Fridman, who in their youth rebelled against the Soviet state and central planning, Mikhail Khodorkovsky initially was a very model of the young Communist bureaucrat. Born in 1963, his rise to power and wealth and inclusion in the "Forbes Five" began in the Komsomol, the Young Communist League.

He graduated from the well-regarded Mendeleev Chemical-Technical Institute in 1986, one year after Gorbachev came to power. In December 1987, Khodorkovsky helped to form the Center for Inter-Industry Scientific and Technical Progress (MENATEP), a catch-all cooperative that sought to finance the work of thirteen of Khodorkovsky's fellow graduates of the Mendeleev Institute. They offered their skills in scientific research, particularly in chemistry, as well as in automation and computerization. One of their main sources of profit, however, stemmed from the buying and selling of computers. In August 1988, the cooperative was reconstituted into the Interbank Organization for Scientific and Technical Progress, also called MENATEP.

MENATEP officially received a charter to open the Commercial Innovative Bank on December 29, 1988, a joint venture with the Soviet Bank Zhilsotsbank. According to some reports, some of the early deposits of the bank were provided by the Komsomol Central Committee. In 1990, the Commercial Innovative Bank was rechartered, again with the name MENATEP, as a joint stock company, and Khodorkovsky became the chairman of the board of directors. It was said to be the first time in seventy years that individuals could openly buy stock in such an entity. To attract investors, Khodorkovsky also made the stockholders members of the MENATEP stockholders' club that was created in August 1991.[22] MENATEP became an active player in acquiring state enterprises when the state began a campaign to privatize state enterprises. MENATEP created a market for the vouchers issued by the state and used them to gain control of many enterprises that had just been privatized. In 1992, the bank created Rosprom as a holding company to oversee its industrial portfolio. While MENATEP directly controls some businesses, particularly in metallurgy and paper manufacturing, most of its forty or so industrial holdings are divided into six categories: chemicals, construction, textile, consumer goods, mining, and oil.[23] Its most prominent oil holding is YUKOS, the country's third largest oil company, which it obtained for a mere $309 million in one of the controversial "Loans for Shares" auctions conducted in 1995.

In May 1997, Khodorkovsky changed his title to become chairman of the board of Rosprom. This allowed him to devote more time to the bank's industrial holdings. Some of his actions have generated considerable criticism, particularly from minority stockholders in Rosprom's subsidiaries. Russia's Federal Securities Commission, for example, investigated the propriety of an $800 million loan that YUKOS took out by putting up as collateral assets in Samaraneftegas, one of its subsidiaries. Minority stockholders in Samaraneftegas also complained that the oil the company produced was sold at a steep discount to YUKOS, thereby transferring the profit on the transaction to YUKOS, with the result that Samaraneftegas operated at a loss.[24] In another instance, Rosprom was ordered to give back two large factories, the Volzhsky Pipe factory and Apatit, a chemical company that it privatized in 1994. The charge is that Rosprom failed to make the investments in particular companies, a condition of the purchase from the state.[25] Khodorkovsky was badly hurt by the combination of the August 17, 1998 currency devaluation and the drop in energy prices. Before the crisis, he had put up 30 percent of the share of YUKOS as collateral for loans for MENATEP from Western banks. As oil prices plummeted, however, so did the value of the stock. Consequently, the Western banks seized the collateral as their own to protect their loans.[26]

Not all of the oligarchs are products of the pre-market era. One of the youngest and, for that matter, newest, to enter the ranks of the oligarchs is Roman Abramovich. For some time, he was probably the least known—regarded almost as a "stealth" oligarch. Because few people even knew what he looked like, in 1999 the newspaper *Versiya* offered a reward to the first person who could find a photograph of him. But while he may have been the new man on the block, Abramovich's rise was rapid and his politics adroit. It was only in 2000, for example, that his name was listed among the ten most influential Russian businessmen. It is widely agreed that he owes most of his success to Boris Berezovsky. Under Berezovsky's patronage, Abramovich managed to win the confidence first of Yeltsin's daughter Tatiana Dyachenko and thus of Yeltsin himself, and then, in a maneuver common to the oligarchs who have survived, of Yeltsin's successor, Vladimir Putin. It was not by chance that Tatiana Dyachenko's husband, Alexei, headed East Coast Petroleum. This was an oil trading company that sold oil purchased from one of Sibneft's refineries, a company created by Berezovsky (and later, as we shall see, controlled by Abramovich).[27]

Abramovich seems to insulate himself from these intrigues. In a show of government favoritism, Putin and the anti-monopoly authorities stood by silently in March 2000 as Abramovich expanded his empire to form RUSSAL (Russian Aluminum), a monopoly, with another oligarch, Oleg Deripaska. Each owns 50 percent of the company's stock.[28] In turn, RUSSAL controls 80 percent of Russia's aluminum output and ranks second in world production. It also owns 25 percent of GAZ, the automobile manufacturer, which produces the Volga automobile and the Gazelle light truck.[29] (Abramovich travels in fast company. Deripaska and another partner, Mikhail Chernoi, as well as Russian Aluminum, were sued in a New York court in late 2000 for, among other things, money laundering, extortion, and attempted murder. Abramovich was not named in the suit.)[30]

Jewish and Non-Jewish "Oligarchs"

Had the Russian economic and political systems not been in flux, it is un-likely that any of the oligarchs we have studied would have achieved a similar degree of power, influence, and wealth. More likely, at least some of them would have been sentenced to jail. Their positions stand in sharp contrast to the non-Jewish oligarchs. We will not go into as much detail about their backgrounds, but each of the five leading non-Jewish oligarchs (at least as of August 16, 1998) owed their success to their positions in the former Soviet economic apparatus, something beyond the reach of their Jewish peers. For that matter, the likelihood is that had the USSR not disintegrated, at least one and probably three of the five non-Jewish oligarchs we will consider would have held the same positions they maintain today. The only difference is that they would have been ministers or vice ministers rather than owners. The best example is Rem Vyakhirev, until recently the president of Gazprom. He had worked his way up the ministry of the gas industry and in 1986 became first deputy minister. When the ministry was transformed into the private firm Gazprom, Vyakhirev remained number two to Viktor Chernomyrdin, who had been the minister and now became chairman of the management board until he was forced to retire in 2001. Vyakhirev took Chernomyrdin's place when Chernomyrdin became deputy prime minister in 1992.

In much the same way, Vagit Alekeprov began work in the petroleum industry and its bureaucracy in 1974. Ultimately, he rose to the post of act-ing minister of fuel and energy. Under his administration, the assets of the ministry were divided up into private entities. Not surprisingly, Alekeprov ended up becoming the president of Lukoil. It probably was more than co-incidence, but Lukoil grew to be the largest of the privatized petroleum op-erating companies; its main assets involved access to three major oil fields, one of which had previously been under Alekeprov's administrative control.

Vladimir Bogdanov, the president of Surgutneftegaz, Russia's second largest oil company, had also been a senior executive in the Ministry of En-ergy and Fuel. He served as general director of the division that, after privatization in 1993, he came to control. The pattern was much the same in the enterprises that managed to avoid coming under control of the banks. The vast majority of new owners had been managing directors during the Soviet era; they then moved into the CEO's chair after privatization, and usu-ally held the largest number of company shares.

Non-Jewish bankers did not move as automatically into their new posi-tions as those who were in control of raw materials and manufacturing en-terprises, but most of them had been spared the socially unacceptable, if not degrading, experiences of operating as *fartsovshchiki*. In other words, they also took advantage of "old boy" insider associations that had been established in the Soviet era. Again, they had links that were unavailable to most Jews.

At least until August 17, 1998, the most prominent and influential Russian banker was Vladimir Potanin, who headed the *Forbes* magazine list of the five richest Russians on June 22 of that year. Born in 1961, Potanin was the son of Oleg Potanin, a senior official in the elitist Ministry of Foreign Trade. This helped ease Vladimir's way into the Moscow Institute for International Relations, an elite school for those headed for work in the Ministry of Foreign Affairs, Foreign Trade, and the KGB. The younger Potanin chose Soiuzpromexport, an organization under the Ministry of Foreign Trade that dealt primarily with the export of nonferrous metals. He worked there from 1983 until 1990, and in 1991, when Gorbachev liberalized the economy, Potanin founded Interros, a cooperative foreign trade institute association that relied primarily on the access and familiarity with the same type of raw materials he had dealt with in Soiuzpromexport. Building on his success and on his accumulation of capital at Interros, he went on to form MFK (in English, the International Finance Company).[31] Calling once again on his connections, he then managed to utilize the funds of Vneshekonombank, the foreign trade bank, to provide capital in 1993 for his new start-up Oneximbank (the acronym for United Export/Import bank) and became its president.

With the help of both Interros and Oneximbank, Potanin built up what was arguably the largest financial and industrial empire in Russia. Unlike his Jewish competitors, he was able in the beginning to rely heavily on his family and his own insider connections.

The only other major non-Jewish banker, Vladimir Vinogradov, also became financially successful by building on his Soviet-era contacts. In fact, he was the only post-Soviet banking oligarch who actually had worked in a Soviet-era bank. Born in 1955, Vinogradov graduated from the Ordzhonikidze Moscow Aviation Institute. He then worked as a senior economist in Promstroibank, a Soviet state bank, and in October 1988 founded Inkombank, one of the country's first wholly private commercial banks, serving as chairman of the board of management and then becoming its president. Inkombank was established as a private limited partnership, and subsequently was converted into a joint stock bank on March 25, 1991. Several of the country's larger enterprises (at the time state-owned) put up most of the bank's initial capital. In the Russian way, many of the shareholders also became subsidiaries of the bank, including Magnitogorsk Steel, the Babayevskaya candy factory, and Sameko Metallurgy. Until its collapse on Black Monday, Inkombank also had substantial control of various timber operations, the Transneft Oil Pipeline, and the Sukhoi Aircraft Design Bureau, as well as several confectionery manufacturers.

🌐 *The Precariousness of Sudden Mobility*

That Jewish oligarchs had to rely much more on their own ingenuity and less on their connections with officials in the old regime may be impressive and may serve as a measure of just how determined and ingenious they were, but their positions provide no guarantee of the future. The impact of the collapse of the ruble and the moratorium on government debt did not differentiate between gentiles with connections and Jews without. It hit them all and only a limited number of those who had the foresight to move out of government securities before August 17 were spared.

However, if Russian history provides any lesson, it is that the incredible success enjoyed by those who only a short time earlier had been part of a marginal group may not endure. The very fact that so many of the newly rich are Jews, and that even before the economic collapse they were resented as a new, often extravagant class, can make Jews a convenient target. The deep resentment and antisemitism of the tsarist era never completely disappeared, especially in rural areas and among such groups as the Cossacks. Nor should it be forgotten that even within academic departments at institutions, as well as in some writers' groups, antisemitism was a deeply held tenet. Thus, groups from the far right like *Pamyat* targeted some of the Jewish oligarchs even when economic times were relatively good. For example, *Pamyat* mounted a series of demonstrations in front of Fridman's Alfa bank in November 1997, to protest what it claimed were "the bank's anti-Russian activities."[32] "Zionist Banks—Out of Russia" was one of the main slogans.

After Black Monday, the attacks became much louder and frequent. Berezovsky's earlier boast that six of the banks (including five run and owned by Jews) controlled half the country's assets all but guaranteed that if anything went wrong, the banks and their owners would be targeted. Subsequently, many came to understand that his boast was exaggerated, but the damage had nonetheless been done. Is it more than coincidence that the only two oligarchs so far threatened with jail have been Gusinsky and Berezovsky, both of whom fled the country?

Triggered by the economic collapse, the Jewish oligarchs in particular, and Jews in general became the target of venomous attacks not just by fringe groups like *Pamyat,* but by communist Duma deputies, including Albert Makashov in November 1998, and Viktor Ilyukhin in December of the same year.[33] Deputy Ilyukhin, among other charges, accused the Jews of conducting genocide against the Russian people.[34] Their remarks echoed earlier attacks by Nikolai Kondratenko, the elected governor of the southern *oblast'* of Krasnodar.[35] Some Muscovites insist that all of this is background noise and that antisemitism is not new in Russia, or anywhere else, for that matter. But the recurring pattern here—repression followed by an opening of long-closed doors—suggests that just as doors were closed tightly to Jews after being opened widely during the Communist era, so the same could happen again in the near future. Whether or not that openness could have been sustained had the Russian economy not collapsed is debatable. After the collapse of the economy and the preeminent status of the Jewish oligarchs, it is hard to see how a repeat of the earlier repressions can be avoided.

NOTES

1. Thomas C. Owen, *The Corporation under Russian Law 1800–1917* (Cambridge: Cambridge University Press, 1991), 119, 174.

2. Ibid., 116–62.

3. Ibid., 122, 161, 171 (Jews were allowed to own some land in some cities), 173.

4. Ibid., 175.

5. *Washington Post,* October 17, 1997, 1, A-34.

6. *Economicheskaya gazeta,* no. 8 (February 1997): 32.

7. *Rossiiskaya gazeta,* March 14, 1995, 1.

8. *Washington Post,* October 17, 1997, A34.

9. *Izvestiia,* July 1, 1997.

10. *Izvestiia,* September 7, 1997.

11. *The Moscow Times,* April 6, 2001.

12. *The Moscow Times,* March 6, 2001.

13. *The Economist,* April 22, 1995, 69.

14. Ibid., and the *Washington Post,* April 7, 1995, D4.

15. March 7, 1995, 1.

16. *Washington Post,* April 7, 1995, D4.

17. *Boston Globe,* March 13, 1994, A114.

18. *Rossiiskaya gazeta,* November 19, 1994, 3; March 7, 1995, 1.

19. *The Moscow News,* no. 6 (February 10–16, 1995).

20. Paul Klebnikov, *Godfather of the Kremlin* (New York: Harcourt, 2000), 11–15.

21. *The Moscow Times,* August 22, 1997.

22. *Kommersant,* September 2, 1991, 13.

23. *Russian Review,* November 3, 1997, 14.

24. *Interfax,* February 7, 1998; *Financial Times,* July 16, 1998, 2.

25. *The Moscow News,* March 19, 1998.

26. *The Wall Street Journal,* October 12, 1998, A14.

27. *The Moscow Times,* June 1, 1999.

28. *Izvestiia,* February 1, 2001.

29. *Johnson's List,* No. 5018, January 10, 2001, IM8.

30. *Financial Times,* December 20, 2000, 3.

31. *Russian Review,* November 3, 1997, 16.

32. *The Moscow Times,* November 26, 1997.

33. *The Moscow Times,* December 17, 1998.

34. *The Moscow Times,* December 16, 1998.

35. *The New York Times,* November 15, 1998, 3; *The Moscow Times,* November 10, 1998, 1; November 12, 1998, 2 & 8; November 28, 1998; *Jerusalem Report,* November 23, 1998, 64.

SIX

ROBERT J. BRYM

Russian Antisemitism, 1996–2000

The Economic and Political Context

On August 17, 1998, the Russian ruble collapsed. Until then, the government, chronically unable to collect taxes, had been selling ruble-denominated treasury bills to finance expenditures. It had compensated buyers for their fear it would not be able to redeem the bills by offering annual interest rates as high as 100 percent. Then, in mid-August 1998, buyers decided that this arrangement was too risky. They stopped purchasing treasury bills. As a result, the value of the bills (and therefore the value of the ruble) dropped. Domestic banks, which held much of the debt and most of the stock in the ruble-denominated stock market, became insolvent. Prices, especially for imported goods, soared. Because some banks shut their doors, many people were unable to withdraw their savings. Those who had cash bought up as many goods as they could before prices rose still higher. Goods swiftly disappeared from the shelves of stores. By mid-October, the ruble had lost two-thirds of its value and Russia entered its worst financial crisis since the fall of Communism.

Inevitably, President Yeltsin had to apportion blame and give at least the appearance of a fresh start. In particular, reform-minded Prime Minister Sergei Kiriyenko had to go. Unable to replace him with Viktor Chernomyrdin due to resistance in the Duma, Yeltsin agreed in September to a compromise candidate, Yevgeniy Primakov, a man hailed by *Nezavisimaya gazeta* as "the Russian Churchill." Some compromise. Some Churchill. Primakov was linked to the Soviet-era KGB. He is an Arabist who enjoyed close working relationships with Saddam Hussein and Muammar Gaddafi. He is also an ardent opponent of U.S. foreign policy who lacks training in economics; in fact, he had no experience in running an economy or even a business. He quickly established good relations with the Communist-dominated Duma. His early appointments included Yuriy Maslyukov as first deputy prime minister and Viktor Gerashchenko as director of the Central Bank. Maslyukov was the former director of Gosplan, the Soviet-era central planning agency, and Gerashchenko was the director of the Central Bank in the 1980s. Infamous for printing money and subsidizing inefficient state-owned industries, Gerashchenko was once described by *The Economist* as the "world's worst central bank director."

For many parliamentarians and citizens as well, blaming Kiriyenko and replacing him with Primakov did not go far enough. Thus in early October 1998, General Albert Makashov, a hard-line Communist in the Duma, told a television interviewer that the time had come to expel all the Jews from Russia. Later elaborating on this theme, Makashov explained that all of Russia's economic woes were the fault of the Jews, some of whom should be jailed. In early November, his remarks were debated in the Duma. A weakly worded resolution was proposed. It deplored racism and called Makashov's remarks "sharp and bordering on crudeness." Despite its mild tone, the resolution was defeated. Communists and hard-line nationalists rejected it almost unanimously. Even the moderate Our Russian Home party was able to muster fewer than half its members in support of the resolution, which apparently the majority saw as unnecessary or too harsh.

At the end of December 1998, Genadiy Zyuganov, head of the Communist Party of the Russian Federation, issued an open letter explaining his party's position on the Jewish question.[1] It is not Jews *per se* who are the problem, he noted, but Zionists. Zyuganov's definition of Zionism and his analysis of its role in causing Russia's problems are worth quoting at length:

> Zionism [is] a variety of the theory and practice of the most aggressive imperialist circles, which strive for world supremacy. In this respect it is related to fascism. The only difference between them is that Hitlerite Nazism acted under the mask of German nationalism and strove for world supremacy openly, while Zionism . . . acts in a concealed manner. . . . Our people are not blind. They cannot but see that the Zionization of the governmental authorities of Russia was one of the causes of the country's present-day catastrophic situation, of the mass impoverishment and extinction of its population. They cannot close their eyes to the aggressive and destructive role of Zionist capital in the disruption of the Russian economy and in the misappropriation of its national property. They are right when they ask how it

could happen that the key positions in several branches of the economy were seized during privatization mainly by the representatives of one nationality. . . . Among the people there is a growing awareness that the criminal course pursued by the anti-popular and non-national oligarchy, which seized power, underlies all their present-day misfortunes. It is only the restoration of the sovereignty of the people and a resolute change in the social and economic course that will ensure the revival and prosperity of Russia.

Zyuganov insisted that his party was merely anti-Zionist, not anti-Jewish. However, the fact that he could, in virtually the same breath, call the financial oligarchy a "non-national" group *and* a group composed mainly of "representatives of one nationality" suggests considerable confusion in his mind, as indeed in the minds of most Russians, about the difference between Zionists and Jews.

Two Views of Russian Antisemitism

Should we be alarmed by the words of Makashov and Zyuganov or should they be interpreted as the utterings of men who represent only a small, powerless, and marginal minority? More generally, is antisemitism likely to pose a real threat to Russia's Jews in the next few years or can it be dismissed as a movement likely to have few tangible consequences either for Russia's Jews or for the course of political events in the country?

Opinion on the dangers of Russian antisemitism has been divided since the days of perestroika. Nor has opinion been harmonized by the twenty or so sample surveys conducted since 1990 that deal in whole or in part with Russian Jews. For example, in 1994 political scientist James Gibson of the University of Houston concluded his analysis of one survey with the following claims:

1. The tendency to seek Jewish scapegoats has not materialized in Russia.
2. Few Russians perceive Jews as responsible for the problems of the country.
3. The Russians most likely to hold antisemitic views are highly unlikely to influence Russian politics because they come from powerless groups.
4. Few Russians support discrimination against Jews.
5. Antisemitism is no more widespread in Russia than it is in the United States.[2]

I have interpreted the results of several surveys differently.[3] However, rather than reiterate the methodological and theoretical issues that separate Gibson and me,[4] I restrict myself here to examining two of the most recent polls concerning Russian Jews. The first survey was sponsored by the American

Jewish Committee (AJC) and was conducted between January 12 and February 7, 1996, by ROMIR, one of Russia's leading polling firms. The second was conducted by VCIOM, the oldest and perhaps most respected polling firm in the country, between November 20 and 25, 1998, in the wake of Makashov's speeches and the Duma's failure to condemn them. Each poll surveyed a representative nationwide sample of about 1,600 Russian citizens. The two surveys allow us to re-evaluate the optimistic and pessimistic interpretations of Russian antisemitism in the light of current developments. In particular, they provide us with an opportunity to examine what I shall call the "Makashov effect"—the polarization of opinion that occurs when political leaders legitimize antisemitism in a time of crisis. Understanding the Makashov effect will help us to assess the potential of Russian antisemitism over the next few years.

🏵 *The Makashov Effect I: The Disappearing Middle*

The 1996 AJC survey asked numerous questions about Jews. The responses to one of them is shown in the left half of Table 6.1. Respondents were asked: "Do you feel that Jews have too much influence, too little influence, or the right amount of influence in our society?" Fourteen percent replied "too much," 49 percent said "too little" or "the right amount," and 37 percent answered "don't know." In terms of both wording and response patterns, this item is typical of questions posed in other similar surveys. Most surveys show that roughly 15 percent of Russians hold negative opinions about Jews and about a third claim to hold no opinion.

Table 6.1
The Makashov Effect I:
Attitudes Toward Jews, 1996 and 1998 (in percent)

	1996: Pre-Makashov (Jews have too much influence in our society)	1998: Post-Makashov (Agreement with Makashov's speech)
antipathy	14	30
don't know	37	11
sympathy	49	59
total	100	100

The third of respondents who answer "don't know" present a major problem for interpreting the results. The problem occurs because "don't know" almost certainly means different things to different respondents. For some, "don't know" implies apathy or utter lack of interest. For others, it implies ambivalence or inconclusive grappling with issues. For still others, it implies distrust or refusal to reveal sensitive or controversial opinion. Much hinges on which of these social types actually predominates. If the great majority of "don't knows" is apathetic, the level of antisemitism in Russia is probably much the same as in many other countries, East and West. If, on the other hand, most Russians answer "don't know" because they are debating the credibility of antisemitic statements or because they privately believe such statements but refuse to make their beliefs public, the potential for the growth of antisemitism is greater.

Much of the academic debate about the level of antisemitism in Russia concerns this very issue. Some researchers have shown that people who answer "don't know" also tend to support anti-reform, Communist, or extreme-nationalist ideas and personalities. They conclude that many of the "don't knows" are potential or "closet" antisemites. Other researchers have shown that people who answer "don't know" on questions concerning Jews also tend to answer "don't know" on other questions; these interpreters conclude that most of the "don't knows" are apathetic.[5] In both cases, the analysis is indirect and the inference uncertain.

The 1996 and 1998 surveys allow us to take a different analytical tack. Instead of correlating "don't know" responses with responses to other questionnaire items, and inferring the meaning of the correlations, we can compare what happens to "don't know" responses under both normal and crisis conditions. The situation in early 1996 was about as normal as it gets in post-Communist Russia. The ruble was stable, goods were on the shelves, there was relative stability of senior political personnel, and prominent elected officials were not broadcasting inflammatory remarks about Jews and thereby legitimizing anti-Jewish sentiment. In late 1998, the situation was just the opposite. Following Makashov's speeches, fewer than 30 percent of Russians polled in the VCIOM survey believed that his statements should *not* be the subject of debate in the Duma.

I surmise that the political and economic crisis of late 1998, together with the legitimization of public debate on the Jewish question, had different effects on the different types of respondents who answered "don't know" in normal times. Specifically, deeply apathetic respondents tended to remain apathetic; ambivalent respondents were inclined to take a stand; and distrustful respondents were likely to "come out of the closet" and state their true views. I therefore expect the response pattern to questions concerning the Makashov affair to depend on whether most of the "don't knows" were apathetic, on the one hand, or ambivalent and distrustful, on the other. In the former case, the distribution of responses in the midst of a crisis would look much the same as the distribution in normal times. In the latter case, the number of "don't knows" would fall. Like a bar magnet placed on a tray of iron filings, the crisis would polarize opinion around the extremes.

Comparing the left and right halves of Table 6.1, we see that the crisis of late 1998 did indeed function like a bar magnet. When respondents were asked in 1996 how much influence Jews have in society, 37 percent said they don't know. When respondents were asked in 1998 about whether they agree with the contents of Makashov's speeches, only 11 percent said they don't know. Economic and political unrest, coupled with Makashov's speeches and the highly publicized inaction of the Duma, apparently polarized opinions. Fully 30 percent of Russians who had heard about Makashov's speeches agreed that Jews should be jailed or expelled for their alleged role in causing Russia's ruin. This suggests a level of anti-Jewish feeling considerably higher than the roughly 15 percent typically measured in the midst of non-crisis situations.[6]

✡ The Makashov Effect II: The Widening Gap

Apart from the issue of "don't knows," most survey research on Russian Jews has been plagued by the problem of weak and inconsistent effects. True, some surveys show that age, education, income, political affiliation, and other variables are associated with some responses to particular items on questionnaires about Jews. It is sometimes said, for example, that antisemitism is concentrated among older, poorer people with little formal education and should therefore not be viewed as a serious threat to Russian Jewry. Often, however, such associations are found only for *some* of the questionnaire items about Jews; other surveys fail to replicate the findings; predicted associations are in the opposite direction from those that are discovered; and even when they are in the predicted direction, associations typically explain little of the variation in responses to the item on the questionnaire.

Some of these problems are illustrated in Table 6.2, which reproduces data from the 1996 AJC survey. Comparing older and younger Russians, the less-well-off and the more well-to-do, the better-educated and those without much formal education, and the employed and the unemployed, we find small and in some cases negligible differences between these subgroups. Moreover, contrary to what one might expect—and contrary to what is intermittently reported in the literature—antisemitic attitudes are slightly more common among *younger* Russians, those with *higher* education, and those who are *employed* than among older Russians, those with little formal education, and those who are unemployed.

Table 6.2.
*"Do you feel that Jews have too much influence, too little influence,
or the right amount of influence in our society?"*
(percent "too much," 1996)

Age	
18–43	13.9
44–93	13.6
Income	
< 45,000	12.0
45,000 +	15.4
Education	
< PTU	14.8
PTU +	12.3
Employed	
no	12.0
yes	16.0

It seems, however, that weak and inconsistent effects are more common under normal conditions, like those of early 1996, than under crisis conditions like those of late 1998. In a crisis period, *political* variables in particular have bigger effects on antisemitic attitudes. Thus, as Table 6.3 shows, in 1996 antipathy toward Jews was just as widespread among democrats as it was among supporters of the Communist and extreme nationalist parties. Similarly, antisemitism was just as common among those who believed Russia was headed in the right direction as among those who believed it was headed in the wrong direction. By late 1998, however, anti-Jewish sentiment was twice as common among supporters of the extreme nationalist and Communist parties, and among people who believed Russia was headed in the wrong direction, than among democrats and people who thought Russia was headed in the right direction. As Table 6.4 illustrates, the Makashov effect not only clarified the minds of respondents who normally claimed not to hold opinions about Jews, but it also sharpened differences among political groups on the Jewish question (see also Table 6.5).

🕎 Conclusion

In sum, the economic, political, and social crisis that hit Russia in August 1998 had discernible effects on public opinion about Jews. In the context of economic instability and political uncertainty, some political leaders were partly successful in mobilizing the public around the Jewish ques-

ROBERT J. BRYM

Table 6.3.
American Jewish Committee Survey (ROMIR),
12 January–7 February 1996 (n = 1,581)
"Do you feel that the following groups have too much influence,
too little influence, or the right amount of influence in our society?"
(Jews, in percent)

Group	Too Little	Right Amount	Too Much	Don't know/ No answer	Total*
Total	21	29	14	37	101
Age					
18–29	25	34	14	28	101
30–39	20	27	13	40	100
40–49	24	29	19	28	100
50–59	18	27	15	39	99
60+	19	27	9	45	100
Education					
Elementary	17	28	11	44	100
Secondary	23	28	16	34	101
Higher	24	35	13	28	100
Presidential Preference					
Democratic	21	29	11	39	100
Comm/Patriotic	21	28	17	34	100
Russia's Direction					
Right	21	35	13	32	101
Wrong	22	28	15	35	100
DK/ NA	17	25	10	48	100

* Does not always equal 100 due to rounding.

Table 6.4.
The Makashov Effect II: Antipathy toward Jews by Presidential Preference,
1996 and 1998 (in percent)

Democratic	
1996: Pre-Makashov	11
1998: Post-Makashov	23
Communist/Patriotic	
1996: Pre-Makashov	17
1998: Post-Makashov	43

Table 6.5.
All-Russian Center for Public Opinion Research Survey (VCIOM),
20–25 November 1998 (n = 1,600)
"What do you think about Makashov's speeches?"

Group	Sympathetic	Disagree	Don't Know	Total*
Total	30	59	11	100
Age				
18–29	26	64	10	100
30–39	26	61	12	99
40–49	28	60	12	100
50–59	42	50	8	100
60+	28	60	12	100
Education				
Elementary	38	35	27	100
Secondary	31	58	11	100
Higher	22	71	7	100
Presidential Preference				
Democratic	23	67	10	100
Comm/Patriotic	43	44	13	100
Russia's Direction				
Right	17	72	12	101
Wrong	33	57	10	100
DK/NA	19	62	18	99

* Does not always equal 100 due to rounding.

tion. As many who had not previously articulated their positions took a stand, some became more supportive of the Jews, but more became negatively predisposed. And, perhaps ominously, the forces both pro and con aligned themselves to an unprecedented degree with particular political parties and personalities.

Lessons of History and Future Prospects

In concluding my analysis, I want to draw out some implications that will be relevant over the next number of years. Before doing so, however, it will prove useful to take a more historical perspective. In particular, I want to comment on the connection between public opinion and state policy concerning Jews in the Soviet era.

In principle, anti-Jewish actions—employment restrictions, emigration quotas, attacks on Jewish property, physical assaults on Jews—may result from state policy, public opinion, or a combination of the two. It is evident that anti-Jewish sentiment among the public formed a deep reservoir throughout the twentieth century. However, state policy was usually decisive in determining the intensity of anti-Jewish action. Consider just three historical episodes:

1. The more than 1,500 pogroms that broke out in Ukraine and Belarus between 1917 and 1920 were in general suppressed by the Red Army, and the Jews under Lenin achieved unprecedented upward mobility, partly because Jews tended to be loyal to the Bolsheviks and partly because they were a relatively highly educated group, in a society that had lost much of its educated elite in war and revolution. Jews were urgently needed by the state, and were therefore protected and even favored so long as they were prepared to forego business activities and non-socialist forms of communal autonomy, including religion.

2. By 1930, Russian and other non-Jewish groups had made rapid strides in education and Jews were not as desperately needed as they had been just a decade earlier. More important, Stalin had embarked on a policy of building "socialism in one country" instead of world revolution. His principal tools: a monolithic Party, a highly centralized economy, a homogeneous culture, and the constant fear of foreign threats in the public mind. The Jews stood in the way of his policy. After all, they still enjoyed semiautonomous cultural institutions. They enjoyed strong ties to relatives and friends in the United States, Palestine, and elsewhere. As a creative intellectual elite, they represented a challenge to cultural and political uniformity. Therefore, Stalin found it necessary to eradicate Jewish institutions, eliminate Jewish communal leaders, and stage propaganda campaigns and trials against groups composed mainly of Jews.

3. By about 1970, the Jews had become largely redundant to the labor requirements of the Soviet state. The leadership realized that Jewish emigration could help the state achieve certain useful goals, including ridding the country of troublesome dissidents and paving the way to increased trade with the United States. Hence the relaxation of restrictions against emigration. By 1980, however, labor shortages were becoming widespread in the European part of the USSR and a growing number of hard-liners were beginning to fear the loss of technical labor power. In this context, emigration restrictions were re-imposed. It was only when perestroika and the collapse of Communism transformed the labor short-

age into an unemployment problem that the emigration movement picked up steam again.[7]

These three episodes suggest that the Soviet leadership was able to manipulate anti-Jewish action pretty much at will. Anti-Jewish action might be suppressed, as it was from 1917 to 1924; it might be elicited, as it was from 1930 to 1953; or it might be turned off, then on, then off again, as it was from 1970 to 1991. In all three cases, the level of anti-Jewish action depended more on the leadership's policies and perceived needs than on the level of anti-Jewish sentiment in the Russian population.

I think the situation today is broadly similar. The fate of Russian Jewry depends less on the level of anti-Jewish sentiment in the general population than on the policies and perceived needs of the people who control the Duma and especially the presidency.[8] Just like the Soviet-era leadership, Russian political leaders today can choose to dry up the country's ample reservoir of anti-Jewish sentiment or can draw on it for their own sustenance.[9]

At the time of this writing (early 2002), two factors render the situation of Russian Jews less precarious than it was as recently as 1999. First, following the December 1999 elections, the Communists no longer dominate the Duma. For the first time in a decade of free elections, a pro-government bloc holds the balance of power. Antisemitism may still be an option for the Communists, but in their weakened state they pose less of a threat to the Jews. Second, the continuing war in Chechnya has diverted public attention from the "Jewish problem." Ethnic animosity and nationalist sentiment are still widespread in Russia, but they are increasingly directed against Islamic separatists and peoples from the Caucasus, not Jews.

On the other hand, the resignation of Boris Yeltsin at the end of 1999 and the victory of Vladimir Putin in the March 2000 presidential election inserted a big unknown into the equation. Putin was a senior KGB spy, and just a few weeks before Yeltsin appointed him prime minister in August 1999, he was seen placing flowers on the grave of his former boss, Yuri Andropov, the former Soviet leader who headed the KGB for fifteen years. He has taken a hard-line stance on Chechnya and expressed the need for a strong, "paternalistic" Russian state. Thus far, however, Putin has gone out of his way to demonstrate publicly his support for Jewish culture and religion, showing up at Jewish holiday celebrations and synagogue dedications and embracing the Hasidic Chabad leadership which has been trying, largely successfully, to wrest control of Russian Jewry's religious institutions.[10] However, as the Makashov affair suggests, playing the Jewish card in a time of crisis is likely to remain an option in Russian politics for some time to come.

🌀 *Postscript*

Largely in reaction to the economic and political events of 1998, the flow of Jewish migrants from Russia to Israel more than doubled in 1999, reaching 31,100. In 2000, however, the rate of emigration to Israel fell 40 percent. The downward trend continued the following year. In the first half of 2001, only 4,820 Jews left Russia for Israel, indicating that the rate of emigration to Israel in 2001 was less than a third the 1999 rate. Meanwhile, the rate of emigration to the United States, Germany, and other Western countries remained stable in 1999 and 2000, at roughly 14,500 Russian Jews per year.[11]

The second Palestinian Intifada undoubtedly dissuaded many Russian Jews from moving to Israel. However, the decline in Russian-Jewish immigration began well before this latest uprising, suggesting that much of the decline in emigration rates was the direct result of an easing of tensions in Russia itself. Relative stability returned to the country after Yeltsin's last years in office and the Russian economy improved dramatically in 2001 and the first half of 2002. Moreover, Russian-Jewish communal life has flourished, providing an increasingly attractive alternative to emigration for some Russian Jews. As Chaim Ben-Yaakov, Russia's chief Reform rabbi, said in 2001:

> The Jews of the CIS . . . know there are very wonderful things about Israel, but that there are also big problems: Culture problems, human relations problems, weather problems, and, of course, security problems. Meanwhile, the economic situation in Russia has stabilized. Some Jews have businesses and are doing well. They ask themselves why they should take the risk and start from scratch.[12]

Or in the words of Berl Lazar, chief rabbi of the Chabad movement in the former Soviet Union:

> It is no longer a source of shame to be Jewish in Moscow, or, for that matter, in Russia. Being Jewish is in style. Nowadays, Jews are seen as being identified with the free professions, with financial prosperity, with education. We're advertising Passover matza all over Moscow, under the banner of "Matzot from Israel." If we had put up advertisements like that a few years ago, people would have told us it was liable to cause a pogrom.[13]

Without in any way minimizing the significance of these encouraging signs, I think it would be wrong to assume that the Makashov affair was an aberration and that antisemitism has no future in Russia. Antisemitic counter-trends still were running strong in 2000 and 2001. For example, in 2000 a popular Russian television anchor asked his viewers if they believe Jews use Christian blood to make matzoh during Passover. He found the answers split about 50–50. In the same year in Ryazan, south of Moscow, masked men stormed into a Jewish school and vandalized the building as they shouted "Death to the Yids" while terrified children and teachers huddled together. Meanwhile, the newly elected mayor of Kursk, a city of half a million, proclaimed his victory "a success over the Jewish conspiracy—the filth" and proceeded to rail against the "Jewish oligarchy" and the *Va'ad*, the Federation of Jewish Organizations of Russia.[14]

Alexander Mikhailov, the mayor in question, concluded his diatribe by claiming that President Putin is sympathetic to his antisemitic opinions. Of course, this claim may lack substance. Still, Putin refused to condemn Mikhailov, perhaps fearing that doing so would alienate his supporters in the pro-Communist "Red Belt" south of Moscow, long considered a bastion of antisemites. Some Duma deputies demanded Mikhailov's removal from office, but no legislation made it to the floor. As is usual in Russia these days, the government did nothing to combat an outbreak of antisemitism.[15] This suggests that antisemitism remains part of Russia's cultural repertoire, ready to be invoked under the right political circumstances.[16]

NOTES

I am indebted to Larisa Kosova of VCIOM in Moscow for her assistance in obtaining the 1998 data set referred to in this paper, and to David Singer of the American Jewish Committee in New York for permission to re-analyze data from the 1996 AJC survey. Zvi Gitelman kindly provided useful comments on a draft version. Funding was generously provided by Robert Johnson, Director of the Centre for Russian and East European Studies at the University of Toronto, and Michael Marrus, Dean of Graduate Studies at the University of Toronto.

1. Genadiy Zyuganov, "Statement by the Chairman of the Central Committee of the Communist Party of the Russian Federation" (29 December 1998), on the World Wide Web at http://www/fsumonitor.com/stories/122998zyug.shtml (January 20, 1999).

2. James L. Gibson, "Understandings of Anti-Semitism in Russia: An Analysis of the Politics of Anti-Jewish Attitudes," *Slavic Review* 53 (1994): 805–806.

3. Robert J. Brym and Andrei Degtyarev, "Anti-Semitism in Moscow: Results of an October 1992 Survey," *Slavic Review* 52 (1993): 1–12; Robert J. Brym, "Anti-Semitism in Moscow: A Re-examination," *Slavic Review* 53 (1994): 842–55; Robert J. Brym, "The Spread of Anti-Semitism in Moscow on the Eve of the 1993 Parliamentary Election," *East European Jewish Affairs* 24, no. 1 (1994): 31–37; Robert J. Brym with the assistance of Rozalina Ryvkina, *The Jews of Moscow, Kiev and Minsk: Identity, Anti-Semitism, Emigration* (New

York: New York University Press, 1994); Robert J. Brym, "Russian Attitudes Towards Jews: An Update," *East European Jewish Affairs* 26, no. 1 (1996): 55–64.

4. On which see Brym, "Anti-Semitism in Moscow: A Reexamination"; Brym, "Russian Attitudes Towards Jews."

5. Brym, "Anti-Semitism in Moscow: A Reexamination"; James L. Gibson, "Misunderstandings of Anti-Semitism in Russia: An Analysis of the Politics of Anti-Jewish Attitudes," *Slavic Review* 53 (1994): 829–35; Ellen Callaghan, "Alienation, Apathy, or Ambivalence? Don't Knows and Democracy in Russia," *Slavic Review* 55 (1996): 25–63.

6. I say "suggests" advisedly. Actually demonstrating the Makashov effect would require a longitudinal research design. It might be claimed that I exaggerate the Makashov effect because many apathetic respondents were filtered out by the screening question asking whether they had heard about Makashov's speeches. However, the level of apathy among those who did not hear about the speeches seems to be significantly *lower* than the level of apathy in the entire sample. Thus, in the entire sample, 31 percent of respondents did not support any particular presidential candidate or said they would not participate in elections, but among those who did not hear about Makashov's speeches, the figure was only 24 percent.

7. Brym with Ryvkina, *The Jews of Moscow,* 66–75.

8. Similarly, in the former Yugoslavia, ethnic conflict in the early 1990s was most intense not where ethnic prejudice was relatively high (e.g., Macedonia) but where ethnic elites were highly successful in mobilizing the population to help them maintain or gain power (e.g., Bosnia). See Dusko Sekulic, Garth Massey, and Randy Hodson, "Who Were the Yugoslavs? Failed Sources of a Common Identity in Former Yugoslavia," *American Sociological Review* 59 (1994): 83–97. And during the Holocaust, Jews were killed in their proportionally greatest numbers not where hatred of the Jews was most intense (e.g., Romania) but where the Nazi bureaucracy was best organized (e.g., Holland). See Zygmunt Bauman, *Modernity and the Holocaust* (Ithaca, N.Y.: Cornell University Press, 1989).

9. Some observers, such as Alan Dershowitz, assert that in the current geopolitical and economic environment, Russia could not long resist human rights pressures from the United States and institutions that it dominates, such as the IMF. Based on past experience with Russia and current experience with China, I question the validity of this assertion. See Brym with Ryvkina, *The Jews of Moscow,* 66–75.

10. Robert J. Brym and Larisa Kosova, "The V. Putin Phenomenon: The Morphology and Semantics of Mass Popularity," *Economic and Social Change: Monitoring Public Opinion* 3 (2000): 18–22. [In Russian.]

11. Mark Tolts, "Russian Jewish Migration in the Post-Soviet Era," *Revue Européenne des Migrations Internationales* 16, no. 3 (2000): 183–99; Mark Tolts, "Jewish Population of the Russian Federation, 1989–1999," in Wolf Moskovich, ed., *Jews and Slavs,* vol. 9 [in press]; Mark Tolts, "Jewish Population and Migration in the Former Soviet Union," paper presented at the 13th World Congress of Jewish Studies (Jerusalem, 2001); Mark Tolts, personal correspondence, August 8, 2001.

12. Uriya Shavit, "Staying Put in Moscow," *Ha'aretz* (English Internet Edition), April 6, 2001, on the World Wide Web at http://www3.haaretz.co.il/eng/htmls/1_1.htm (July 14, 2001).

13. Ibid.

14. Lev Gorodetsky, "Russian Gov't Not Doing Enough against Anti-Semitism, Reports Find," *Jewish Telegraphic Agency* (February 11, 2001), on the World Wide Web at http://www.jta.org/story.asp?story=6999 (August 8, 2001); Phil Ittner, "Concern in Russia over

Anti-Semitism Outbreak: Some Say Putin Could Do More," *San Francisco Chronicle,* February 14, 2001, A14, on the World Wide Web at http://www.sfgate.com/cgi-bin/article.cgi?file=/chronicle/archive/2001/02/14/MN73287.DTL&type=printable (August 8, 2001).

15. Gorodetsky, ibid.

16. Markus Mathyl, "The Rise of Political Anti-Semitism in Post-Soviet Russia," *Anti-Semitism Worldwide 1999/2000,* on the World Wide Web at http://www.tau.ac.il/Anti-semitism/99–2000/mathyl.htm (July 14, 2001).

RECONSTRUCTING
JEWISH COMMUNITIES

Part Three

SEVEN

❧

MARTIN HORWITZ

The Widening Gap between Our Model of Russian Jewry and the Reality (1989–99)

This chapter is based upon my experience working in Russia and Ukraine over the past seven years, where I observed the new Jewish communal structures, investigated the problems and potential of their organizations, and made small community grants to their newborn community groups. The "widening gap" of my title comes from constantly being struck by the vast difference between the questions asked me about that life, or raised in both the press and in scholarly articles, and the changed reality of that Jewish life.

Because my attempts to describe the two opposing cliffs abutting this gap and the process of erosion that seems to have created it were provoked partially by the wording of a call to the conference at which this chapter was first presented, I shall start by examining the language and its presuppositions in the conference proposal.

❧ Jewish Life After the USSR: A Community in Transition

The organizers of the conference held at the Davis Center for Russian Studies at Harvard University in February 1998 proposed that "Jews in Russia have had their ups and downs. Periodically they have been openly accepted in positions of influence in the arts and business and even on occasion in government. This openness usually occurs in the aftermath of a major shift in regime or at a time of stress, as for example right after the Bolshevik revolution or during World War II. At other times Jews have been the victims of spontaneous as well as organized anti-Semitism."

I believe that almost every sentence in this paragraph *initially* seems correct, but upon examination the statements are either basically wrong or prompt misleading generalizations.

Let us take the sentences in order: "Jews have had their ups and downs. Periodically they have been openly accepted in positions of influence in the arts and business and even on occasion in government." First, it is precisely in the arts that Jews have almost always been accepted in positions of influence (with the exception of the years 1948–50, when Soviet politburo member Andrei Zhdanov terrorized the intelligentsia). *Business* as understood in a capitalist sense did not officially exist during the Soviet period. Jews were always "over-represented" in almost all professional and administrative fields because they generally lived in urban environments and had a powerful desire for education. They were even on occasion highly visible in the government—here the word *periodically* is misleading, but basically it too reveals the irrelevance of trying to use these factors as "clues" to the "state of post-Soviet Jewry." Such factors might have provided useful clues when outside observers were dealing with the closed system that Soviet society presented to the world, but they certainly are obsolete gauges for evaluating the community as it has evolved over the past decade.

Back to our quotation: "This openness" occurs in the aftermath of a "major shift in regime" or at a "time of stress, as for example right after the Bolshevik revolution or during World War II." Again, a closer look reminds us that the circumstances are now more complicated. Since August 1991, there has been no *regime* in the sense that the term has traditionally applied to Russia or Ukraine. Russian politics has its unique nature, as does British or American or Danish or Nigerian politics, but there is no solid, fixed regime whose "shifts" in policy depend on an inner battle with some kind of "stress" to that entire system.

Finally, I must challenge the old concept that considers the nature and amount of antisemitism, some of which is "organized" and the other "spontaneous." It should be stressed that antisemitism in Russia—the country where the word *pogrom* originated, is not just a concept. It is an emotional, knee-jerk reflex, an automatic aid that brings attention, engenders a political effect inside the United States, and even raises money to hold conferences. But the question about whether the pogroms were spontaneous or organized really reflects the thinking of analysts of tsarist Russia. In evaluating the period from 1917 until 1991, I cannot think of analytically useful examples of "spontaneous anti-Semitism." Official Soviet government and Party policy's antisemitic elements, yes. But even these were not specifically "organized." The concept reflects old thinking that can lead to confusion if one regards the appearance of an antisemitic publication, statement, or even act of vandalism as signaling a change in policy somewhere higher up. Though it is true that some Jews living in Russia also react this way depending upon their age, for scholars studying Russian society, adherence to this paradigm may signal the use of a long outdated conceptual model.

One final example: It is the issue raised as to whether the region's Jews will establish their own explicit identity and their own communal institutions. By 1993, Jews had actively created these institutions, benefited from them, or were indifferent to them. The point of decision had long passed.

What has changed to make our old model, our old paradigm, our old questions so outdated and inadequate? What has changed to render so much of our writing on this subject less and less relevant?

Before providing the data accumulated during my personal experience as a grant-maker during the past decade and more, I shall back up my critique of the outdated mindset and scholarly and journalistic agenda regarding Jewish life after the fall of the Soviet Union. The following list of unnoticed facts and unstudied topics about Russia and Ukraine will add weight to my argument.

Fact 1. Since 1991, more than 70 young specialists have graduated from accredited institutions in Moscow with master's-level degrees in Jewish studies. They include:

1996   17 from Project Judaica at the Russian State University for the Humanities
1997   10 from Maimonides University
1998   14 from Maimonides University; 25 from the Jewish University of Moscow; 9 from Project Judaica.

All of these graduates have a decent knowledge of Modern Hebrew, Yiddish, biblical Hebrew, and Aramaic. They are familiar with modern Jewish history, ancient history, Jewish literature, philology, sociology, and linguistics. In addition, they have some familiarity with classical Jewish texts (*Tanakh, Mishna*). Utilizing materials acquired from three conferences for younger scholars in 1996, 1997, and 1998, they have published three collections of their work.

Fact 2. The number of Jewish schools in the FSU in 1991 was 149; in 1997 it was 264. In 1991, 4,815 Jewish students attended these schools, including

13 in kindergarten; in 1997, the numbers were 10,699, including 32 in kindergarten.[1]

Fact 3. Since 1993, the Teachers Seminar at St. Petersburg University has held six serious annual, week-long seminars for teachers in Jewish schools. A total of 455 teachers have attended these seminars.

Fact 4. The Second CIS Student Scholarly Conference published its proceedings in July 1998 under the name *Tirosh* ("New Wine" in Hebrew), containing twenty-eight papers selected from submissions in twenty-two cities. The authors, who ranged in age from nineteen to twenty-nine, were all from the Jewish University in Moscow, Solomon University in Kiev, University of Rostov on Don, the Russian State University for the Humanities (RGGU), and Moscow State University. The papers were in the areas of Art, Philosophy and Religious Thought, Inter-ethnic Cultural Contacts and Parallels, Ancient and Medieval Jewish History, History of Eastern European Jewry, and Contemporary Jewry.[2]

Fact 5. Serious Russian-language publishing of books of Jewish interest in fields ranging from Judaism to Jewish history, philosophy, or belles lettres was virtually nonexistent until the early 1990s. However, a serious bibliographical bulletin, circulated both by mail and online from St. Petersburg, registered 105 titles in 1996 and 122 in 1997.[3]

Fact 6. A survey has not been taken of the total number of concerts, plays, and cultural evenings of Jewish content in a selection of Russian and Ukrainian cities, but had one been taken in 1998, it would have shown thousands of cultural events of Jewish cultural significance, with an approximate attendance of at least a quarter million Jews. For post-Soviet Jews, such events are as significant as an American overflow High Holiday service or a mass celebration of Talmud study in Madison Square Garden in New York.

Fact 7. The Russian Jewish Congress granted over $15 million in 1997 in the fields of religious programming, social and cultural activities (including publications), primary and secondary education, secular higher education and research, religious higher education, and regional programs for areas outside of Moscow. The Congress had branches in forty-six cities as of 1998.

Even a cursory view of these phenomena points to a series of research topics that have so far gone unstudied, while the microscopic attention to the monitoring of antisemitism and emigration continues to dominate attention. Areas of potential interest could include (1) the self-image and consciousness of Jews actively working in Jewish communities and institutions; (2) the views of the generation of the 1970s that actually did "stay on"—they could be asked what has changed for them both personally and for Jews around them; (3) a comparative psychological study of Jews of the same age, education, and "Jewish interests" living in Russia, Ukraine, Israel, the United States, and Germany; (4) a study of the incremental growth of local support to Jewish institutions in both Russia and Ukraine, comparing both large cities and small towns; (5) an investigation of the commonplace adult Jewish statement: "Our children are not the same as we were—they are different Jews, different people, with different worldviews and different interests." We need to know whether this is true and why.

⊛ The New Reality

Three elements have radically changed the world in which not only Jews but all residents of Russia now live, think, and act: (1) there is no longer any single, determining role played by the "Party and the government"; (2) the resulting open space, dating even from 1989, has been enthusiastically entered and occupied by Jews whose institutions have moved rapidly toward building something like a "Jewish community"; and (3) the major external force shaping Jewish public life has become international Jewish organizations with ideological, religious, or cultural agendas of their own.

A short look backward is enough to remind us of these changes. In 1989, before the many newly formed Jewish cultural organizations were organized into a single Soviet-wide organization called the *Va'ad*, Jews were scattered in many isolated local organizations and were forbidden to communicate with each other. Even rabbis and religious congregations could not communicate among themselves: they had to deal only with Moscow. As a result there was no Soviet-wide public existence for Jews. This context exists no longer. And the artificial and suffocating Soviet nationality policy, coupled with a Russian and a Communist Party monopolization of all social and cultural life, also no longer exists. In its place, especially since the disappearance of the Soviet Union in 1991, is an open public space, fought over and even partially dominated by new political and economic powers. Nonetheless, it is a space whose limits are openly discussed and criticized by those who are active within it. Within this new open space, the emerging Jewish reality is much more determined by its own initiative and leadership and the domination of foreign Jewish structures, both American and Israeli, with overwhelming resources, than by any aspect of domestic Russian political policy.

Here I should like to submit the observations and the experiences upon which I base my call for a new look at our models of Russian Jewry.

I base these conclusions on my experience in making small community grants over the years 1991–2002. The Jewish Community Development Fund in Russia and Ukraine provided more than 240 grants to over thirty communities during this period.[4] Although some of the grants were made to groups who came into being as structures because of their first grant, I consider that these figures reflect a significant cross-section of actual reality, a small but significant part of a larger whole, in the Jewish community life of Russia and Ukraine.[5]

The areas of activity in which grants were made reflect both the breadth and variety of this new Jewish life. They include the following:

- Jewish kindergartens
- Day schools and Sunday schools
- Choirs, musical ensembles, Klezmer festival/seminars, Yiddish song performance, and groups collecting Jewish artifacts and historical documents
- Local and national radio and television broadcasts
- Support for the distribution of Jewish newspapers in regions not usually served
- Holocaust research, documents, and teachers aids, focusing on the hitherto unexamined history of Nazi genocide on Soviet territory
- Publishing of veterans' memoirs from World War II, "Memory Books," teacher-composed educational materials
- "Culture bus" programs designed to spread cultural activity from a regional center to smaller areas of Jewish settlement (Ukraine)
- Local structures providing home care for the aged; a children's *Tzedakah* (charity) group modeled on the Pioneers, only using Maimonides for its Oath; Hillel youth groups bringing communal Passover *Seders* to provincial cities, with a follow-up Sabbath program using the same methods; training seminars for volunteers and consultants attempting to spread the Jewish volunteer experience into the northwest region of Russia
- Recently we have supported a variety of Internet community projects combining the training of representatives from local schools, welfare centers, and music groups; performing searches for these groups; and using Web pages to make the existence of their Jewish community life visible to the rest of the Jewish Internet world.

Of special interest are projects that connect Jewish interests with the larger goal of combating xenophobia of all kinds. Two projects are noteworthy: the publishing of the first edition of the *Diary of Anne Frank* in Ukrainian, which has been in wide demand from groups ranging from local libraries to military colleges [*sic!*], and a "Climate of Trust" multiethnic group in St. Petersburg that has met for two years to discuss general strategies for combating xenophobia.

Can we make any generalizations from this list of groups and projects? I believe that this newly revived, growing, and largely unstudied and officially unnoticed Jewish life can be categorized as follows:

1. Education is the major channel for creating a "New Russian Jew," with the Jewish school as a central communal institution. The attitudes of young Jewish children and youth are very different from those of their parents, and the children bring their knowledge of history, holidays, and often Shabbat home to their parents (their schools often hold classes for adults as well). The Jewish kindergarten and the Jewish school are often the major Jewish institutions in the community providing a field for active participation, leadership, and even the beginnings of fundraising.

The area of higher education in St. Petersburg, Moscow, and Kiev has seen a growing number of scholars and teachers who are active in Jewish studies in state institutions of higher education, as evidenced by the topics and the level of papers given at the yearly Sefer Conference of Judaic Studies in Moscow (these activities supplement the publishing and research activities at the three Jewish universities — more properly called institutes of Jewish studies). While the purpose of these conferences was originally primarily to "nurture" and encourage teachers and scholars at all levels, the conference in February 1999 had over 150 papers delivered in three days, many of which were at the level of presentations found in most other countries.

2. Culture (including music, theater, dance, and art). There are no statistics available for easy analysis here. The relative significance of Jewish culture (compared to Jewish religious observance) is a separate topic in itself. I should merely point out here that it is the consensus among serious Jewish activists and among those working in the former Soviet Union over the past decade that there is a constant demand for Jewish books, concerts, theater, and art. Serious Russian-speaking Jewish intellectuals all over the FSU are beginning to conceptualize and describe the specific identity that is formed around Jewish culture.

3. The Holocaust and the influence of the experience of World War II. The existence in almost every Jewish community of Jewish war veterans groups, the publishing of serious memorial books, and, most importantly, the research, publications, and teacher training of the Holocaust Research Center in Moscow headed by Ilya Altman point to the importance of this topic in the self-knowledge and self-understanding of the larger Jewish community.

4. Jewish youth. The growth of at least two generations of Jewish youth who have experienced open celebrations of Jewish holidays, attendance at Jewish schools, and an environment of open, public Jewish activity has produced a Jewish youth quite different in attitudes and sensibilities from its parents. This topic remains to be studied in detail. I offer an anecdote to illustrate:

A six-year-old girl who regularly attends the *Adayin Lo* kindergarten is riding a bus with her mother in St. Petersburg when she sees a newly built apartment building: "Look Mama, see the balcony! What a nice place to build a Sukkah on Sukkot!" The mother is about to shush the child and tell her not to talk about such things in public, when she remembers that, "No, this is good," and just smiles.

5. The steadily increasing emergence of local financial support for local Jewish communal institutions. The most obvious evidence is seen in the emergence of the Russian Jewish Congress, with offices not only in Moscow but also with branches in forty-five other Russian communities. Several smaller structures exist also in Ukraine. From our own data, I can add that at the Jewish Community Development Fund we have begun to demand 15 percent local funding for any project in Russia and have seen the beginnings of local support in Ukrainian Jewish communities. There, too, institutions are beginning to find that support, though with great difficulty.

6. Religious life in synagogues. I have left this point for last for two reasons. In my opinion, synagogues are far less at the center of Jewish communal life than in any other country in the world, for a variety of reasons. However, the small but slowly increasing growth of Jewish life that takes place within synagogues with "community center" elements is quite characteristic of the new Russian Jewry.

🌼 Conclusion

If my perception of a widening gap between our perceptions and the emerging Jewish reality is accurate, the following changes in Western Jewish action and attitude should be seriously considered.

Jewish organizations should drastically re-orient their policies toward supporting institutions and processes that really create new Jewish life. Organizations such as the American Joint Distribution Committee, private funders such as the Schusterman Family Foundation, local Federations in American Jewish communities, Israeli institutions such as the Jewish Agency, the Pinkus Fund, the Ministry of Education, and Lishkat Hakesher (Liaison Office of the Israeli Prime Minister's Office) should rethink their beliefs about what constitutes valid "Jewish life."

Scholars, writers, and journalists should make a conscious effort to discard outdated stereotypes based on inadequate assumptions of both the context and the tendencies of the new Jewish life. We must begin to study and write about this new Jewish life as it *is* and not as we are used to understanding it.

I end with the words of Yosif Zissels, who has been a Ukrainian Jewish leader for the past decade and longer. I would hope that our future actions, writing, and speech would make his words obsolete: "We used to be the Jews of Silence because we were afraid to speak; now we are the Jews of Silence because other Jews will not listen to us.

"We knew that we were ignorant and had been robbed of knowledge and tradition. But we thought that together with you, with your help we would recover our sense of independent Jewish self and community. Not to be treated as objects of what you thought we should be or do, but as autonomous subjects."

NOTES

Martin Horwitz is director of the Jewish Community Development Fund in Russia and Ukraine (JCDF), a project of the American Jewish World Service that was initially begun in 1993 by the Nathan Cummings Foundation and the Moriah Fund to support Jewish renewal and Human Rights groups in these countries at the grassroots community level. It has since been joined by the Hilda and Jacob Blaustein Foundation, the Grinspoon Charitable Trust, the Steven Scheuer and Alida Brill Scheuer Foundation, and a devoted group of smaller funders.

1. Zhenya Lvova and Ilana Roitman, eds., *Jewish Schools in the Former Soviet Union, 1997/98* (St. Petersburg: Petersburg Jewish University, 1999).

2. Personal communication from Matvei Chlenov.

3. Personal communication from Alexander Frenkel, editor of *"Narod knigi v mire knig,"* St. Petersburg.

4. Personal communication from Alexander Frenkel, editor of *"Narod knigi v mire knig,"* St. Petersburg.

5. None of these grants is the result of a simple paper application followed by a decision. Each one came as the result of one or two visits to the city or town, where I often stayed not in a hotel, but a home; a meeting with all active Jews in the community; a follow-up session with the group asking for support; discussion of the situation as seen both by activists and ordinary Jews; and, often, similar discussions with non-Jewish human rights activists.

EIGHT

※

SARAI BRACHMAN SHOUP

From Leadership to Community: Laying the Foundation for Jewish Community in Russia

In 1991, in his introduction to *Jewish Culture and Identity in the Soviet Union* edited by Yaacov Ro'i and Avi Becker, Edgar Bronfman counseled world Jewry to take decisive and concrete action in response to Mikhail Gorbachev's reform efforts. He wrote, "If we do not want to lose [Jews in the Soviet Union] as Jews, we must teach them to be Jews. . . . To carry out this task, Jews in the West must . . . send rabbis and teachers to the Soviet Union from everywhere in the Diaspora and from Israel. We must send books and other Jewish educational materials. We must 'twin' Jewish communities in the West and Israel with communities in the Soviet Union."[1] In other words, Bronfman advised, we must take advantage of the open gates and flood the region with Jewishness, making every attempt to transmit a meaningful Judaism to the Jews of the former Soviet Union.

It was good advice when Mr. Bronfman wrote it, and in a generic sense, his appeal is still relevant. Indeed, although much progress in Jewish development in the former Soviet Union has been made since 1991, enough work remains for a small army of rabbis and teachers and truckloads of books.

When read in today's context, however, this call to action has proved insufficient to re-create Jewish communities in Russia. Despite significant efforts by distant funders and on-the-ground organizations alike, there is no definitive Jewish community or Jewish leadership in Russia.

It is a deceptive phenomenon: Russia, with a Jewish population of 300,000–400,000, has strong pockets of involved Jews in a multitude of Jewish projects. In the combined republics of the former Soviet Union, there are more than 30 Jewish day schools, 150 Sunday and supplementary schools, 60 local Jewish newspapers, and four or five university-level Jewish Studies programs.[2] According to a 1997 survey of 3,300 Russian and Ukrainian Jews, almost 30 percent of Russian Jews at least occasionally participate in Jewish activities.[3] In addition, most Jews (two-thirds in Russia) report some awareness of the existence of Jewish organizations.[4]

Yet delving further, it seems that the participation and awareness reported must be very superficial. The survey results provide evidence that most Jews know very little about what the various Jewish organizations actually do.[5] Even more telling, the survey shows that awareness of foreign organizations is higher than that of domestic Jewish communal groups,[6] and those who intend to emigrate from the FSU are more highly represented among the Jewishly active than are those who have no plans to leave.[7]

The late Daniel Elazar, a leading expert on world Jewish communal development, wrote that in the modern Diaspora, "community is built on a fluid . . . base, with a high degree of self-selection,"[8] and that, as a result, "participation actually defines the limits of the community."[9] Although the definition of a Jewish community has become increasingly complicated in our time, it is nonetheless clear that the majority of Russian Jews do not feel a part of one, and for reasons we shall explore later, a good number are even suspicious of the motivations of the organized Jewish bodies.

Whether Jewish leadership exists is an even murkier issue than the definition of community. For our purposes, a leader can be defined very generally as one with a vision (an "ideal and unique image of the future")[10] and action plan, and he or she has been given the stage to lead. Given that understanding, I suggest that many of us who been involved in Jewish work in Russia would have trouble identifying very many such broad-thinking individuals or authority figures.

The tack taken for the past decade or so needs some revision. If Western Jewish organizations active in Russia want to stimulate the development of a Jewish community and Jewish leadership, they must reconsider the roles they are playing and become attuned and react appropriately to three discrete but interrelated phenomena.

First, Russian Jews—and Russians in general—are increasingly wary of Western transplants. The Russians' decade-long capitalistic experiment, viewed widely as an import from the West, has left them in a crisis of direction and leadership. In addition, as several leaders of Western organizations noted in interviews with me, Russian Jews have tired of being treated as "junior partners" by their Western funders.

Second, both history and modernity probably have had a deeper effect on Russian Jews and their ability to develop Jewish communities than many Western actors have realized. It is illuminating to examine the historic—Russian and Soviet—understanding of "community" and specifically "Jewish community," and also to look at the various models for leadership inherited from the Soviet era, as well as those paradigms now conveyed to it from the West. Since we are dealing with creating a community from the ground up, it is also helpful to elucidate the general structural development that the world Diaspora Jewish community has taken in recent times. The latter allows us to appreciate that community-building today is nowhere an easy task; studying the Diaspora also lets us speculate about how the particularities of Russian Jews' historical experiences and influences might affect Jewish community development there.

The leadership void, economic upheaval, and issues of pride have together created a novel situation, one that dictates that the Jewish world must take a new approach. Especially for the younger generation, the recent turn of events in Russia has launched "mental revolutions" that, like all revolutions, may yield exciting new ideas and ways of thinking but may also breed devastating confusion about values, morals, and meaning. If the Soviet paradigms for community and leadership had already at least in theory been overturned, their replacements, which were standards borrowed from the West, are now being examined with more skepticism than before. For the most creative and motivated young Russian Jews, the consequences are potentially radical. While their parents weathered other crises, it is possible that for the young adults with just hazy memories of the Soviet era, the current climate will inspire innovative ways of thinking and new approaches to identity-forming that are neither "Soviet" nor "Western" in origin.

The paradox of the troubles that have slowed Russia's development is that they may speed up Jewish identity development even as, on an individual level, they effectively cancel all accepted and traditional notions of community, leadership, and even Jewishness. We in the West who are dedicated to bringing Jewish culture back to Russia must be open to new ideas and new types of leadership that emerge, especially from the younger generation. As the wielders of coveted funds, we also have to be on the lookout for innovation and to be particularly reflective about funding decisions. All of us functioning as "funders" or "developers" must view our jobs as an awesome charge in which the choice of "favorites" can have a direct impact on the future Jewish community of Russia.

⊛ Development of Community and Leadership Concepts

History provides Russian Jews with very little on which to draw as they go about setting up their Jewish communities. They are essentially starting anew; and this is so for three reasons. First, although there was significant Jewish communal development in pre-Soviet Russia, there was never any truly cohesive or planned Jewish community, either in tsarist Russia or the Russian Republic of the Soviet Union. In fact, only twice in the nearly two hundred years that Jews have lived in Russian-dominated lands have there been attempts—both with questionable success—to establish a Jewish communal superstructure.

The second reason involves a muddled understanding of leadership. Over the past century, the definition of a leader has been so completely manipulated and undermined by changing political realities and the paradoxes of living under Communism that members of the younger generation, at this moment in particular, have no choice but to develop their own definitions of leadership.

Third, during pre-Soviet times, nearly all Jewish activity took place within Jewish ghettos or hamlets in the Pale of Settlement, the border within a border where the Jews under Russian rule were required to live for nearly 125 years (officially, from 1791 to 1915). In a setting where all one's neighbors were Jews, the concerns about identity and the understanding of "community" were by necessity different from those that predominate in a more integrated environment. It is the voluntary character of today's Diaspora Jewish communities, making everyone "Jews by choice," that distinguishes Jewish life in the Pale of Settlement from its manifestations today —whether in St. Petersburg, Prague, London, or New York. In the modern era, Daniel Elazar concludes, "the first task of each Jewish community is to learn to deal with this freedom. This task is a major factor in determining the direction of the reconstitution of Jewish life in this generation."[11]

Thus, one must differentiate between past and present Russian-Jewish communities. It must be understood that, first, Russia has never had a Jewish communal "umbrella" nor a viable attempt to establish an all-inclusive Jewish communal structure. Second, there seems to be serious confusion about what a leader should be. One must appreciate the utter newness of Jewish community-building to Russia; this appreciation should sensitize Western organizations to the need to consider the focus of their work carefully.

⊛ Jewish Communal Structures

During tsarist times, the Jewish community never managed to create a comprehensive structure. This was a result of the prohibition against Jewish organizing and continual harassment of the Jews by both the Russian authorities and the local populations, combined with internal dissension and increasing emigration. There were, however, many Jewish political and social organizations that served the Jewish community, although usually in ways that advanced their organizations' particular ideologies. The Jewish socialist movement, the Bund, and the assimilationist Society for Dissemination of Enlightenment among the Jews in Russia (OPE) were two of many organizations that were able to gain strength as movements by providing educational and welfare services to the general Jewish population.[12] It is clear why an overarching community body was never formed: none of the major competing ideologies of the day—Zionism, assimilationism, socialism, and resettlement/emigration—were particularly conducive to Russian-Jewish community-building. And the vast majority of Jews outside the political activist loop, who resembled the fictionalized characters in *Fiddler on the Roof,* were very occupied with their own small *shtetl* communities, with the daily tasks of feeding their families, and the private and public observance of religious traditions.[13]

Yet, the revolutionary period in Russia, with the hope of freedom from tsarist tyranny that accompanied it, inaugurated a brief flowering of Jewish communal life. During a seven-month period of 1917, under the provisional government, remarkable progress indeed was made in organizing the Jewish community.[14] By the summer of 1917, the Jewish community was already planning an all-Russian Jewish Congress for December 1917. The Congress never took place, for by then the Bolsheviks were in power and already had begun to curtail Jewish grassroots organizational efforts.

During Communist times, when the *Evsektsii,* or Jewish sections of the Communist party, became the central address for Jewish issues, all indigenous Jewish organizations were forced to dissolve. For more than fifty years, the Jewish community consisted primarily of a few officially sanctioned cultural institutions. In the 1970s, an underground Jewish life arose, but it centered primarily on the issue of emigration, not on building Jewish life in the USSR. When it became clear that the Soviet government intended to hold firm to a limited emigration policy, the "dissident" movement diversified, giving rise to Jewish cultural gatherings and study groups focusing on Judaism, Hebrew, and Jewish history. Although these groups could be considered as actors of a sort in Jewish communal life—the first since 1917—they never became organized institutions. As such, these groups provided neither a foundation nor suitable models for Jewish communal development in post-Soviet times.

It is not surprising, therefore, that, after the introduction of glasnost and perestroika in the late 1980s, the first effort at Jewish communal organization was the formation of an umbrella group entitled the *Va'ad*, a name taken not from Russian, but Polish Jewish history.[15] Since it did not have a Jewish communal heritage of its own, Russia could only attempt to replicate one of Poland's highly developed structures.

Sadly, the *Va'ad* has been ineffective as a unifying structure. Partly because of the collapse of the Soviet Union, and partly because of leadership and financial problems, it has taken a back seat to the Russian Jewish Congress (RJC), the organization established in January 1996 by Jewish businessmen as a Jewish lobbying and support group. Although the RJC and its most active figures are well known in the West, and it strives to represent the Jews of the Russian Federation, according to the 1997 survey, the RJC is less well known in its native land than are three foreign Jewish organizations—the Jewish Agency, the Joint Distribution Committee, and the Chabad-Lubavitch movement.[16]

In their 1997 survey, Chervyakov, Gitelman, and Shapiro observe that those who were interviewed were highly critical of the activities of the Jewish organizations. The subjects also generally felt mistrustful of these structures, especially the indigenous Jewish groups. Endeavoring to get to the roots of Russian and Ukrainian views about community organizations, the study's authors propose that because organizational bodies are usually associated with the state, people of the former Soviet Union expect these groups to bear full responsibility for the community's welfare (and thus are disappointed when the organizations' mandates do not include all the services that the Communist state purported to provide); and, second, are conditioned to be suspicious about any structure that "officially" represents the Jewish population.[17] If the government-backed Jewish authority of the Soviet era could not be trusted, many must think, why should we trust the official Jewish organs today?

This is probably the most plausible explanation for the criticism and distrust. Whatever the reason, the fact is that tensions remain between the Jewish population and the community structures. We have no reason to believe that the Russian-Jewish population has yet overcome its historical disinclination to developing effective communal structures.

🕎 *Models for Jewish Leadership*

The Jews of Russia today are influenced by at least three models of leadership: general Russian Soviet, Jewish Soviet, and Western. The co-existence of three very different paradigms by itself may generate some understandable confusion. Add to that the necessary complexity of Russian thinking in these chaotic times, causing simultaneous endorsement and disparagement of each model, and the definition of leadership becomes a virtual cacophony.

The notions of leadership transmitted during Russian and Soviet times are themselves anything but simple. Stereotypical Soviet leaders had the following profile: they were distant leaders who spoke in platitudes, conveyed neither charisma nor conviction, and generally were supervisors rather than actors. The average citizen both relied on and feared those in positions of authority.

The suspicion about "provider" organizations and figures, imparted by past political systems that persisted for years as the Russian government went through crises of leadership, is a reflection of the jumbled image that the former Soviet citizen has about authority. The reluctance to trust anyone or anything completely may in fact be a significant obstacle to the development of leaders, and also to the emergence of true adherents. To complicate matters further, however, there still appear to be remnants of a yearning for a fast and simple definition of the leader—the strong, central, fear-evoking ruler who can be counted on for unmistakable authority. The powerful and popular current mayor of Moscow, Yuri Luzhkov, conveys that image, as do a number of other rising Russian politicians, perhaps including President Vladimir Putin.

The other relevant remnant of Communist leadership is the paradoxical but correspondent lack of confidence in the idea that any ordinary individual can possibly make a difference. Clearly, there are ramifications of such an ingrained sense of societal order for emerging leadership.

Soviet society engendered complex mental states. Robert Tucker coined the phrase "cross-thinking" to describe the state in which a Soviet citizen creates a clear distinction between public expression and private understanding.[18] Expanding Tucker's definition to imply even greater complexity seems to me more apt: Communism produced a situation in which even one's *internal* understanding of reality was confused. Such cross-thinking cannot disappear overnight. All of these lingering ghosts of the Soviet era have backed Russians into a corner, leaving open few avenues from which legitimate leadership may emerge. In such an environment, the emergence of strong local or national Jewish leaders is difficult.

The Jewish dissident provided a sharp contrast to the Soviet leader: For those who remember them, the Jewish dissidents provided images of men and women strong in their convictions, often highly articulate, and readily accessible to followers and students. Although dissident activities and secret Jewish lives cannot be considered general Jewish community structures, they did become "communities" for a small number of people and symbols of a community for a larger group. As such, their leaders provided some of the only models for Jewish leadership to come out of the Soviet era.

The third leadership model comes from the West. The Jewish dissident "type" probably provides a pretty good approximation of the Western leader in that charisma, attractiveness, skill, and drive were all important qualities. Perhaps this explains in some small part why Western Jews so easily and eagerly took on the dissidents' battles. These leaders' personal qualities, which allowed them to persevere and, in some cases, to reach their goals, resonated with Western sensibilities and notions of leadership. Although there are many types of leaders in the West, it is very likely that the general American ideal of a leader is pretty universal. He or she is the person motivated to lead, possessing the self-confidence and abilities to develop and implement a vision, to make decisions and to handle problems that arise. We see this type in almost all sectors of American society—political, religious, social, and intellectual. As a result of television, travel abroad, and Western investment, the American conception of leadership has infiltrated Russia. Its level of influence, and the ways in which the Western image has intermingled with Russian and Soviet ideas, is interesting to explore.

What are the characteristics, for example, that have propelled the Russian "oligarchs"—the nation's top tycoons—to leadership? Marshall Goldman's chapter in this book explains their meteoric rise and their backgrounds. It is clear that a combination of financial success, technical expertise, and personal drive expanded their influence beyond the commercial and into the communal and political spheres. Yet, as an article in the *Economist* observed, the typical oligarch is an "opportunist who cannot look beyond the short term. . . . In the West, such a man might be a lobbyist or a fixer. He certainly lacks the ability to be a tycoon."[19] In other words, the oligarchs are part-Soviet, part-Western. I imagine that to truly understand the motivations of the several tycoons who are also active in Jewish causes—for their interests cannot be pure opportunism—would be to gain insight into highly complex personalities and understandings of leadership.

At a leadership-training workshop in Moscow, I was told that the participants, all in their twenties, were asked to draw pictures of themselves as leaders. Drawings included someone telling others "Let's go!"; a captain of a ship; a lonely and tragic person; something "other" or "different"; figures centering on communication; figures centering on warmth and support; and someone "igniting" others with ideas. Most of these images seem to impart a highly Westernized view of leadership (with the possible exception of the "lonely" and perhaps the "other" images): inspirational, forward-thinking, consensus-building, motivational.

In role-play at the same seminar, however, the most dominant issues were shown to be trust and confidence in the motivations of the program and the program leaders, in organized institutions, in other participants, and in the individual's own abilities.[20] Also significant to understanding their perceptions of leadership is to note an observation from an earlier meeting with many of the same people. When asked to engage in a "teaching" exercise, the vast majority tended to a more instructional, and less motivational, approach.[21] It seems that the intellectualized images of leadership for most of these up-and-coming-leaders were closely in line with Western notions (it is also possible that they were aware of what the Western-trained seminar instructors wanted them to think about leadership). Nonetheless, they had neither internalized the values nor could escape from attitudes inculcated by the culture in which they lived.

I am not proposing that people who may be called leaders of the Jewish community in Russia do not exist. Certainly, individual "communities" have leadership, or else they would not persist, and there are also individuals who can be said to represent larger group interests in some way. The point here is that unlike in the West, there is no clear understanding of a leader's characteristics or role. This, in turn, must have an effect on personal development, relations between individuals, relationships between individuals and institutions, and communal development in general.

World Jewish Communal Structures

It is increasingly true that diaspora Jews, if they feel Jewishly committed at all, feel that they are so by choice rather than simply by birth. Not that an organic tie does not underlie the fact of their choice, but birth alone is no longer sufficient to keep Jews within the fold in an environment as highly individualistic and pluralistic as the contemporary world. . . . The Jewish communities in the diaspora are not communities of fixed boundaries.[22]

The community's organizational successes may obscure its failure to mobilize most Jews to take their Jewishness with utmost seriousness.[23]

In his book *People and Polity: The Organizational Dynamics of World Jewry,* Daniel Elazar examined the dilemmas and limitations inherent in Jewish community-building in the modern age. His model is eminently applicable to the situation in Russia, and for this reason, in addition to others already cited, it is likely that Jewish community development in Russia will be as difficult as in other parts of the world, if not more so. However, it is also possible that the crisis of community-building, if not avoidable, can be muted if foreign organizations doing work there take certain steps to allow the Russian Jews, especially certain highly creative leader-types, greater independence in deciding the future of their community.

The "unboundedness" of the Jewish community, as described by Elazar, has permitted many of the modern debates about legitimacy, authority, influence, unity, and leadership. High rates of intermarriage in the Diaspora have made resolution of these issues seem particularly urgent and contentious. The American Reform movement's decision concerning patrilineal descent is an example of one response to this issue that has brought some of the most delicate "boundary" issues into the open.

In Russia, debates about boundaries have not begun to rage as in the West. Yet the lack of communal structure and the paucity of leadership in Russia, combined with the existence of a highly assimilated population, would seem to play directly into Elazar's model. Indeed, in a society in which a third of the people of pure Jewish heritage (and closer to half for people of partly Jewish origin) are marrying non-Jews,[24] the boundary problem is as great as in the West. In some ways, though, Russia's task is different from, and much harder than, that of other countries because having been separated from Judaism and Jewish culture for so long, fewer Jews than in the United States or Europe feel an "organic tie" to their Jewishness. In addition, historic and more recent manifestations of antisemitism may provide significant disincentives to Jewish affiliation, especially among the part-Jewish.

Yet precisely because the community is so undeveloped, one can also imagine a scenario in which Russia is able to shield itself from some of the difficulties other modern societies face in defining and building Jewish community. Russian Jews are advantaged by the fact that they are starting over. They have the capacity, the numbers, and the authority—who is to stop them?—to define boundaries as they wish, to create communities in their own styles, and to fashion leaders under their own definitions. Russian Jews have been separated physically and mentally from their Western relatives for so long, and are disaffected enough with the West, that they may possess the spirit and boldness to chart their own course in creating a Jewish community, a Jewish leadership, and even a Judaism. In addition, whereas history is thoroughly unhelpful in providing Russian Jews with communal structures, it furnishes abundant examples of intellectual and religious innovations as well as maverick thinkers on whose traditions Russian Jews are free to draw.

To many, this scenario will be unacceptable, implying as it may a direct threat to *klal Yisrael,* the united Jewish community. Should Russian Jews pursue their own course, issues of unity with the rest of Jewry will indeed arise. Arguing for Russian-Jewish self-expression does not necessarily mean that the issues that are already fracturing the Jewish people in the United States and Israel are irrelevant to the Russian situation. Indeed, despite the greater fluidity that characterizes the boundaries of the modern Jewish community, one cannot ignore the importance of boundary definitions, in the interest of the future of Judaism. Few would argue with the statement that the most pressing Jewish issue today is the need for the international Jewish community to attempt to reach consensus on lines of demarcation that somehow manage to recognize both the importance of tradition and the special circumstances of our current era.

Any endeavor to come to such a resolution must take Russian Jewry into account. But just as Russia's history and understanding of community and leadership are unique, so should be the solution to the problem of Russian communal development. The suggestion here is that Russian Jews should be given the freedom to be Jews—and Jewish leaders, in their own ways—forming their own movements and organizations. The alternative may in fact be no Jewish community at all.

A Role for Western Organizations

Western organizations have a responsibility to take their work seriously, to understand the power their dollars carry, to recognize the need to develop indigenous Russian models, and to make the inevitable imposition of their Western perspectives as innocuous as possible. Because of the many obstacles to community-building that this chapter has discussed, I would argue that Western organizations should concentrate more on cultivating future leaders rather than on building institutions or organizations. To this end, one model for implementation could be a Russian-Jewish version of the MacArthur Foundation's "genius" grants.

If it is indeed survival of Jewishness that we are seeking, promise lies in the emergence of creative, visionary leaders. In an informal survey of a number of the Western organizations doing work in Russia, I found that most programs included "leadership development" components and that a good number of these leadership programs focus on skills and qualities that are deemed important to their particular organizational goals.

Although we must accept that Western investors cannot possibly be completely objective, the following type of proposal may make it possible to avoid rendering judgment on people and projects and thus may encourage truly indigenous leaders to emerge.

Every year, the John D. and Catherine T. MacArthur Foundation makes no-strings-attached grants to "exceptionally talented and promising individuals who have shown evidence of originality, dedication to creative pursuits and capacity for self-direction."[25] The MacArthur Foundation says that it "identif[ies] individuals whose creativity has been especially pronounced, those with promise of benefiting from the award, and of then benefiting society. These individuals exemplify human possibility."[26] The uniqueness of the Fellows Program, commonly known as the "genius grants," lies in its underlying premise—that there is great merit, and potential reward to society, in removing the constraints that financial needs put on individual creativity. It is similarly of great merit to take risks on individuals.

Imagine if an organization or individual undertook to make "genius grants," and provided back-up guidance, to the most promising Russian-Jewish individuals. Such an award could be viewed as seed money or venture capital for intellectual, social, artistic, or religious endeavors. It would be an exciting experiment, but one that, I acknowledge, would not be as low risk as the MacArthur grants seem to be. Whereas MacArthur makes awards to individuals who are known, at least within their own circles, for their work, the Russian grants would have to be to individuals whose creativity is, at least in part, unproven. Because of the risk involved, there would be the additional challenge to the grant-maker of not resorting to "favorites."

Although I do think the idea might be worth developing further and giving a test run, I propose it more as a motivational dream than as a proposal for action. It is meant to illustrate a type of role for the Western Jewish organization that promotes new leadership and ideas as the foundation for Jewish communal development, and is as encouraging as possible of the award recipients' autonomy. The invitation is open to other Western funders to engage in discussion on the viability and exact form of such a project.

Helping to conceive of a new Jewish community and leadership and, possibly, a new Judaism, is an admirable, but not an easy, task. I prefer to view Diaspora Jews as the nineteenth-century Jewish historian and philosopher Simon Dubnow did, as necessarily members of a larger non-Jewish community, and Jews' persistence in such an environment as a thoroughly "puzzling and complex phenomenon."[27] Living with contradictions is an unavoidable fate of the Diaspora Jew. As such, it is unlikely that there is any foolproof formula for creating Jewish community, except perhaps for promoting creative thinking about Judaism and the Jewish future.

NOTES

The author was Program Director at the Charles and Lynn Schusterman Family Foundation, established in 1987, which funds programs that enhance and enrich Jewish life in the U.S., Israel, and the Former Soviet Union. The Schusterman Foundation has been the major funder of the FSU's Hillel program, established in a partnership between the Foundation, the American Jewish Joint Distribution Committee, and Hillel: The Foundation for Jewish Student Life on Campus. The Schusterman Foundation is also active in other Jewish development projects in the FSU through the JDC.

1. Yaacov Ro'i and Avi Becker, eds., *Jewish Culture and Identity in the Soviet Union* (New York: New York University Press, 1991), xviii.

2. Valeriy Chervyakov, Zvi Gitelman, and Vladimir Shapiro, "Emerging Jewish Identities and Communities in Post-Soviet Russia and Ukraine: A Dynamic Analysis," unpublished manuscript, July 1998, 4.

3. Ibid., 39–40.

4. Ibid., 31.

5. Ibid., 35.

6. Ibid., 36.

7. Ibid., 39.

8. Daniel J. Elazar, "Jewish Communal Structures Around the World," *Journal of Jewish Communal Service* 74, no. 2 (Winter/Spring 1997/8): 127.

9. Ibid., 24.

10. Edwin A. Locke, *The Essence of Leadership: The Four Keys to Leading Successfully* (New York: Lexington Books, 1991), 49.

11. Daniel Elazar, *People and Polity: The Organizational Dynamics of World Jewry* (Detroit: Wayne State University Press, 1989), 34

12. Zvi Gitelman, "Jewish Communal Reconstruction in the Former Soviet Union," in Peter Y. Medding, ed., *Values, Interests and Identity: Jews and Politics in a Changing World: Studies in Contemporary Jewry, An Annual* (New York: Oxford University Press, 1995), 140.

13. Nearly every Jewish town had Jewish communal structures that existed primarily to accomplish necessary religious functions for the local population.

14. See Zvi Gitelman, *Jewish Nationality and Soviet Politics* (Princeton: Princeton University Press, 1972), Chapter 2.

15. From the sixteenth to the eighteenth centuries, the *Va'ad arba aratsot,* or Council of Four Lands, unified Jews in the Polish-Lithuanian empire. Of course, at that time Jews were barred from residence in the Russian Empire.

16. Chervyakov, Gitelman, and Shapiro, 35.

17. Ibid., 43–44.

18. Robert C. Tucker, *Political Culture and Leadership in Soviet Russia* (New York: W.W. Norton & Co., 1987), 185.

19. "Beyond the Throne," *The Economist,* September 12, 1998, 76.

20. Personal interview with Reuven Gal, October 26, 1998. The reference is to the JDC's Leadership Training Program, an experimental initiative funded by the Schusterman Foundation. The program's first workshop took place October 22–25, 1998.

21. My notes from participation in the interview process for the JDC's Leadership Training Program, August 27–30, 1998.

22. Elazar, *People and Polity: The Organizational Dynamics of World Jewry,* 50.

23. Ibid., 11.

24. Chervyakov, Gitelman, and Shapiro, 11.

25. MacArthur Foundation Web site, November 1998.

26. Ibid.

27. Simon Dubnow, *Jewish History: An Essay in the Philosophy of History* (Philadelphia: The Jewish Publication Society of America, 1903), 27.

NINE

❦

ALANNA COOPER

Feasting, Memorializing, Praying, and Remaining Jewish in the Soviet Union: The Case of the Bukharan Jews

When asked how they arrived in Central Asia, most Bukharan Jews[1] answer by telling a story that unfolded "long, long ago" of a ruler in Bukhara who invited Jews from Persia to join his court. In one version of the tale, the ruler invited the Persian Jews to weave golden carpets for his palace in Bukhara. In another, he invited ten Persian Jews, each an expert in a different craft, to serve as court artisans. In still another version, the ruler of Bukhara invited a Jewish doctor from Persia to his palace to treat his ailing wife. When the wife was cured, the ruler requested that the doctor remain in Bukhara. The doctor agreed only on condition that ten Jewish families be allowed to join him.

Although the details of these stories differ, their basic theme is consistent. The ancestors of the Bukharan Jews arrived from Persia many generations ago. They settled in Bukhara, which became the center of Jewish life in Central Asia; hence they acquired the name "Bukharan Jews." Only later did they spread out to other cities such as Tashkent and Samarkand.[2]

Historians offer no corroboration for this folk legend. The historical record, however, confirms that Bukharan Jews are indeed a branch of Persian Jewry and that they have a centuries-long history in the area that, between the fifteenth and the early twentieth century, was called the Bukharan Khanate.[3]

Using Soviet census information, scholars have estimated that in 1989, between 35,000 and 40,000 Bukharan Jews were living in the former Soviet Union.[4] The overwhelming majority were in the Central Asian republics of Uzbekistan and Tajikistan. In addition to the Bukharan Jewish population in these two republics, there was a significant Ashkenazi Jewish population which, in 1989, numbered approximately 60,000.[5]

Compared to the Bukharan Jews who have a centuries-long history in Central Asia, the Ashkenazi Jews are recent arrivals. They began settling in the area in the late nineteenth century when Russian rule extended into the region. During the Second World War, they flooded into the area after escaping or being evacuated out of their homes in Eastern Europe.

Unlike most of the Jews in the former Soviet Union, and most notably unlike the Ashkenazi Jews in Uzbekistan, the Bukharan Jews did not assimilate to any significant degree in the Soviet era. In 1962, an estimated 34 percent of the Ashkenazi Jews in Tashkent were married to non-Jews, whereas only about 8 percent of the Bukharan Jews in Tashkent were married to non-Jews.[6] Additionally, the Bukharan Jews in Central Asia maintained a low level of acculturation to Soviet norms, one indicator of which is language. In 1979, almost 90 percent of the Ashkenazi Jews in Samarkand declared Russian, as opposed to Yiddish, to be their mother tongue. In the same year, only 17.3 percent of the Bukharan Jews in Samarkand declared Russian, as opposed to Tajik (an Iranian language), to be their mother tongue.[7]

Since the dissolution of the Soviet Union, the Bukharan Jews have emigrated en masse from Central Asia. Today the number of Bukharan Jews remaining in Tajikistan is estimated at a few hundred and the number in Uzbekistan is no more than 3,000.[8] Those who have emigrated have resettled primary in Israel (mostly in Tel Aviv and its outskirts) and in New York (mostly in Queens and Brooklyn).

Maintaining Low Levels of Acculturation and Assimilation in the Soviet Era

Sergei Poliakov's book *Everyday Islam* (1992),[9] which focuses on religious and traditional life among the general Central Asian population, provides an important contextual background for understanding the situation of the Bukharan Jews in Central Asia during the Soviet era. Poliakov was a professor at Moscow State University and a life-long member of the Communist party. His book, which is laden with Marxist ideology, portrays Central Asian society as stagnant and backward, explains the root of the region's social problems, and offers recommendations for transforming the society into one which is modern and just.

While Poliakov's ideological argument is not relevant to the discussion here, much can be gleaned from his claim that in Central Asia there was a strong link between low levels of urbanization and industrialization, and the maintenance of the traditional organization of society during the course of Soviet rule. People had little incentive to leave their home villages and towns in search of employment, education, or high culture. As a result, extended kinship networks never became nuclear. Even in Tashkent, Uzbekistan's capital and the largest city in Central Asia, the Uzbeks tended toward traditional social patterns throughout the Soviet era. For example, according to data gathered as part of the 1979 census, 85 percent of the Uzbeks living in Tashkent thought it necessary to obtain their parents' permission before marriage, and only 6 percent of the married Uzbeks living in Tashkent had married non-Uzbeks.[10] Both these statistics are indicators that marriage decisions were not being made by individuals as individuals; rather that they were made by individuals in the context of the group of which they were a part.

This pattern is important if we are to understand the structure of the Bukharan Jewish family in Central Asia. Almost every Central Asian city and town that was home to a Bukharan Jewish community had a Jewish *mahalla* (residential quarter). Throughout the Soviet era, Jewish populations remained concentrated in the *mahallas,* which continued to function as centers of Jewish life. Within the *mahalla,* living arrangements were patrilocal. That is, when a man would marry, he would bring his bride into his parents' home. Groups of brothers would live with their mother, father, wives, and children in the same household. This residential pattern, which remained dominant throughout the Soviet era, reinforced the strength of the extended family structure

The following section discusses the strong overlap between social organization and religious life. I contend that because the traditional social structure of the Bukharan Jews remained intact, Jewish identity and practice also remained intact.

🌸 *Jewish Practice and Identity among Bukharan Jews in the Soviet Era*

I asked Bukharan Jews living in Central Asia to state why they are special or different from other Jewish groups. When I asked them which qualities make their group unique, they often gave me answers such as the following:

> What is unique about the Bukharan Jews is that we kept our religion and our Torah. Ninety percent of what the Torah says, we do—which is much more than the Russian Jews and the Polish Jews.

and:

> The Bukharan Jews never changed their nationality [on their passports].
> The Ashkenazi Jews hid their nationality. But the Bukharan Jews always
> said, "We are Jewish."

Instead of distinguishing themselves by referring to particular ethnic
customs and traditions, Bukharan Jews in Uzbekistan characterize themselves
as unique for remaining practicing Jews and retaining a strong sense of
Jewish identity throughout the Soviet era. In effect, the Bukharan Jews are
not explaining what marks them as distinct from all other Jewish groups.
Rather, they are explaining what distinguishes them from the other Jewish
group with whom they have been in contact; that is, the Ashkenazi Jews in
Uzbekistan. Being a Bukharan Jew meant, they explained to me, being a
"pure" Jew. Being an Ashkenazi Jew, on the other hand, meant being a "Russian Jew," which is an oxymoron in the Soviet lexicon. According to Soviet
terminology, a Jew is a Jew by nationality. So if a Jew is from Russia, or if
a Jew is from Uzbekistan, he or she is still just that—a Jew from Russia, or
a Jew from Uzbekistan. A person cannot be a Russian Jew or an Uzbek Jew
unless he or she is the product of an intermarriage between a Russian and
a Jew, or between an Uzbek and a Jew.

Nevertheless, the Bukharan Jews use the term *Russian Jews,* rather than
Ashkenazi Jews, to refer to the Jews from Eastern Europe. This choice of terminology is value laden. The implication of the term *Russian Jews* is that they
are not *chistiye evrei,* that is, they are not "real" or "pure" Jews. Rather, they are
half-breeds. According to the Bukharan Jews, the Ashkenazi Jews did not retain their Jewish identity. They married non-Jews, hid their identity on their
passports, and did not maintain Jewish practices and traditions, whereas the
Bukharan Jews remained practicing Jews throughout the Soviet period.

How were they able to maintain their religious adherence? One way of
addressing this question is to examine Bukharan Jewish institutional life.
Indeed, an accepted approach to understanding Jewish life in the former
USSR is to take note of the numbers of synagogues, schools, Jewish theater
groups, and Jewish newspapers to measure the extent of Jewish identity
and practice. This approach is generally linked to a study of Soviet policy,
based on the premise that during periods when policies were lenient, institutions were active and Jewish life flourished. By contrast, in periods when
religious restrictions were tightened, institutional life declined, and as a result Jewish practice waned and Jewish identity weakened.

Merely examining formal religious institutions and Soviet policy is not
adequate, however, for evaluating the populations of Central Asia, Bukharan

Jews included. Families did not adopt nuclear structures, and their extend-ed kin network remained strong. As a result, religious practice and identity were maintained. A case study of one particular ritual will illustrate the in-separable nature of religious life and social life among the Bukharan Jews. An analysis of the Jewish memorial service demonstrates that despite the fact that the Soviets suppressed religious institutional life, the religious life of Bukharan Jews continued to flourish because the fabric of their social orga-nization was not torn.

Memorial Services

Memorial services are held in honor of the deceased each evening for a week after an individual's passing. While this practice is common among Jews the world over, Bukharan Jews continue to hold such services once a week even *after* this first week. If, for example, an individual passes away on a Tuesday, memorial services would be held in his or her honor each Tues-day of that month. After that first month, and continuing throughout the entire first year after the death, memorial services would be held once a month. If an individual passes away on the fourteenth of the month, me-morial services would be held in his or her honor on the fourteenth of each month during that year. An additional memorial service is held to com-memorate the end of the first year of mourning. Added together, during the first year of an individual's death, a total of twenty-one memorial ser-vices are held in his or her honor. Such services continue to be held annu-ally on the anniversary of the individual's death as long as people are still alive to remember the person.

The services are generally held in the home of the individual who has passed away. When an elderly parent passes away and leaves behind married children, at least one of the deceased's children (most often a son) is usually living in the house where the deceased had lived. Guests who attend the event, therefore, are gathered in the home of the deceased, but they are si-multaneously gathered in the home of the person's living sons. During the first week after an individual's passing, the primary mourners are prohib-ited from taking any responsibility for financing or preparing the memo-rial services. Subsequent memorial services are funded by the sons, and the sons' wives prepare the food that is served at the event. While the daugh-ters of the deceased and other female relatives often participate in prepar-ing the meals, it is not considered their responsibility to do so.

Memorial services take place in spacious dining halls. Tables and benches are arranged in a U-shaped formation, echoing the arrangement of the furniture in the Bukharan Jews' synagogues. In the home where the memorial service is being held, and in the synagogues as well, religious and community leaders sit at head tables, located at the base of the "U." In the synagogues, the ark that holds the Torah scrolls also forms part of the base of the "U." At memorial services, a picture of the deceased hangs on the wall just behind the religious dignitaries and seems to take the place of the ark.

Male guests and relatives attending the memorial services sit at the tables along the legs of the U-shaped formation. The women who attend the event, like the women who attend synagogue services, sit at tables located at the ends of the "U," or in an adjacent room.

🌼 The Order of the Service

The event begins with *mincha* and *ma'ariv* (the daily afternoon and evening services). Interspersed during the services, segments of the Zohar, a medieval mystical text, are read and a *hashkavah* ("rest in peace")[11] is said in honor of the deceased. These segments of the service are conducted by the religious dignitaries who sit at the front of the room.

All the men in attendance participate in the prayer services. For some, this means reading the service quietly to themselves as the *Hazzan* [Cantor] leads out loud. Many others, however, do not know the service by heart and are unable to read from the prayer books. Regardless, all men stand together at appropriate spots, sit down together, and respond to the *Hazzan* by saying "amen" at the appropriate junctures.

After the prayer service, speeches in honor of the deceased are delivered. These are generally given by the religious and community leaders. A range of topics is appropriate for these speeches: some may speak about the weekly Torah portion or the upcoming holiday, making little or tenuous reference to the deceased. Others may reflect on the life of the deceased, admiring his or her personal qualities and accomplishments. Some may talk about a historical or contemporary situation involving the Jewish community. Still others may cover all these topics in one speech.

An elaborate meal is then served. The food and the order in which it is served follow a strict pattern. First, the untouched sweets that had been placed on the table before the guests' arrival are cleared. Raw greens and radishes are then served. These vegetables are followed by fried fish flavored with garlic and coriander, served with fried dough. The main dish is then presented: *Osh palov,* a common Central Asian rice and meat dish. Finally, fruits make up the dessert. Upon conclusion of the formal meal, the guests rise from the table and leave.

🕎 *The Meaning of the Memorial Service*

Analysis of the memorial service demonstrates how the rite serves both as a medium for religious practice and as a way to reinforce the structure of kinship organization. Both are inextricably woven together.

Looking at the event from a religious perspective, the central elements involve the prayer services and the religious teachings imparted by the rabbis. But if we regard the event as a social phenomenon, the religious elements might be seen as secondary; indeed, they also might have been easily concealed from Soviet authorities. It might be said that friends and relatives had gathered together not to pray, but rather to remember the deceased over an elaborate meal. The religious nature of the service could have been concealed not only by food, but also because prayer books were generally not used. The religious leaders who knew the prayers from memory would lead the service; the other men followed simply by standing or saying "amen" in the appropriate spots, having no need for religious props. Additionally, religious messages imparted during the services could have been hidden. While the rabbi *could* use the event as a forum to deliver religious instructions and teachings, he could also naturally switch from Torah teachings to eulogizing the deceased.

There is no indication that these components of the service were chosen consciously to conceal the religious nature of the service. Nevertheless, they allowed the tradition to continue throughout the Soviet era. Despite restrictions placed on religious institutional life, the custom of communal prayer was perpetuated. On account of one individual's death, men gathered to pray communally twenty times during the course of one year. Multiply twenty by the annual number of deaths in a community, and add to that sum the yearly services that are held for individuals who had passed away even decades before. The total number of death rites, ironically, contribute to yielding a vibrant and active religious life.

When analyzing the rite, it is important to note that at an experiential level, for people who are themselves taking part in the memorial service, the religious nature of the event is totally intertwined with other social aspects of the event. The rite, for example, serves as a public demonstration of the transference of family property from father to son. During the first week of mourning, when relatives and friends come to the house of the deceased, the son does not take upon himself the role of host. This practice is, of course, not unique to Bukharan Jews. Its Jewish universality may be explained by the fact that it is rooted in *Halacha* [Jewish law]. The practice may also be explained as a means to cater to the psychological needs of mourners who are grappling with the recent death of a close family member.

However, there is also a sociological context, grounded in the particularities of the case of the Bukharan Jews. The home, which was once governed by the deceased parent, seems to still belong to that parent during the liminal first week that follows death. While his parent's presence is still so strongly felt, the son is unable to assume the role of host. During the memorial services that are held subsequent to the first week of mourning, the son does take the role of host upon himself. Thus, he proclaims his command and ownership of the space. At the same time, the fact that the service is held in memory of the parent, in the home that used to belong to the parent, and that the parent's picture hangs in a central location all serve as a reminder that the house once belonged to the parent. While the son comes to be recognized as the owner of the home this position is understood to be temporal, as it is not divorced from his family's history. Though the home is his, it is still innately connected to his father, and even to his grandfather.

The nature of the bond between a woman and her parents is also articulated through the locale of the memorial service. When a woman's parents die, she participates in the mourning services held in their honor, but the services are held in her brother's house rather than her own. While the memorial services are forums for mourning and remembering, they are also forums for articulating social bonds and their significance. A daughter is raised with the knowledge that she will leave the family home, move into her husband's family's home, and facilitate the perpetuation of his lineage. A son is raised with the knowledge that family property is transmitted through him and that he will carry on the lineage through his own sons. Inheritance, which is symbolized in the memorial service, is an expression of the guardianship of the family line.

The memorial service is a means not only of articulating the roles of daughters and sons in relationship to their parents, but also of articulating the daughter-in-law's role in her relationship to her parents-in-law. The daughter-in-law has primary responsibility for preparing the meals for her deceased parents-in-law, just as she was primarily responsible for caring for them while they were alive. The daughter of the deceased, in turn, who does not hold primary responsibility for the care of her elderly parents, does take primary responsibility for the care of her husband's elderly parents—with whom she lives.

I attended a memorial service, held in honor of a woman named Miriam, one year after her death. During the course of the event, I asked one of the guests why it was that Sara, who was Miriam's daughter-in-law, was preparing the event, rather than one of Miriam's two daughters. The guest answered: "[The event is being held here] because Miriam lived with Sara in this house, and she died in this house." The guest continued, "Sara has been in mourning [this past year]. This event is for her to give honor to her mother-in-law and also for the other women to tell Sara that [now that the year is over she should] come out of mourning and be happy."

Regardless of the nature of their personal relationship, a daughter-in-law takes on the role of primary mourner for her parents-in-law, and acts out this role by hosting their memorial services. It is significant that she herself does not decide what food to prepare or how it should be served. Both the menu and the order in which it is presented follow a strict pattern that is repeated by the hostess at all such events. The meal is not an expression of her particular creativity, tastes, culinary capabilities, or aesthetic sensibilities. Nor is the meal an expression of the value that the particular hostess places on the particular relationship that she had with the deceased. Rather, it is a means for the hostess to articulate her formal social relationships and her adherence to the communal norms that dictate how that relationship should be articulated.

I have used the case of the memorial practice to demonstrate the extent to which religious practice was tied to social organization in the Bukharan Jewish community before the break-up of the Soviet Union. The two are so bound that daily afternoon and evening services came to be inextricably woven into the experience of death rites. The obligation to pray at certain hours was not experienced as part of an abstract and universal system of religious law. Instead, each prayer service was connected to memories of an individual, and each prayer service took place not in a "house of worship" but rather in a home—a place with deep connections to individuals and families. Finally, each prayer service took place among a network of participants who came together not as a congregation, but rather as kin.

The Dissolution of the Soviet Union and the Transformation of Jewish Identity and Practice of Bukharan Jews

When the Soviet Union dissolved and the shackles of Communist restrictions were shattered, the Bukharan Jews began to emigrate en masse. Bloody riots in Dushanbe (Tajikistan) and in Andizhan in 1990 were among the initial sparks that ignited massive emigration. Speaking to a *Jerusalem Post* reporter, a Jewish leader in Samarkand articulated the community's fear. "After the collapse of Nabiyev's government [in Tajikistan] there is great concern among our people that [President Islam] Karimov [of Uzbekistan] could also be vulnerable. . . . Islamic fundamentalism is already very strong in such areas of Uzbekistan as the Fergana Valley. . . . If violence breaks out between Tajiks and Uzbeks in Samarkand, the Jews will get caught in the middle. We are very frightened about what might happen."[12]

This initial wave of panic ended when President Karimov created an environment of relative economic and political stability in the early 1990s. Under his tightly controlled government, there has been little antisemitism.

Today in Uzbekistan, not only is Jewish expression tolerated, but institutional life has also been permitted to blossom. Since Uzbekistan gained its independence, emissaries and funds have been allowed to pour into the country. The Joint Distribution Committee, Chabad-Lubavitch, the Israeli government, the Jewish Agency, the Bnei Akiva Youth Movement, and the Midrash Sephardi Yeshiva are among the contributing organizations. Working sometimes together and sometimes against one another, these various organizations have helped local Jews build and run Jewish schools, cultural centers, newspapers, adult education programs, and summer camps. They have helped arrange shipments of matzoh for Passover, kosher slaughtering, and aid programs for the poor. These programs are targeted toward Bukharan Jews and Ashkenazi Jews alike.

While these types of religious activities have helped to build communities and strengthen Jewish awareness among other groups of Jews from the former Soviet Union, the Bukharan Jews have not had the same experiences. Because communal structures have eroded as a result of massive emigration, and because the newly established religious institutions are created and run by outsiders, religious life in many ways has become divorced from the organic social whole of what it once was a part, even under Communism.

Before the break-up of the Soviet Union, the Bukharan Jews' definitions of Judaism had been woven into the local social fabric and into the norms particular to Central Asia. Interestingly, however, Bukharan Jews did not see their local version of Judaism as a variant of Judaism. Rather, they understood their version of Judaism to be authentic. Being a Bukharan Jew did not mean being a member of a unique group in the Diaspora. Instead, it meant being a *chisty evrei,* a real Jew, a pure Jew.

Now the localized version of Judaism has to contend with the new definitions to which it has been exposed. Since their reunion with the wider Jewish world, those few Bukharan Jews who remain in Central Asia, and all those who have immigrated have had to confront the challenge presented by newly introduced global definitions of Judaism. This is a particularly difficult and confusing challenge because emissary organizations represent versions of Judaism that claim to be general and abstract. Sometimes these versions are at odds not only with the Bukharan Jewish version, but with the versions presented by the other emissary organizations. As a result, Bukharan Jews today struggle to negotiate a renewed view of Judaism that encompasses their localized under-standings as well as the various abstract versions that they now confront.

NOTES

1. This term refers to Central Asian Jews who are not of Eastern European origin.

2. According to Benjamin of Tudela's travel reports, there was a significant Jewish community living in Samarkand in 1168. This community was decimated in 1598 by a local Khan. Most of the survivors fled to Bukhara. Not until the nineteenth century did Jews begin returning to Samarkand. For further information on the demographic shifts of Samarkand's Jewish population, see Itzhak Ben-Zvi, "The Jews of Bukhara," in his *The Exiled and the Redeemed* (Philadelphia: Jewish Publication Society of America, 1957), 72–74; Walter Fischel, "The Secret Jews of Persia: A Century-Old Marrano Community in Asia," *Commentary* 7 (1949): 31; Giora Fuzailov, *MíBukhara LíYerushalayim* (Jerusalem: Misgav Yerushalayim, 1995), 58; Mikhael Zand, "Bukhara," in *Encylopaedia Judaica Yearbook* (Jerusalem: Keter Publishing House, 1975), 184; Mikhael Zand, "Bukharan Jewry and the Russian Conquest of Central Asia," *Pe'amim* 35 (1988): 52–55.

3. Ben-Zvi, "The Jews of Bukhara"; Mikhael Zand, "Hityashvut hayehudim b'asia hatichonit biymai kedem uviymai habainayim hamukdamim," *Pe'amim* 35 (1988), 4–23.

4. Baruch Gur, *Daf Matzav Mispar 4: Uzbekistan* (Jerusalem: Jewish Agency for Israel, Unit for the CIS and Eastern Europe, 1993), 4; "Bukharan Jews," in *Encyclopedia Iranica* (London: Routledge and Kegan Paul, 1990), vol. 3, 531.

5. Gur, *Daf Matzav Mispar 4*.

6. Mordechai Altshuler, "Some Statistics on Mixed Marriages among Soviet Jews," *Bulletin on Soviet and East European Jewish Affairs* 6 (1970): 31.

7. Mikhael Zand claims that the Bukharan Jews speak a distinct Jewish dialect that he labels "Judeo-Tajik." The Bukharan Jews currently living in Uzbekistan, however, tend to refer to their language simply as "Tajik," which is widely spoken by the large population of ethnic (non-Jewish) Tajiks living in the area. When asked to characterize their language, the Bukharan Jews do claim that they speak with a smattering of words taken from Hebrew and with an inflection that their neighbors can detect as "Jewish." For census references, see M. Zubin, "Yehudai mekhoz Samarkand bishnat 1979: skira statistit," *Pe'amim* 35 (1988), 170–77.

8. This figure was established through conversations in 1997 with community leaders in Samarkand, Bukhara, and Tashkent (the cities in Central Asia with the largest Bukharan Jewish populations) and with representatives of the local Jewish Agency branch offices.

9. Sergei Poliakov, *Everyday Islam: Religion and Tradition in Rural Central Asia* (Armonk, N.Y.: M. E. Sharpe, 1992), xvi.

10. Yu. V. Arutyunyan, *Uzbekistan: stolichniye zhiteli* (Moskva: Rossiiskaia Akademiia Nauk, 1996), 186, 194.

11. This prayer is popularly recited among Sephardim.

12. Walter Ruby, "As Strife Rises So Should Aliya from CIS," *The Jerusalem Post,* May 21 (1992).

TEN

❦

YOHANAN PETROVSKY-SHTERN

The Revival of Academic Studies of Judaica in Independent Ukraine

❦ Origins: Institutes of Jewish Integration

Jewish studies in Ukraine embody an intrinsic paradox. Ukrainian-Jewish studies have a history but do not have historic continuity. Several notes illuminating this paradox are in order.

The nineteenth-century process of Jewish integration created two important institutions of higher Jewish learning that operated in Ukraine. First, the Zhitomir Rabbinical College was established in 1847 and opened in 1850.[1] It had four-year and two-year programs aimed at preparing a new type of rabbi able to deal with communal issues. According to a decree of Nicholas I, genuine communal leaders (*dukhovnye ravviny,* "spiritual rabbis") had to be substituted by Crown rabbis, who would be state-paid and state-controlled bureaucrats. The Zhitomir Rabbinical College, the only one in Russia besides Vilna, contributed greatly to Russian-Jewish culture. A number of outstanding Jewish thinkers, journalists, and writers came from among its students and faculty. Yet because the traditional Jewish community rejected the implanted leadership of Crown rabbis, the College did not reach its intended goal. It was closed and in its stead the Zhitomir Institute of Jewish Teachers was established in 1873.[2] A by-product of the Great Reforms, it did not survive the period of liberalization in Russia under Alexander II; after twelve years it too was shut down. For some fifty years, no institutes of higher Jewish learning existed in Ukraine, nor were there scholarly institutions or programs offering Jewish studies. Thus, for example, Professor Afanasii Bulgakov (father of the famous Russian writer Mikhail Bulgakov), who taught the history of religions at Kiev University in the fin de siècle period, was absolutely ignorant of biblical Hebrew or classical Jewish sources.[3] Between the closure of the Teachers Institute and the growth of new scholarly endeavors during the early Soviet period, there was a fifty-year gap in the continuity of academic and scholarly Jewish studies.

However, some initiatives still were taken by a number of prominent Ukrainian intellectuals. Their contribution was by no means consistent, nor did it have serious cultural repercussions within the Jewish community. Nonetheless, it would be unfair to disregard it. Of particular importance were the efforts of Mykola Drahomanov and Ivan Franko to introduce Jewish historical and philosophical studies into Ukrainian scholarship. Their efforts resulted in quite a number of scholarly essays and literary pieces, pivotal for the further development of Ukrainian-Jewish cultural dialogue. It was probably under the influence of their attempts that the Zionist leader Vladimir Zhabotinsky, imbued with nationalistic fervor, issued his appeal to revive national Ukrainian culture. Once Jewish studies were again allowed in Ukraine in 1991, Jewish intellectuals, sympathetic to the cause of Ukrainian statehood, drew attention to the Ukrainian Nationalist–Zionist dialogue of the turn of the twentieth century. Zhabotinsky's book of essays, published in Kiev in 1991, translated into Ukrainian and edited by Israel Kleiner, was a milestone in the continuation of this dialogue.[4] It sold out immediately.[5]

🏵 Soviet Yiddish Institutions

During the 1920s and 1930s, Jewish studies in Ukraine were particularly important for Jewish studies as a whole in the Soviet Union. Zvi Gitelman has analyzed the travails of the *Evsekstsiia*,[6] and Abraham Greenbaum has drawn a comprehensive picture of the development of Jewish research institutions.[7] I will summarize the most important issues in this regard and briefly trace them against the Ukrainian backdrop.

The All-Ukrainian Academy of Sciences of Ukraine (*VUAN*), established immediately after the October Revolution, created within it the so-called Jewish Commission on History and Ethnography, *Ievreis'ka istoriko-etnohrafichna komisiia,* headed by a brilliant scholar, Ilia Galant. The *Komisia* emulated the well-known Society of Jewish History and Ethnography that had been operating in St. Petersburg from 1908. The "Galant Commission" organized a number of expeditions to the former *shtetlekh* in the Pale of Settlement and collected a wealth of primary documents on nineteenth-century Russian-Jewish history. Its two-volume collection of works, published in 1929, has remained an indispensable source for researchers of the traditional Jewish community of nineteenth-century Ukraine.[8]

Yet the *Weltanschauung* of the commission was frowned upon by Soviet authorities. Galant himself was too interested in Jewish folklore, hasidism, and communal history to be tolerated by the new Soviet academic policy, a policy based on the principles of class struggle. In 1929 the commission was dismantled, almost simultaneously with the closure of the OPE—Society for the Enlightenment of the Jews (*Obshchestvo rasprostraneniia prosveshcheniia sredi evreev Rossii*) in Leningrad and other important Jewish institutions that had a suspect pre-revolutionary background.[9]

But Kiev was more fortunate. The Communist Party decided to transform Kiev into an unparalleled center of culture of the "victorious Jewish working masses." Unlike "bourgeois" Hebrew, Yiddish was considered the genuine language of the Jewish proletariat. Stripped of any trace of Hebrew influence and orthographically distorted, it was to be the language of a new Jewish culture. The Institute of Proletarian Jewish Culture opened in 1929 in Kiev. Headed by the ambitious Iosef Liberberg, it had a number of scholars on staff, including the Yiddish linguist Nahum Shtif. Liberberg managed to obtain the greater part of the OPE book collection and a number of valuable documents and manuscripts from the Society for Jewish History and Ethnography, which was later transferred to Kiev from Leningrad. The library of the institute could have become a valuable source for generations of scholars to come. But the enormous potential of its collection was not developed, as the institute targeted Yiddish culture and concentrated its research on how to incorporate Yiddish language classics into the literature of socialist realism. Hebrew manuscripts were by and large ignored. No matter how narrow the scope of the institute was, however, we should acknowledge the presence of modified Jewish studies in its curriculum.[10] The general shift in orientation of Jewish studies could be observed in other cities of the Soviet Union as well. Yisroel Sosis in Minsk was forced to switch to the history of the Jewish revolutionary movement; Yekhiel Ravrebe in Leningrad could not publish anything on Hebrew or Aramaic linguistics;[11] and Moyshe Beregovsky, a famous musicologist from Kiev, had to go from the study of pre-Revolutionary Yiddish folklore to that of contemporary Yiddish songs of the "Soviet Jewish masses."[12]

With the politically motivated closing of the institute in 1934 and Liberberg's exile to Birobijan, a new organization emerged to continue the tradition of Jewish studies. It was established at the Academy of Sciences of

Ukraine and operated through 1948 under the Cabinet of Jewish Culture.[13] Folklore, linguistics, and literature were among its major research objectives. Ilia Spivak contributed to the research of Yiddish classics (Perets and Sholom Aleichem) and Yiddish socio-linguistics (Yiddish during the Great Patriotic War). The Cabinet operated under comparatively favorable circumstances since Kiev in the thirties was a center of Soviet Yiddish culture. Leyb Kvitko, Itsik Fefer, and David Hofshtein—the leading Yiddish *literati* of the period—created an environment of intense Yiddish cultural life in Kiev, of which the Cabinet was a part. Inseparably linked to the destiny of the Soviet Jewry, the Cabinet was abruptly shut down in the 1948 anti-cosmopolitan campaign, its members arrested, and Spivak tortured to death.

The purges of late Stalinism dealt a terrible blow to Jewish studies in Ukraine. Its last major figure was Saul Borovoy in Odessa, an unsurpassed researcher of the Hebrew response to the Khmel'nyt'skyi campaigns. He survived miraculously and switched his field to political economy. Having come back from exile in early 1956, Moyshe Beregovsky, by now the leading authority on Jewish musical folklore, was not able either to publish his monograph or teach anything relevant to Jewish studies at the Kiev conservatory.[14] At the time of this hiatus in Jewish academic research, there also appeared the most vicious antisemitic publications, such as *Iudaiizm bez prykras* ("Judaism Unembellished") by the notorious Trofim Kychko, published under the aegis of the Ukrainian Academy of Sciences.[15] Consequently, when in the late 1980s and early 1990s a new generation of researchers expressed curiosity about Jewish subjects, no one was available in Ukraine to instruct them, except a small number of elderly schoolteachers able to teach introductory Yiddish.

University Judaica in Ukraine and Russia: A Comparison

The contemporary situation for Jewish Studies in Ukraine should be seen in a broader context. It is useful to compare it with the conditions that promoted the revival of Jewish studies in Russia. Such a comparison will highlight the specific features of the revival in Ukraine that set the latter apart from developments in Russia (mainly, Moscow and St. Petersburg). Unlike Ukraine, Russia had always retained a high profile in academic biblical and Oriental studies. The Institute of Asian and African Languages at Moscow State University, the Institute of Oriental Studies of the Academy of Sciences in Leningrad, and the Oriental Department at the Leningrad University all operated from the 1960s through the 1980s. Certainly those institutions, which had prepared a variety of rank-and-file military interpreters as well as Soviet intelligence service officials, had a number of associates who potentially knew and could teach Hebrew, if not Israeli studies, for example, Dmitri Prokofiev, who taught contemporary Hebrew Literature at the Jewish University in Moscow. Those institutions prepared or sheltered a number of top-level scholars, such as Igor Diakonov, I. Sh. Shifman, and Klavdia Starkova, who passed the tradition of Semitic studies on to Igor Voevutsky, Yuri Vartanov, and Shimon Yakerson (the latter two taught during the 1998–99 academic year at the Jewish University in St. Petersburg and at the Biblical Center of the Russian State University for Humanities). Having been secluded within the four walls of their scholarship, those scholars became immediately available for teaching biblical and Israeli studies, comparative Semitics, Hebrew and Aramaic, and the history of Jewish booklore to a wide audience of students and scholars, once opportunities presented themselves.

Underground Zionist-minded Hebrew teachers from among the refuseniks, a rather small yet salient group in Moscow in the 1970s and 1980s, were another source of teachers of Hebrew and elementary Jewish studies at higher educational establishments in Russia once it became possible to teach these subjects. Lev Gorodetsky, a well-known Zionist from the Russian underground and one of its most prolific Hebrew teachers, today administers the Biblical Center, associated with Project Judaica, at the Russian State University for Humanities.[16] The religious underground represents another success story. Pinchas Polonsky and Ze'ev Dashevsky from the religious Zionist *"Makhanaim"* group taught several talented Torah teachers who later joined Rabbi Adin Steinzaltz's yeshiva, *Mekor Khaim,* in Moscow.[17] The underground circle of Rabbi Eliyahu Essas developed another stream of religious education (Shlomo Gendelman, one of the participants of that circle, today administers the Department of Jewish Studies at Touro College in Moscow).

Finally, Russia had a not insignificant number of Jews who worked in the field of humanities at the Academy of Sciences in the Soviet Union. Once they were offered an opportunity, they expanded their professional skills to Jewish studies and succeeded in establishing themselves as high-rank Jewish intellectuals, lecturers, and researchers of Jewish subjects. Mikhail Chlenov, Rashid Kaplanov, and Viktor Kelner from Moscow and St. Petersburg are typical representatives of that group.

By contrast, Jewish studies in Ukraine could not be based on similar groups. Nowhere in Ukraine were there academic institutions that taught Hebrew, Bible, or Oriental studies. Ukraine had no Zionist-minded dissidents able to teach Hebrew; the religious underground was unimaginable in the large cities of Ukraine and could survive only somewhere in the periphery, where it would have no impact on the urban cultural environment. There were few Jewish scholars associated with the Academy of Sciences, and most of them were in natural sciences or medicine. Access to the humanities was completely restricted and was characterized not even by a *numerus clausus;* rather, a *numerus nullus* prevailed. In the period between 1962 and 1985, there were no Jewish students at the Department of Philology and the Department of Journalism of Kiev State Shevchenko University; in the same period three Jewish students were officially registered as Ukrainians at the Department for Romance and German Philology (including the author).

Under these circumstances, how was it possible to revive Jewish studies in Ukraine? Who could assume responsibility for that effort? The main source of the revival came from an influx of high-ranking researchers and professional technical workers with strong humanitarian motivation. Mikhail Kalnitsky, perhaps the best expert in local Jewish history; Yosif Zissels, an outstanding communal leader; and Leonid Finberg, a leading expert in Jewish sociology, had formerly been engineers. At the end of the 1980s, a group of scholars came to the surface—predominantly in Western Ukraine—who had belonged to the prewar generation of scholars and embodied either Polish-Ukrainian or Austrian-Ukrainian intellectual traditions. They had kept silent for decades, concealing their knowledge of Hebrew and Yiddish, and had taught other subjects. Finally, in the early 1990s, they were able to contribute to Jewish studies. Some, like Marten Feller from Drohobych, became heads of newly organized Jewish educational establishments. Others, like Yakov Khoniksman from Lviv, remained prolific independent researchers. A major cadre of new educational leaders was formed by a middle-rank Jewish intelligentsia consisting largely of former schoolteachers and communal leaders. At the same time, there was a higher level of professional interest in Jewish studies at the nationalistic Ukrainian Universities, among them Kyiv-Mohyla Academy or Lviv State (Ivan Franko) University. Driven by their own professional curiosity, and lacking support from Jewish scholars or political leaders, several professors at these institutions introduced topics on Jewish history and Jewish civilization into their curriculum. Those features could not but create a profile of Jewish studies peculiar to Ukraine.

🕎 Starting from Scratch: Trends in Jewish Studies

The revival of Jewish studies immediately after Ukraine achieved independence in 1991 had political, social, and cultural implications. In the view of some, Jewish studies were to provide a counterbalance to both Russian chauvinistic attitudes toward authentic, rather than Soviet-imposed, Ukrainian culture, and to the Russian political antisemitism of the Soviet period.[18] Ukrainian-Jewish relations in the 1990s were based on the "principle of negative parallelism." When Russia hurried to establish new relations with the United States, Ukraine expedited its relations with Israel. When Russia seemed to be looking for new strategic partnerships with Arabic countries, Ukraine was discussing a missile-carrier program with Israel.[19] Russia was indifferent to the rise of antisemitism, whereas Ukrainian President Leonid Kravchuk was the only political leader from the FSU who attended the European Conference on Antisemitism in Brussels.[20] In Kiev in September 1991, Kravchuk publicly expressed remorse on behalf of the Ukrainian people for atrocities committed against Jews by Ukrainians during World War II.[21] Interestingly, among the most important propellants of the Ukrainian-Jewish revival in the 1990s was the claim shared by Ukrainians and Jews that they had been similarly oppressed by the dominating Russian culture and by forced Russification. Both Ukraine and Israel were perceived as national states that emerged from statelessness and from a situation in which both lacked political rights.[22] Hence the salient governmental support of Jewish endeavors, at least amongst intellectuals and the ruling elite.

Looking back at the past decade, one can identify three major streams in Jewish studies in Ukraine. While two of them, Holocaust and local studies, may be found in both Ukraine and Russia, the other, which might be called "revisionism," is a typically Ukrainian phenomenon. The revisionist trend should be understood against the backdrop of the Ukrainian-Jewish and Ukrainian-Israeli political dialogue that I have called "A Ukrainian-Jewish Utopia."[23] Though the people to be mentioned would not consider themselves revisionist in Jewish studies or historical scholarship, their intellectual production could be characterized as such. To understand the main issues raised by the revisionists, it is useful to examine the presentations at Ukrainian-Israeli and Ukrainian-Jewish conferences or to summarize dozens of interviews given by Ukrainian and Jewish public figures. First, the revisionists rewrite Ukrainian-Jewish history, and tend to acquit Ukraine retroactively of guilt for harm caused to Ukrainian Jews. Bohdan Khmel'nits'kyi in the seventeenth century, they argue, targeted Poles, not Jews. The 1881 pogroms were orchestrated by Russian authorities and the 1904 pogroms by the Black Hundreds. Semen Petliura, leader of the Ukrainian Rada in the period of the Civil War (1918–21), behaved properly to Jews and was sympathetic to Zionism, while the pogroms of 1919 were unleashed by the White General Anton Denikin's army. The famine of 1932 in Ukraine (*Holodomor*) was not perpetrated by Communist Jews who wanted to pay back the Ukrainians for the Civil War pogroms; rather, it was a campaign of anti-Ukrainian genocide orchestrated by the Kremlin.[24] In addition, the revisionists reinterpret Zionism by stressing its utility as a model for the emergence of Ukrainian statehood. Ukrainians, like Jews, went through dark centuries of national oppression. Due to historical circumstances, the sense of statehood (*derzhavnist'*), the languages (Hebrew and Ukrainian), and national dignity of both peoples were consigned to oblivion. Yet Zionism changed the Jewish profile. In the course of some fifty years, Jews managed to regain national dignity, rebuild a state, and revive their language. If Ukrainians could make use of the Zionist experience, what patterns of Jewish political and cultural development should they accept, and which should they reject? In this connection, Zhabotinsky's concern for the fate of the Ukrainian language, whose decline he deplores, serves as an indispensable epigraph for Ukrainian-Jewish relations.[25] According to the revisionists, those relations have always been friendly, based on mutual understanding of a similarity of national destinies. Lesia Ukrainka, Ivan Franko, and Mykola Hrushevsky's philosemitism is cited as the best example of those attitudes. Those relations have become even more intense due to the common fate of Jewish and Ukrainian dissidents who became friends in the Soviet *Gulag* system.[26]

Quite a number of prominent Ukrainian intellectuals are revisionists, including Vadim Skurativs'kij, Taras Vozniak, Omelyan Prytsak, Ivan Dziuba, Mykhailo Riabchuk, Larysa Skoryk, and Yaroslav Dashkevich.[27] The "Jewish side" is represented by Marten Feller,[28] Leonid Finberg,[29] and Semion Gluzman.[30] Liberal-minded Ukrainian and Ukrainian-Jewish intelligentsia might be considered the audience for their ideas. Though many of their ideas are not sustainable from a scholarly point of view, they have a serious impact on the general intellectual environment in Ukraine and create conditions for the further development of Jewish studies. Mention should be made of the Ukrainian language, which has again, as in the twenties, become the language of scholarly expression, especially for the "revisionists." Ukrainian has therefore reappeared on the stage of European Jewish studies.

An interest in local history is another trend in Ukrainian-Jewish studies. Using primary sources found in local archives, researchers have produced a wealth of data on urban nineteenth- and twentieth-century Jewish history. Galician Jewish scholars, aware of renowned predecessors such as Shlomo Buber or Meir Balaban, have made outstanding contributions to Ukrainian-Jewish local history.[31] Yaakov Khoniksman, the oldest Yiddish-speaking historian in Ukraine and professor of economy at the Lviv Polytechnic Institute, has published half a dozen monographs and brochures on the history of Jews in Galicia, Lviv, Drohobych, and Boryslav. He also has compiled the first two-volume edition of the history of Jews in Ukraine.[32] His younger colleague, Vladimir Melamed, has published a scholarly monograph on the socio-political history of the Jewish community in Lviv.[33]

Attempts have been made to trace specific historical aspects of certain regions and localities of Ukraine. Among these are popular publications of dubious scholarly value[34] and serious collections of articles and documents, such as histories of the Jews in the Crimea or on the communal religious life in postwar Kiev and Lviv.[35] A group of researchers from Zaporizhzhia organized a number of conferences in the early 1990s devoted to the history of Jews in southern Ukraine, an area particularly important for economic and commercial breakthroughs during the second half of the nineteenth century.[36] Mikhail Kal'nitskii published perhaps one hundred articles on the history of Jews in Kiev, heavily supporting his points though his own archival research.[37] When synthesized in a monograph, his study may drastically reshape our vision of the Jewish history in Kiev, hitherto viewed predominantly through the prism of the Beilis case. Though focused on internal grassroots Jewish history, researchers of local history nevertheless contribute to broadening our knowledge of the historical background of Ukrainian Jewry. However, the lack of knowledge of twentieth-century English-language scholarship and almost complete ignorance of Hebrew and Yiddish language primary sources prevent many researchers from successfully establishing themselves as serious scholars by the standards of Jewish studies in the West and Israel.

The third trend, which studies the Holocaust, is even more popular among Jewish researchers due to its political resonance and the immediate accessibility of sources. Though there was official avoidance of the subject under the Soviet regime, this topic is by no means purely academic for Ukrainian Jews. About one and a half million Soviet Jews were murdered during World War II, and many Jewish families in Ukraine remember their relatives who perished. A number of groups and independent researchers are dealing with this subject. Headed by Yuri Liakhovitsky, the group *Drobnitskii Iar* in Kharkiv monitors antisemitism in contemporary Ukraine, publishes source-based historical surveys of the Holocaust, collects data on survivors, and criticizes neglect of the subject by the authorities. In their scholarly productions, these groups clearly intend to blame Ukrainian nationalism and its proponents who collaborated with the Nazis as the foremost instigators and executors of the "final solution."[38] One can make a plausible argument that some of the independent Holocaust study groups in Ukraine use their subject to attain political and social importance within the Jewish community and attract the attention of the Ukrainian authorities; in my experience, Holocaust studies are used as an instrument of struggle for power in the Jewish community in Ukraine at large.

The agenda of those groups that work within established Ukrainian institutions is quite different. Such groups include the Cabinet of Jewish Culture, re-established by Ivan Kuras, the Ukrainian vice-premier, at the Ukrainian Institute of National Relations and Political Science (formerly the Communist Party Institute). Their approach to the Holocaust omits any mention of the part played by the Ukrainian population in mass murders. These "Crown scholars" depict the Holocaust as the systematic extermination of the Jewish population on Ukrainian territory, perpetrated by the Germans.[39] Needless to say, these views represent latent revisionism. Recently, Zhanna Kovba, a freelance researcher from Lviv, attempted to impose a revisionist approach on Holocaust studies. Her monograph, which deserves a separate critical assessment, is an eloquent demonstration of the nonproductive, if not dangerous, perspective of a mythological revisionist outlook on the Holocaust.[40] Kovba characterizes relations between Jews and Ukrainians in Galicia in the prewar and war periods as products of fruitful cooperation, if not of spiritual rapprochement, interrupted by the Nazis who alone bear responsibility for the Holocaust. According to Kovba, anybody who does not agree with her statement should be considered either a Ukrainian, Jewish, or Polish extremist, or a corrupt journalist (see note 40). To summarize, Ukrainian Holocaust researchers and research groups have offered an extreme form of what might be called either "anti-[Daniel] Goldhagen" or "pro-Goldhagen" versions of the Holocaust in Ukraine. Evidently, there is yet a long way to go until those groups abandon their mythological approach to historical reality.

Mention should be made of a general shift in Ukrainian-Jewish scholarship. In the late 1990s and early part of our new decade, there has been a tendency to move away from the major trends described above—local history, revisionism, and Holocaust studies. An important breakthrough is indicated by the recent publication of a number of books by *Dukh i Litera* Publishers (together with the Judaica Institute of Ukraine). These address the general reader and integrate Jewish-Ukrainian issues into a broader context of modern Jewish scholarship.[41]

🌣 *Judaica between Politics and Economics*

Higher Jewish education in Ukraine has seen a variety of expressions and has passed through a number of different stages in the past decade. In the first stage, which was the briefest and not unexpected, former antisemites and party functionaries of Ukrainian universities approved of the idea of having a branch of Jewish studies established at institutes of higher Jewish learning. By "Jewish studies" they usually meant the teaching of Hebrew, not Jewish civilization. This approach was by no means an enthusiastic attempt to introduce Jewish studies into the curriculum. Rather, in my judgment, it was a servile gesture aimed at matching the new pro-Israel stance of the first independent Ukrainian government. Teaching Hebrew was politically fashionable. The West was astonished and a new generation of students swiftly got used to the idea. However, for the most part, as reflected by programs at the Institute of Ukrainian Studies at Kiev Shevchenko University, directed by a former Communist, Professor Kononenko, this campaign remained a pipe dream that produced no results. Hebrew was introduced into the curriculum as a spoken language of a national minority group in Ukraine!

During the second, more stable phase, Ukrainian intellectuals—mostly of dissident liberal or nationalistic backgrounds—welcomed the inclusion of Jewish studies courses in the curricula of Ukrainian universities on a regular basis. In some cases, they even endorsed the establishment of Jewish research groups at the universities. Consequently, those groups were able to offer specific courses on Jewish studies. One of the first such research groups was established in the industrial city of Zaporizhzhia. Later, Lviv University and Kiyv-Mohyla Academy offered introductory courses on Jewish philosophy and history.[42] In most cases, the courses were taught by liberal-minded intellectuals who had no special educational background in Jewish studies (like Pistryi at Kiyv-Mohyla Academy), but they felt that humanities without a hint of Jewish studies would be a deficient field of study. The trend of teaching courses related to Jewish history, literature, and culture or including lectures on relevant topics into the syllabi may yet become the most important factor for developing Jewish studies in Ukraine. At this point, however, it is too early to analyze the impact on Ukrainian university students.

The third stage saw a renaissance of Jewish teacher training. During the first three years of Ukrainian independence, some 150 teachers of Jewish origin, teaching Russian literature or mathematics at provincial schools, embarked on a program to teach elementary Jewish tradition and history. They were joined by a hundred Israel-oriented young people, who had learned the basics of Hebrew at seminars sponsored by the Jewish Agency. By 1994, sixty-five Sunday Jewish schools in Ukraine were teaching three major subjects up to three times per week: Jewish tradition, history, and introductory Hebrew. Although there was great communal demand for that type of teaching, there was a shortage of qualified teachers. The problem was partially solved in 1993 with the establishment of a Ukrainian Center for Jewish Education, which worked along with the Ukrainian Institute for Education

Management. It was the first full-time, Ukraine-wide Jewish higher educational establishment, and it provided training for over two hundred Jewish teachers working at fourteen full-time and sixty-five Sunday Jewish schools.[43] Six to seven annual seminars, with some eighty teachers coming for two weeks of intensive (ten hours per day) training, contributed to radical changes in Jewish secondary education. The center was particularly attentive to the needs of distant provincial schools in towns such as Bershad, Poltava, Sumy, Berdichiv, Haysin, Kirovohrad, and Donetsk. In the early 1990s, before foreign rabbis (by and large hasidim of the Chabad and Karlin-Stolin groups) established themselves as communal leaders, a public opinion poll conducted by the center had demonstrated that it was the local Jewish school—not the synagogue or Jewish Cultural Society—that was considered the communal Jewish center par excellence. In 1994, the center introduced a teachers college program that prepared some twenty-five licensed Jewish teachers for Ukrainian Jewish schools and colleges. Ninety percent of those who taught at the college (former mathematicians and engineers) had graduated from Israeli programs of intensive training. To some extent they were attracted by the relatively high salaries of the Ukrainian Center for Jewish Education—it more than doubled the salaries paid by the Jewish Agency or American Joint Distribution Committee to local Jewish tutors. Before it experienced a tremendous economic blow in 1996 from which the Va'ad of Ukraine (its major sponsor) could not recover, the center contributed to yet another breakthrough in higher Jewish education: the Department of Jewish Studies at the International Solomon University in Kiev.[44]

In the Ukrainian-Jewish revival, the story of the International Solomon University (ISU), which has some 650 students, is by far the most complicated. It is considered by its rector, Dr. Alexander Rosenfeld (an economist), to be the only Jewish university in Ukraine. On the other hand, Ukrainian-Jewish leaders, along with Israeli universities, claim that ISU is not a Jewish institution, since fewer than 10 percent of its students are Jewish. The higher educational authorities of the state attempt to discredit ISU, whose tuition is half that of Kiev Shevchenko University, especially when one factors in "hidden costs" such as payment for "tutoring" to the faculty members who prepare the admissions examinations, a standard procedure inherited from Soviet times. Private Ukrainian institutions tried to cooperate with ISU, but its strange status as a "small business" rather than an academic institution forced them to abandon their efforts. Both foreign and domestic Jewish communal institutions such as the Va'ad, the American Joint Distribution Committee, or the Jewish Agency for Israel (*Sokhnut*) have fought for a share in ISU for about a decade, with no apparent result. However, ISU students—Ukrainians, Russians, and Jews—consider their educational institution to be Israel-oriented. When participating in city-wide competitions for young intellectuals or in athletics, they use the Israeli flag as their symbol. Nevertheless, ISU remains an oddity, having no particular intellectual, political, or cultural orientation, and lacking interactions with the Jewish international and domestic milieu.

ISU was established in 1992 by three men—a plumber, a building manager, and a physicist—as a small business. The administrators of the university never concealed the economic rationale behind the project. Tuition ranged between $150 and $300 (today it is between $600 and $1,000) depending on the department. No scholarships were offered. The majority of the high-quality staff were Jewish instructors at Kiev's higher educational institutions, mostly at the Polytechnic Institute. Six departments were established— New Technologies (Computers), Physics and Mathematics, Law, Humanities, Biology, and Sociology. Judaic studies were limited to two hours per week of Yiddish or Hebrew and two hours of Jewish history, taught exclusively by the department of humanities. Yiddish was taught by a native speaker and former schoolteacher. According to several ISU faculty and students with whom I spoke, in the two-semester courses on Jewish tradition—for which Rabbi Ya'akov Dov Bleich, Chief Rabbi of Ukraine, assumed responsibility—only two lectures were actually delivered.[45] Jewish history was represented by two courses, "Jewish Resistance in Ukraine during the Great Patriotic War" and "Jews in the Bolshevik Party." The first was taught by Ster Elisavetsky, a former schoolteacher and Holocaust researcher, the second by Froim Gorovsky, professor of scientific Communism and a Communist Party leader from the Polytechnic Institute. This situation struck some as intellectually and morally questionable.

No matter how minimally the ISU leadership wished to have Jewish studies incorporated into its curriculum, the Ukrainian Center for the Jewish Education proposed establishing a Department of Jewish Studies at ISU. The center offered its premises, staff, and financial backing to implement this goal. After a year of sophisticated intrigues and international pressure, the university leadership gave its reluctant consent. The Department of Jewish Studies was established in 1994 and was immediately supported by international Jewish political organizations, major Jewish foundations, and local Ukrainian institutions. Financial support came predominantly from the Va'ad of Ukraine, headed by Yosif Zissels. The department offered intensive courses in Hebrew, Bible, Semitic languages, Yiddish, introduction to Jewish literature and philosophy, introduction to Judaism, history of the ancient Middle East and Greece, Jewish art, Israeli studies, and English.

The department also hired some twenty tutors, of whom five were university professors holding doctorates, seven professionally trained Hebrew tutors, and two senior researchers of the Academy of Sciences of Ukraine. Half the department's students were exempt from tuition; the rest paid just one-fourth of the tuition required by the university. The department attracted scholars from Canada, Germany, Israel, and the United States who taught for one or two semesters. Moreover, it targeted students from the university at large, providing Hebrew and Jewish history (six hours per week respectively) to students from the humanities and sociology departments. The Jewish studies section planned to become the intellectual center of the university, but its situation changed drastically with the financial breakdown of the Va'ad.[46] Unable to provide for its own financial needs, the Va'ad had to withdraw its investments from higher education. Neither the American Joint Distribution Committee nor the Jewish Agency (represented by the Pinkus Foundation, which was established to support higher Jewish education) was eager to intervene to provide assistance. Unsympathetic to the cause, the ISU leadership dismantled and re-organized the department. The students, who had then to pay the required annual tuition irrespective of their financial resources, were transferred to other departments. By 1998, the Department of Jewish Studies had ceased to operate. Regular classes in Hebrew and a somewhat modified and improved version of Jewish history remained the only Jewish subjects taught at the university. Random lectures from foreign visitors could not substitute for consistent instruction in Judaica. Kievan intellectuals used to joke in the seventies: "The nearer one gets to Kiev State University, the farther he is from the scholarship." Today one may say with a mixed feeling of disappointment and regret, "The nearer to ISU the farther from Jewish studies."

🕎 Judaica or Judaism?

Given the complex character of Jewish studies in Ukraine, how is it possible to characterize contemporary trends? I would argue that Ukrainian-Jewish intellectuals are a semiassimilated elite who, by and large, are distant from the Jewish community, a community that I understand as an organized entity, which includes religious, cultural, and educational communal institutions.

In the beginning of the 1990s, the paramount task was to establish institutions that could provide Jewish studies and function as a liaison between Jewish intellectuals and the Jewish community. St. Petersburg and Moscow have followed this path by creating a network of programs, universities, and centers that manage to bring together the community and intellectuals engaged in teaching and learning Judaica. They also have succeeded in creating a network of Judaica scholars, Jewish and non-Jewish, brought together under umbrella organizations like the International Center for Teaching Jewish Civilization "Sefer" [the coordinating organization for academic Judaica in the FSU], or the Jewish Heritage Society (both Moscow-based).[47] This rapprochement has produced a new generation of Jewish leadership able to assume responsibility for local communal and cultural development.

Ukrainian-Jewish leadership has failed to do this. In an oblique way, it has contributed to widening the gap between the Ukrainian-Jewish community and Ukrainian-Jewish intelligentsia, even more than in the early 1990s. Intellectuals, who were able to do their research and teach students at the Universities, could not reach out to the community. Looking for the recipients of their ideas, local Jewish intellectuals had to offer their knowledge and skills to Ukrainian non-Jewish institutions of higher learning. Jewish intellectuals went to teach non-Jews and lost the stimulus to deepen their own knowledge of Judaica. Simultaneously, the Jewish community turned its back on its intellectual resources. As a result, the Ukrainian-Jewish community did not manage to produce a viable generation of new Jewish leadership. Thus, in a silent, undeclared war between those advocating the academic teaching of Judaica and those promoting communal teaching, both sides lost. Communal and religious leaders remain aloof from or ignorant of developments in Ukrainian or even Russian cultures, and Jewish intellectuals remain largely ignorant of Jewish traditions and culture.

Several examples will illuminate this situation. Established in 1997 in Kiev, the Ukrainian Institute of Judaica (*Instytut Iudaika Ukrainy*) is an intellectual center for Jewish publication and research.[48] Its conferences, organized annually since 1992, attract most Jewish intellectuals involved in research on Jewish history and culture in Ukraine.[49] Its publications range from the high-standard bilingual literary journal *Yehupets*, to proceedings of conferences, and to a series of scholarly publications on Ukrainian-Jewish history.[50] The institute also monitors the social and political situation in Ukraine, collects oral history, organizes public opinion polls, and promotes Ukrainian-Jewish political dialogue. The intellectual elite, *literati*, and public figures involved in the work of the institute could without any exaggeration be dubbed the *crème* of the Ukrainian-Jewish intelligentsia. I should admit, however, that the weakest area of the Institute of Judaica, unfortunately, is Judaic studies. The staff knows neither Jewish languages nor "Jewish traditions" (a post-Communist euphemism for Judaism), and the understanding of Jewish history and culture is superficial, biased, and does not go beyond modern Ukrainian-Jewish political history, Russian-Jewish literature, or Holocaust studies. It is interesting that Kyiv-Mohyla Academy, the private Ukrainian university with the highest standards of teaching, invites several scholars of the Institute of Judaica to teach at its premises on a temporary basis. Yet Jewish institutions, in other words the "community," do not.

The younger generation has rejected academic Judaica, preferring to get its Jewish education at the yeshivas like *Aish ha-Torah,* communal centers like *Makor,* or Rabbinical establishments like *Machon,* the two-year program of Progressive Judaism (all of which are Kiev-based).[51] Vinnitsa, Odessa, and Lviv have a network of communal institutions for local Jews. "People's universities" in Dniepropetrovsk and Kharkiv, sponsored by religious institutions (such as Chabad) or Western organizations (including "the Joint"), provide the same sort of community-based forms of education for people of all ages. However, few young people involved in the operation of those institutions are interested in pursuing careers as teachers of Judaica, in managing Jewish education, or in doing scholarly research in the field of Jewish studies. The young generation looks at Judaica studies as the prerogative of older age groups. It is as if the young are saying: "Let the assimilated elite do Judaica; we would rather try—or play—Judaism."

Ukrainian Jews are rapidly losing their potential to establish a tradition of Jewish studies that can survive and be passed on to the next generations. The natural decline and slow emigration that will sweep the present Ukrainian-Jewish elite will leave nobody behind. One may argue that the same process, for different and diverse reasons, is taking place in the general Ukrainian milieu. Indeed, though Ukrainian-Jewish intellectuals experience the same decline as their Ukrainian brethren, the Jewish case seems to be irreversible. Another half-century rupture in Ukrainian-Jewish studies will be the logical outcome of this process.

🪬 *Conclusions*

In the last ten years of the twentieth century, Jewish studies in Ukraine were a manifestation of the rebirth of Ukrainian-Jewish life. Due to unique historical, political, and cultural circumstances, of which the most important was the absence of a living scholarly Judaica tradition, Ukrainian-Jewish studies underwent a process of development different from that of Russian Judaica. Ukrainian independence also cast its socio-political pattern on the development of Jewish studies. Major trends have included the re-definition of the Ukrainian-Jewish heritage, the renewal of research on local Jewish history, and the study of the Holocaust. A number of valuable contributions to scholarship were made by scattered groups of researchers and even more by independent scholars. In the early 1990s, Jewish higher education could not meet the needs of the Ukrainian Jewry. By the middle of the decade, however, unparalleled forms of studies in Judaica were introduced that served both the community at large and students in higher education in particular. Yet because of frictions between intellectual and communal leadership, the Ukrainian-Jewish community failed to establish an efficient system of higher Jewish learning, and thus jeopardized the future of the Ukrainian-Jewish intellectual elite.

NOTES

This essay is a part of a broader topic, "Ukrainian-Jewish Utopia," that I developed as my presentations at the University of Toronto (November 24, 1994), Columbia University (December 6, 1994), and Harvard University (May 4, 1998).

1. For more detail, see E. Melamed, "Iz istorii Zhitomirskogo ravvinskogo uchilishcha," in *Evrei v Rossii. Istoriia i kul'tura. Sbornik nauchnykh trudov [Trudy po iudaike. Istoriia i etnografia. Vyp.* 5], ed. D. A. Elyashevitch (St. Petersburg: Petersburg Jewish University, 1998), 118–43.

2. Isaac Levitats, *The Jewish Community in Russia, 1844–1917* (Jerusalem: Posner and Sons, 1981), 47, 53–54.

3. M. Zolotonosov, *Master i Margarita kak putovoditel' po kul'ture russkogo antisemitizma* (St. Petersburg: INA Press, 1995), 58, n.39.

4. Volodymyr Zhabotyns'kyi, *Vybrani statti z natsional'noho pytannia,* ed. Israel Kleiner (Kyiv: Respublikan'ska asotsiatsia ukrainoznavtsiv, 1991).

5. The same was the fate of Israel Kleiner's book on the parallelism of Ukrainian and Jewish nationalisms. See Israel Kleiner, *Vladimir (Ze'ev) Zhabotyns'kyi i ukrain'ske pytannia* (Kyiv, Toronto, and Edmonton: Kanads'kyi Instytut Ukrains'kykh Studii, 1995).

6. Zvi Gitelman, *Jewish Nationality and Soviet Politics. The Jewish Sections of the CPSU, 1917–1930* (Princeton: Princeton University Press, 1972).

7. Abraham Greenbaum, *Jewish Scholarship and Scholarly Institutions in Soviet Russia, 1918–1953* (Jerusalem: Hebrew University, Centre for Research and Documentation of East European Jewry, 1978).

8. *Zbirnyk prats'. Ievreis'ko-istoryko-arkheohrafichna komisiia.* Vyp. 1, 2 (Kyiv: Vseukrains'ka Akademiia Nauk, 1928–29). About this edition see Saul Borovoi, *Vospominaniia* (Moskva-Ierusalim: Evreiskii Universitet v Moskve, "Gesharim," 1993), 185–86.

9. V. Khiterer, "Evreiskaia istoriko-arkheograficheskaia komissiia Vseukrainskoi Akademii Nauk (VUAN)," in *Ievreii v Ukraini. Istoriia, kul'tura, tradytsii* (Kyiv: Natsional'na Akademiia Nauk Ukrainy, Instytut Natsional'nykh Vidnosyn i Politolohii, 1997), 78–89.

10. The strange history of the Institute is detailed in Zachary Baker's "History of the Jewish Collections at the Vernadsky Library in Kiev," *Shofar* 10, no. 4 (1992): 31–48. Contemporary sources that discuss the Institute include I. Khinchyn, "Zavdannia yevreis'koi marksivs'koi istoriohrafii i arkhivna sprava," in *Arkhiv radians'koi Ukrainy* (Kharkiv,

1933), 171–82; I. Khinchyn, "Z dosvidu orhanizatsii evreis'koi arkhivnoi sektsii na Ukraini," *Arkhivna Sprava* 1(12) (Kharkiv, 1930): 13–18; and several articles in Yosef Liberberg, ed., *Bibliologisher zamlbukh* (Kharkiv, 1930). For recent sources see Binyamin Lukin, "Archive of the Historical and Ethnographic Society: History and Present Condition," *Jews in Eastern Europe* 1(20) (Jerusalem, 1993): 45–61; Nikolay Senchenko and Irina Sergeeva, "Jewish Scholarly Institutions and Library Collections in Kiev After 1917: A Brief Historical Sketch," *Soviet Jewish Affairs* 2 (1991): 45–50.

11. Avraham Greenbaum and Mikhail Beizer, "Yehiel Ravrebe: Jewish Poet and Scholar," *Jews and Jewish Topics in the Soviet Union and Eastern Europe* 1(17) (Jerusalem, Spring 1992): 30.

12. Mark Sokolianskii, "Dolgo i schastlivo," in Saul Borovoi, *Vospominaniia* (Moscow-Jerusalem: Evreiskii Universitet v Moskve, "Gesharim," 1993), 12–14.

13. O. B. Berenstein, "O sud'be kabineta evreiskogo iazyka i folklora," in *Pam'iataty zarady zhitiia* [Proceedings of the Round Table Discussion devoted to the 40th anniversary of the destruction of the Jewish Anti-Fascist Committee (JAFC)] (Kiev, 1992), 83–88.

14. Eda Beregovskaia, "M. Ya. Beregovskii: zhizn' i sud'ba," *Arfy na verbakh. Prizvanie i sud'ba Moiseia Beregovskogo* (Moscow-Jerusalem: Evreiskii Universitet v Moskve, "Gesharim," 1994), 17–18.

15. On Ukrainian antisemitism in the context of the new Russian Cold War antisemitism, see Mordechai Altshuler, "Soviet Jewry: A Community in Turmoil," in Robert Wistrich, ed., *Terms of Survival: The Jewish World since 1945* (London: Routledge, 1995), 195–230.

16. Lev Gorodetsky's basic textbook on biblical Hebrew is currently being prepared for publication.

17. For updated information on this organization, see http://www.machanaim.org (April 2002).

18. For the bibliographical account of this trend see V. Levin, "Jewish Topics in Ukrainian Literary Journals, 1990–1991," *Jews and Jewish Topics in the Soviet Union and Eastern Europe* 3, no. 19 (Jerusalem, Winter 1992): 52–61.

19. David Makovsky, "Ukraine Makes Offer for Satellites," *Jerusalem Post*, July 16, 1994, 2.

20. *Jerusalem Post*, May 24, 1992.

21. *Jerusalem Post*, January 11, 1993.

22. This was a commonly accepted view of the majority of the Ukrainian state and public figures interviewed by Sheldon Kirshner (with whom I worked as an interpreter) of the *Canadian Jewish News* in the fall of 1992. Among those interviewed were Dmytro Pavlychko, Head of the Parliament Foreign Affairs Commission; Yuri Shcherbak, at that time in transition from the position of the Minister of Ecology to the first Ukrainian Ambassador in Israel; Ivan Drach, Ukrainian poet and MP; Larysa Skoryk, MP; and others.

23. Public lecture at the Ukrainian Research Institute, Harvard University, May 4, 1998.

24. See, for example, Yaroslav Dashkevich's remarks in "Materialy mizhnarodnoii naukovoii konferentsii 'Problemy ukraiins'ko-evreis'kykh vidnosyn'," *Svit*, no. 3–4 (1991): 25–26; by Ivan Dziuba in his "Z orlynoiu pechalliu na choli" (Preface), in I. Kleiner, *Vladimir (Zeev) Zhabotyns'kyi i ukraiins'ke pytannia* (Kiev-Toronto-Edmonton: Instytut Ukrains'kykh Studii, 1995), 21–22; and Larysa Skoryk in Sheldon Kirshner, "Jewish-Ukrainian Relations Shaky," *Canadian Jewish News*, December 10, 1992, 16.

25. See Zhabotinsky, "*K voprosu o natsionalizme. Otvet g. Izgoevu*," 1904; "Urok iubileia Shevchenko" (1911), in Z. Zhabotinskii, *Felietony* (Berlin: Zaltsman, 1922), 186–99. One of the most important publications in this general line of argument is "Ukraina: iudei, hebrei,

ievreii," in Taras Vozniak, ed., *Nezalezhnyi kul'turolohichnyi chasopys,* no. 8 (Lviv, 1996), which features articles, translations, and publications from Paul Celan, Franz Kafka, Martin Buber, S. N. Eisenstadt, Abraham Kook, Abraham Joshua Heschel, Shmuel Yosef Agnon, and Ze'ev Zhabotinsky. This issue of *Chasopys* also offers several brilliant intellectual insights into Ukrainian-Jewish cultural relations. See especially V. Rossman, "Dvi kontseptsii vybranosty, abo neistorychni zauvahy na istorychni temy," 64–89; Myroslav Marynovych, "Ukrains'ko-ievreis'ki stosunky v svitli konfliktolohii: pershe nablyzhennia," 19–29; Taras Andrusiak, Ukrains'ko-Zhydivs'ka peredvyborcha koalitsiia 1907 roku," 57–69; Taras Vozniak, "Tsivilizatsiia ochikuvannia," 98–113.

26. Among them, the families of Yaroslav Dashkevich and Yosif Zissels.

27. This new revisionist outlook of Ukrainian-Jewish relations in historical perspective suffused most of the articles and reports on the subject. See, for instance: "Do ievreis'ko-Ukrain'skoho forumu v Izraili," *Suchasnist',* no. 8 (Kiev, serpen' 1992), 49–127; see especially Yaroslav Dashkevich, "Problematyka vyvchennia ievreis'ko-ukrains'kyx vidnosyn (XVI–pochatok XX st.)," 49–54; Izrail Kleiner, "Uroky vtrachennykh mozhlyvosteii," 55–75; Mykhailo Riabchuk, "Vsesvitnia 'zhydo-mason'ska zmova' ta perspektyvy antysemityzmu na Ukraini," 110–15. For later discussion along the same lines, see "Narod i natsia," *Filosofs'ka i sotsiolohichna dumka,* no. 5–6 (Kiev, 1994): 130–64.

28. Marten Feller has provided an in-depth revision of Jewish-Ukrainian cultural relations during the last two hundred years. Marten Feller, *Poshuky, rozdumy i spohady ievreia, iakyii pam'ataie svoikh didiv, pro ievreis'ko-ukrains'ki vzaiemyny, osoblyvo zh pro movy i stavlennia do nykh* (Drohobych: Vidrodzhennia, 1994).

29. A renowned Jewish-Ukrainian intellectual, Leonid Finberg, has been especially efficient in organizing Ukrainian-Jewish dialogues on political, cultural, and scholarly levels. Yet in the course of the discussion of an earlier version of this essay at the Davis Center/Harvard University conference on February 15, 1999, Finberg himself acknowledged that the "revisionists" push the issue of Ukrainian-Jewish historical relations to the other extreme in order to counterbalance the negative outlook of previous scholarship, both Ukrainian and Jewish.

30. For Semyon Gluzman, his personal friendly relations with Ukrainian nationalists who were political prisoners of the Soviet Gulag system were of paramount importance. See his memoirs: S. Gluzman, M. Marynovich, and Z. Antoniuk, *Lysty z voli* (Kiev: Sfera, 1999).

31. Shlomo Buber, *Anshe shem* (Jerusalem, s.a. [1967–68]); Buber, *Kiryah nisgavah hi ha-ir Zolkva* (Krakow, 1903); Majer Balaban, *Dzieje Zydow w Galicyi i w Rzeczypospolitej krakowskiej, 1772–1868* (Lwow: Nakl. Ksiegarni Polskiej B. Polonieckiego, 1914); Balaban, *Herz Homberg i szkoly jozefinskie dla zydow w Galicyi 1787–1809* (Lwow: Nakl. spolki wydawn, "Kadimah," 1906).

32. Yakov Khonigsman and Alexander Naiman, *Evrei Ukrainy (kratkii ocherk istorii),* Chast' 1 (Kiev: Ukrainsko-finskii institut menedzhmenta i biznesa, 1992). See also Ya. Khonigsman, *Yanovskii Lager'. Kratkii istoricheskii ocherk* (Lvov: L'vovskoe obshchestvo erveiskoii kul'tury im. Sholom-Aleikhema, 1996); Ya. Khonigsman, *Katastrofa l'vovskogo evreistva* (L'vov: L'vovskoe obshchestvo erveiskoii kul'tury im. Sholom-Aleikhema, 1993); Ya. Khonigsman, *600 let i dva goda spustia. Istroria evreev Drohobycha i Borislava.* (L'vov: Bnei-Brit "Leopolis," L'vovskoe Obshchestvo evreiskoi kul'tury, 1997).

33. Vladimir Melamed, *Evrei vo L'vove (XIII–pervaia polovina XX veka)* (L'vov: Sovmestnoe Ukrainsko-Amerikanskoe predpriiatie TECOP, 1994).

34. R. I. Goldstein, ed., *Materialy k istorii evreiskoi obshchiny Dnepropetrovshchiny (k 200-letiiu osniovania obshchiny)* (Dnipropetrovs'k: VPOP "Dnipro," 1992).

35. E. Solomonik, ed., *Evrei Kryma. Ocherki istorii* (Simferopol'-Ierusalim: Mosty, 1997); Mikhail Mitsel', *Obshchiny iudeiskogo veroispovedaniia v Ukraine. Kiev, L'vov: 1945–1981 g.* (Kiev: Sfera, 1998) [*Biblioteka Instytutu Iudaiky*].

36. *Evreiskoe naselenie iuga Ukrainy: Istoriia i sovremennost'. Tezisy k nauchno-prakticheskoi konferentsi, 17–18 oktiabria 1991 g.* (Zaporozhie: Zaporozhskii Gosudarstvennyi Universitet, 1991); *Ievreis'ke naselennia Pivdnia Ukrainy: Doslidzhennia i dokumenty,* vyp. 1 (Zaporizzhia: Zaporiz'kyi Derzhavnyi Universytet, 1994).

37. His most recent publications include *Jewish Sites of Kiev: A Historical Map* (Kiev: Institut Iudaiki, 1998). See also Mikhail Kal'nitskii, *Sinagoga Kievskoi Iudeiskoi Obshchiny. Istoricheskii ocherk* (Kiev: Institut Iudaiki, 1996).

38. Yu. Liakhovitskii published some 121 documents that demonstrate the rampant antisemitism of local Ukrainian authorities in Kharkiv during the Nazi occupation. See Yu. Liakhovitskii, *Zheltaia kniga. Svidetel'stva, fakty, dokumenty,* vyp. 3 (Kharkov: Biblioteka gazety "Bensiakh," 1994), 13–69. Other publications of the "Drobnitskii Iar" group include Yu. Liakhovitskii, *Poprannaia mezuza. Kniga Drobnitskogo Yara,* vyp. 1 (Khar'kov: Osnova, 1991); idem., *Holocaust na Ukraine i antisemitism v perspektive* (Kharkov: Bensiakh, 1992).

39. Anatolii Podolskii, *Genocide of the Jewish Population of the Middle Dnepr Region in the Years of German Occupation, 1941–1944* (Moscow: Jewish Heritage Society, 1995) [Preprints and reprints Series, no. 18].

40. Zhanna Kovba, *Liudianist' v bezodni pekla. Povedinka mistsevoho naselennia Skhidnoii Halychyny v roky "ostatochnoho rozv'iazannia ievreis'koho pytannia"* (Kyiv: Instytut Iudaiiky, 1998). On the basis of anecdotal evidence, Kovba makes several far-fetched statements: on the tolerance toward Jews in Galicia in the 1930s (p. 29); and on the tolerant attitude of Galician Ukrainians to Jews in 1941–43 (pp. 95–98). She resorts to a typical Soviet-style reference to the anonymous ("certain") scholars as well as to the powerful and again, anonymous, groups interested in stirring up national hatred, while criticizing previous Holocaust scholarship. "The materials that I have worked through and analyzed allow me to claim, that both [Jewish and Ukrainian nationalist historians—YP-S] base their assumptions on myths and stereotypes that are cultivated and spread by certain (*deiakymy*) extremist-biased activists of Jewish, Ukrainian or Polish origin, or by those who are carrying out orders of the outside groups" (203–204). For a more balanced approach to the issue by a Ukrainian historian, see Yaroslav Hrytsak, "Ukraintsi v anty-ievreis'kykh aktsiiakh u roky druhoi svitovoi viiny," *Nezalezhnyi kul'turolohichnyi chasopys,* no. 8 (L'viv, 1996): 60–68.

41. See Vadim Skuratovskii, *Problema avtorstva "Protokolov Sionskikh Mudretsov"* (Kyiiv: Dukh i Litera, Biblioteka Instytutu Iudaiiky, 2001); Simon Markish, ed., *Rodnoi Golos: stranitsy russko-evreiskoi literatury kontsa XIX—nachala XX v.* (Kyiiv: Dukh i Litera, Biblioteka Instytutu Iudaiiky, 2001).

42. See, for instance, information on the course "History and Culture of the Jewish People" offered at L'viv University: http://www.franko.lviv.ua/faculty/istor.html. Kyiv Mohyla Academy offers "Judaism" as an elective course in the Department of Philosophy. See http://www.ukma.kiev.ua/univ/fac/FHS/departs/philos/f_corg4.htm.

43. For updated information on Jewish schools in Ukraine, see the Web site of the Ukrainian Center for Jewish Education: http://www.jewukr.org/center/ (April 2002).

44. Vladimir Khanin, "Hakhinuch hayehudi be'ukraina," *Yehuday brit hamoetsot bema'avar,* 18, no. 3 (1995): 102–103, 109. The author refers extensively to the archive and the expertise of the Center for Jewish Education.

45. Personal interviews with Professor Grigory Yablonsky, the former ISU rector; Professor Froim Gorovsky, former Dean of the Department of Humanities; Dr. Meir Yusim,

the vice-rector of ISU; ISU students who attended seminars of the Ukrainian Center for Jewish Education; Genia Ziskind, administrator, responsible for the schedule of Chief Rabbi Yaakov Bleich; and Rabbi Yaakov Bleich.

46. The breakdown of the financial activities of the Va'ad had bitter implications for Ukrainian Jews. See, for instance, "Firm Steals Millions from Ukrainian Jews," *Milwaukee Journal Sentinel,* October 26, 1995, 3. It also caused a political uproar in Israel. See, for instance: Batsheva Tsur, "Jewish Agency, Government Sued by Ukrainian Immigrants," *Jerusalem Post,* May 29, 1996, 6.

47. See http://www.jewish-heritage.org (especially the archive of the newsletter "Jewish Studies in Eastern Europe") (April 2002).

48. See http://www.judaica.8m.com.

49. *Ievreis'ka istoriia ta kul'tura v Ukraini. Materialy konferentsii. Kyiv, 22–23 lystopada* 1993 (Kyiv: Asotsiatsiia ievreis'kykh orghanizatsii ta obshchyn Ukrainy, Asotsiatsia Iudaiky, 1994).

50. Among the most interesting publications of the Institute of Judaica are: *Yehupets, Khudozhnio-publitsistychnyii almanakh,* vyp. 1 (Kyiv: Assotsiatsia Iudaiky Ukrainy, 1995); *Yehupets, Khudozhnio-publitsistychnyii almanakh Instytutu iudaiky,* vyp. 3 (Kyiv: Sfera, 1997); *Yehupets, Khudozhnio-publitsistychnyii almanakh Instytutu iudaiky,* vyp. 4 (Kyiv: Sfera, 1998).

51. Of those young people who graduated the Jewish boys' school in Kiev in 1994 and 1995 and who chose to study at local establishments of higher education, not one went to the then operating Department of the Jewish Studies at the International Solomon University.

ELEVEN

❦

MARK TOLTS

Demography of the Jews in the Former Soviet Union: Yesterday and Today

Since 1989, mass emigration has played a decisive role in the fate of the Jews in the former Soviet Union (FSU). However, the recent levels of assimilation and demographic erosion are not simply consequences of this mass emigration; they have deep roots in the historically unfavorable dynamics of the Jewish population in the Soviet Union. The "demographic collapse" of the Jewish populations of the successor states to the Soviet Union is due mostly to internal trends and was only accelerated by mass emigration.

To understand the main demographic trends among these Jews, we must estimate their numerical dynamics in different parts of the FSU. We shall analyze the dynamics of Jewish emigration from the FSU as well as its directions and selectivity. Mixed marriage and demographic erosion will also be studied. Fortunately, recent statistics contain rich data, on the basis of which we can develop a rather detailed picture of Jewish demographic dynamics in the FSU.[1]

❦ Numerical Decline

The numbers of Jews enumerated in Soviet census data have been entirely dependent on the self-declaration of the respondents. Conceptually, these numbers correspond to what has been defined as the "core" Jewish population.[2] The "core" Jewish population is the aggregate of all those who, when asked, identified themselves as Jews or, in the case of children, were

MARK TOLTS

identified as such by their parents. It does not include persons of Jewish origin who reported another ethnic nationality in the census.

By contrast, the "enlarged" Jewish population includes "core" Jews and their non-Jewish household members. In the FSU today this group is significantly larger than the "core" Jewish population. For example, in the late 1980s the ratio of "core" to "enlarged" Jewish population in Russia was roughly 1 to 1.6, and in Ukraine and Belorussia about 1 to 1.4; on the basis of the 1994 Russian micro-census, the ratio of "core" to "enlarged" Jewish population in Russia was estimated at 1 to 1.8.[3] Thus, the "core" Jewish population is obviously smaller than the total population eligible for *aliyah* according to the Israeli Law of Return which applies to Jews, children and grandchildren of Jews, and their spouses.

Table 11.1.
The "Core" Jewish Population[a] in the FSU, by Republic/Region, 1959, 1989, and 1999, in Thousands

Republic/region	1959[b]	1989[b]	1999[c]	1989 as % of 1959	1999 as % of 1989
Russian Federation	880	570	310	65	54
Ukraine	840	487	145	58	30
Belorussia/Belarus	150	112	27.8[b]	75	25
Baltic States	67	40	18	60	45
Moldavia	95	66	7	69	11
Transcaucasia	99	67	16[d]	68	24
Central Asia	148	138	20	93	14
FSU	2,279	1,480	544	65	37

(a) "Core" Jews at the beginning of the given year, including "Tats."
(b) Census data.
(c) Estimate.
(d) Not including "Tats" in Azerbaijan; on the problem of evaluation of the 1999 Azerbaijan census results, see text.
Sources: 1959 and 1989 Soviet censuses, 1994 Russian micro-census, and the post-Soviet national censuses; vital and migration statistics.

The last Soviet census was taken in 1989, giving us a good base from which to measure Jewish population decreases during the recent period of mass emigration. The first post-Soviet Russian micro-census, which encompassed 5 percent of the total population as of February 14, 1994, presented a new base for the estimate of the "core" Jewish population for the Russian Federation.[4] In 1999, population censuses were conducted in four other countries: Azerbaijan, Belarus, Kazakhstan, and Kirgiziia.

Demography of the Jews in the Former Soviet Union

The recent Jewish population decline has been much greater than it had been over the entire three decades between 1959 and 1989. Estimates show that during the first ten years of the recent mass emigration (1989–98), the total number of "core" Jews in the entire FSU dropped from 1,480,000 to about 544,000 (see Table 11.1).[5] The absolute number of this recent decrease in the FSU as a whole (936,000) was higher than that in the previous three decades (799,000), and of course the rate of this drop (63 percent) was much faster than between 1959 and 1989 (35 percent).

There are great differences between the dramatic decline of the population in Russia and that of the other newly independent states. By the beginning of 1999, the number of Jews in the Russian Federation had decreased to approximately 310,000. During the first ten years of the mass emigration, the Jewish population fell by 46 percent in Russia (that is, a bit more than between 1959 and 1989, when the rate of decrease in the republic was 35 percent). The absolute number of this decrease in Russia (about 260,000) was about one-fifth less than that between 1959 and 1989 (310,000).

Between 1989 and 1999, the number of Jews in the Former Soviet Union outside Russia dropped by almost a factor of four—from 910,000 to 234,000. The estimated absolute number of this recent decrease in the other newly independent states as a whole (676,000) was much higher than in the previous entire three decades between 1959 and 1989 (489,000).

Armenia experienced an especially dramatic numerical decline, and its already small Jewish community has almost disappeared. The numerical decline by 89 percent in Moldavia was very impressive; and in Central Asia and the Caucasus the decrease was by 86 and 76 percent, respectively. Also in Ukraine, the numerical decline was higher than the average for the FSU —70 percent. The 1999 census in Belarus was the first that empirically confirmed the dramatic demographic decline of a sizable Jewish community in the FSU outside the Russian Federation. The census data show that during the ten years following the 1989 Soviet census, the total number of "core" Jews in Belarus dropped by 75 percent.

At the start of the recent mass emigration, Russia's Jews made up 39 percent of the total number of Jews in the FSU. However, between 1989 and 1999 the population decline of Russia's Jewry was only 28 percent of the total Jewish population decline in the FSU. As a result, by the beginning of 1999 Russia's Jews accounted for about 57 percent of the total number of Jews in the FSU. Post-Soviet Jewry is concentrated more and more in Russia. Thus, it is rapidly turning into *Russian* Jewry by place of residence in the FSU.

🏵 Recent Mass Migrations

Migrations are a most important demographic phenomenon among FSU Jewry today. Movements include emigration beyond the borders of the former Soviet Union, as well as resettlement of Jews remaining within the FSU.

EMIGRATION OUTSIDE THE FSU

The movement of large numbers of Jews from the FSU to Israel and the West is a well-known feature of the contemporary Jewish world. The rate of this recent mass emigration has been even higher than the mass Jewish emigration from the Russian Empire had been at the turn of the twentieth century.[6]

According to my estimates, in the ten years between 1989 and 1998, about 1.2 million (post-)Soviet Jews and their non-Jewish relatives left the FSU. This number is more than four times greater than the entire emigration totals from the previous twenty years (Table 11.2).

I have presented figures from available data, in an attempt to estimate the total size of the recent Jewish mass emigration from the FSU for the above-mentioned ten-year period (1989–98) by countries of destination. Many complexities are encountered in making such estimates.

I have based my estimates on the statistics of the countries of destination. For emigration to Israel, *aliyah* data by republics of the FSU from the Israel Central Bureau of Statistics (CBS) have been used, and these are quite accurate (see Appendix 11.1). For emigration to the United States, I have relied mainly upon the statistics of HIAS (Hebrew Immigrant Aid Society); see Appendix 11.2. Immigration figures for other countries (Germany, Canada, Australia, and others) are much less comprehensive and clear, and have been estimated roughly from different sources.

Our estimates show that total emigration peaked in 1990 and 1991, when 90 percent and 76 percent of the emigrants, respectively, went to Israel. From 1992 to 1998, slightly more than half of those who emigrated to countries outside the FSU after the peak of 1990–91 chose Israel as their destination. During the entire first ten years of the mass emigration, the number of Jews and their non-Jewish relatives who emigrated from the FSU to Israel totaled about 770,000, and the percentage of emigrants who arrived in Israel as their country of destination was 62 percent.

For the same ten-year period, the number of Jews and their non-Jewish relatives who emigrated from the FSU to the United States may be esti-

Demography of the Jews in the Former Soviet Union

Table 11.2.
*Emigration of Jews and Their Non-Jewish Relatives from the FSU,
1969–88 and 1989–98, in Thousands*

Year	Total	Thereof to:			Percent of total to Israel
		Israel	U.S.[a]	Germany	
1969–78	177	135	42	...	76
1979–88	117	33	84	...	28
1969–88	294	168	126	...	57
1989	72	12.9	56[b]	0.6	18
1990	205	185.2	6.5[b]	8.5	90
1991	195	147.8	35.2	8.0	76
1992	123	65.1	45.9	4.0	53
1993	127	66.1	35.9	16.6	52
1994	116	68.1	32.9	8.8	59
1995	114	64.8	21.7	15.2	57
1996	106	59.0	19.5	16.0	56
1997	99	54.6	14.5	19.4	55
1998	83	46.0	7.4	17.8	55
1989–1998	1,240	769.9[c]	290.0[d]	114.9	62

(a) Data for 1969–88 include all destinations other than Israel for those who emigrated with Israeli visas; annual data for 1991–98 cover only HIAS-assisted emigrants (see Appendix 11.2).
(b) Departures.
(c) Total does not equal the sum for years due to rounding.
(d) Including emigrants who had not been assisted by HIAS.
Sources: Israel. CBS data and other governmental sources; Mordechai Altshuler, *Soviet Jewry Since the Second World War: Population and Social Structure* (New York: Greenwood Press, 1987), 56; Yoel Florsheim, "Emigration of Jews from the Soviet Union in 1988," *Jews and Jewish Topics in the Soviet Union and Eastern Europe,* no. 2(9) (1989): 30; Sidney Heitman, "Soviet Emigration in 1990: A New 'Fourth Wave'?" *Soviet Jewish Affairs* 21, no. 2 (1991): 13; Madeleine Tress, "Welfare State Type, Labour Markets and Refugees: A Comparison of Jews from the Former Soviet Union in the United States and the Federal Republic of Germany," *Ethnic and Racial Studies* 21, no. 1 (1998): 118; Pavel Polian, "Evreiskaia emigratsiia iz byvshego SSSR v Germaniiu," *Vestnik Evreiskogo Universiteta* 4(22) (2000): 187.

mated at approximately 290,000. The number of Jews and their non-Jewish relatives who emigrated to Germany was lower (about 115,000). However, from 1997 onwards, more emigrants went to Germany than to the United States, making Germany the second-ranking receiving country for Jewish emigration from the FSU.

During the ten-year period from 1989 to 1998, more than 230,000 Jews from Russia and their non-Jewish relatives migrated to Israel (30 percent of the total number of all FSU immigrants to Israel). Over the same period, the recorded number of immigrants from Ukraine to Israel exceeded 240,000 (31.5 percent). Immigrants from Russia to Israel were the most numerous group between 1991 and 1994, but in 1989–90 and 1995–98, more immigrants arrived from Ukraine. During 1989–98, the recorded number of immigrants from Belarus to Israel was 63,000 (8.2 percent of the total number of FSU immigrants to Israel). In this ten-year period, emigration to Israel alone from each region (except the Baltic States) was higher than the entire emigration totals over the previous nineteen years (1970–88; see Table 11.3).

Table 11.3.
Emigration of Jews and Their Non-Jewish Relatives from the FSU to Israel and the U.S., by Republic/Region, 1970–88 and 1989–98, in Thousands

Republic/region	Total, 1970–88[a]	To Israel, 1989–98	To the U.S., 1989–98[b]
Russian Federation	50.4	230.5	70.9
Ukraine	106.7	242.2	121.3
Belorussia	13.8	63.2	32.4
Baltic States	27.3	19.4	7.6
Moldavia	29.4	44.2	15.1
Transcaucasia	41.5	50.8	9.7
Central Asia	21.7	101.1	33.0
Unknown	0.0	18.5	0.0
Total	290.8	769.9	290.0

(a) Including all destinations for those who emigrated with Israeli visas.
(b) Author's estimate for republics/regions is based on the known distribution of emigrants in 1989 and 1991–98, which was adjusted for the total estimated number in the period.
Sources: Altshuler, *Soviet Jewry since the Second World War: Population and Social Structure,* 62; Florsheim, "Emigration of Jews from the Soviet Union in 1988," 30; Table 2 and Appendixes 11.1 and 11.2 of this chapter.

Throughout the years of migration to the United States, Ukrainian Jews made up the most numerous group. In the same ten-year period from

1989 to 1998, according to our estimate, more than 120,000 Jews and their non-Jewish relatives migrated from this republic to the United States (42 percent of the total number of FSU immigrants to the United States). Over the same period, the recorded number of immigrants from the Russian Federation to the United States exceeded 70,000 (24 percent), while about 32,000 Jews from Belarus and their non-Jewish relatives migrated to the United States (11 percent).

Based on these migration figures, we may measure the different levels of emigration from the three Slavic republics of the FSU to Israel and to the United States. During the ten-year period from 1989 to 1998, the recorded migration of Jews and their non-Jewish relatives to Israel, as a percentage of the estimates based on the 1989 Soviet census number of the "enlarged" Jewish population,[7] was as follows: 26 percent for the Russian Federation, 38 percent for Ukraine, and 42 percent for Belarus. For the same period, this indicator of migration to the United States showed more pronounced discrepancies between Russia, Ukraine, and Belarus: these percentages were estimated at 8 percent, 18 percent, and 21 percent, respectively.

Using a different approach, for the period 1990–95, total migration to Israel and the United States was estimated at higher levels from Moldavia, Transcaucasia, and Central Asia than from the Slavic states of the FSU, as well as from the Baltic states.[8] However, we do not know the figures for the distribution of migrants to Germany from the FSU by republic, and our knowledge of the geography of origin of the (post-)Soviet Jewish emigration as a whole is incomplete.

There were also great differences in the levels of emigration beyond the FSU from different parts of the Russian Federation. During the recent mass emigration, Jewish emigration was higher from St. Petersburg than from Moscow and the provinces (outside Moscow and St. Petersburg) as a whole. However, levels of emigration from the North Caucasus and Birobijan were the highest.[9]

The percentage of Jews (by any definition) in this period of migration decreased from the start of the mass emigration through the most recent period, up through 2002. For example, according to official Russian data based on internal passport records,[10] the proportion of Jews among all those who emigrated to Israel fell from 64 percent in the second half of 1992 to 36 percent in 1997 and 31 percent in 1998.

According to the *halachic* (Jewish religious) approach used in Israeli statistics, the proportion of Jews among immigrants was much higher than in Russian statistics for the same period.[11] In 1997, according to official Israeli data, the percentage of Jews among all immigrants to Israel from the FSU was 59 percent, and it was about the same from the Russian Federation.[12] At the start of the recent wave of *aliyah* (in 1990) this percentage among all immigrants to Israel from the FSU was as high as 96 percent.[13]

Younger people are more likely to migrate than others. Among (post-) Soviet Jews, the younger the population, the higher the percentage of intermarriage and the greater the number of offspring of mixed couples. Aggregate *aliyah* data are heavily dependent on the age structure of the "enlarged" Jewish population, and such data cannot show the propensity for *aliyah* of homogeneous and mixed Jewish families.

Actually, the data of the 1994 Russian micro-census show that the "core" Jewish population was much older than the "enlarged" Jewish population. The median ages of these two populations were 56.0 and 46.8 years, respectively. The percentage aged sixty-five and above was 32.4 in the "core" Jewish population and 22.8 in the "enlarged" Jewish population (see Table 11.4).

Table 11.4.

Age Structure of the "Core" and "Enlarged" Jewish Populations[a] in Russia and of All Immigrants from Russia to Israel, 1994, in Percent

Age group	"Core" Jewish population in Russia, 1994	"Enlarged" Jewish population in Russia, 1994	All immigrants from Russia to Israel, 1994
Total	100.0	100.0	100.0
0–14	6.2	13.4	21.0
15–29	9.9	16.4	26.0
30–44	16.5	17.5	20.6
45–64	35.0	29.9	20.2
65+	32.4	22.8	12.2
Thereof 75+	14.5	9.6	3.8
Median age	56.0	46.8	32.0

(a) Ashkenazic Jews only.

Sources: Mark Tolts, "The Interrelationship between Emigration and the Socio-Demographic Profile of Russian Jewry," in Noah Lewin-Epstein, Yaacov Ro'i, and Paul Ritterband, eds., *Russian Jews on Three Continents* (London: Frank Cass, 1997), 153; Evgeny Soroko, "Jewish Households in Russia According to the 1994 Microcensus," Seminar paper discussed at the Division of Jewish Demography of the Avraham Harman Institute of Contemporary Jewry, The Hebrew University of Jerusalem, 1998, Tables A2–A4; Israel. Central Bureau of Statistics, *Supplement to Monthly Bulletin of Statistics,* no. 9 (1995): 97.

For the same year, the median age of all immigrants to Israel from the Russian Federation was 32.0, or twenty-four years less than the "core" Jewish population of the country of origin; the percentage aged sixty-five and above among immigrants was only 12.2 percent. Especially low was the share of immigrants aged seventy-five and above; it was only 3.8 percent, or fewer by a factor of about four than in the "core" Jewish population of the Russian Federation.

These data clearly show the highly selective character of emigration by age—the emigrants are much younger than those who remain. This is a very important factor for the future of the Jewish communities in the FSU. Moreover, the level of Jewish identity is also an important indicator.[14] Obviously, emigration is higher among the more strongly identifying Jews, and these are the ones who have left—and are still leaving—the FSU.

RESETTLEMENT WITHIN THE FSU

During the 1990s, migratory movements other than mass emigration affected the number of Jews in the different parts of the FSU. These movements mostly involved migration to and from the Russian Federation, and we are fortunate to have statistical information about their patterns.[15]

In 1989–98, according to official Russian data, 20,577 Jews arrived in the Russian Federation from other parts of the FSU, and 14,637 Jews emigrated to other parts of the FSU. Thus, the recorded migratory balance for Russia's Jews with other parts of the FSU was positive, totaling 5,940 (see Table 11.5).

The data show that in 1989–91, Russia's Jews had a slightly negative migratory balance (864) with other parts of the FSU. But between 1992 and 1998, the registered migratory balance was positive, totaling more than 6,800.

In 1989–91, before the dissolution of the Soviet Union, Russia's Jewish migration balance was negative with all parts of the country except Transcaucasia and Central Asia. Since 1992, immigration of Jews from the Baltic States and Moldavia to Russia has exceeded Jewish emigration from the Russian Federation to these republics. Since 1994, Russia has had a positive Jewish migration balance with the Jews from Ukraine.

Two regions have been the principal sources of immigration to Russia: Transcaucasia and Central Asia. These two regions are the most conflict-ridden areas in the FSU. Accordingly, in some cases emigration to Russia has simply been a means for Jews to escape ethnic conflicts and wars. For example, in 1989–98 the registered Jewish migration from Azerbaijan and Georgia to the Russian Federation consisted of about 7 percent of the total number of Jews in each republic (not including part of the Mountain Jews who were recorded as "Tats" [see note 5]), according to the last Soviet census of 1989. During that period, Russia's positive migration balance was approximately 3,400 for

MARK TOLTS

Table 11.5.
Registered Migration of the Jews in Russia with Other Parts of the FSU, 1989–1998

	1989–91[a]	1992–94	1995–98	1989–98[a]
Immigration	7,900	7,080	5,597	20,577
thereof from:				
Ukraine	3,400	2,314	1,986	7,700
Belorussia	900	417	300	1,600
Baltic	300	406	199	900
Moldavia	350	310	234	900
Transcaucasia	1,350	1,652	1,453	4,450
Central Asia	1,600	1,981	1,425	5,000
Emigration	8,764	4,065	1,808	14,637
thereof to:				
Ukraine	4,700	2,445	940	8,100
Belorussia	1,300	666	304	2,250
Baltic	500	105	50	650
Moldavia	650	227	92	950
Transcaucasia	650	164	190	1,000
Central Asia	1,000	458	232	1,700
Balance	-864	3,015	3,789	5,940
thereof with:				
Ukraine	-1,300	-131	1,046	-400
Belorussia	-400	-249	-4	-650
Baltic	-200	301	149	250
Moldavia	-300	83	142	-50
Transcaucasia	700	1,488	1,263	3,450
Central Asia	600	1,523	1,193	3,300

(a) Author's estimates for regions, sum of which does not equal the (published) total due to rounding.

Sources: Appendixes 11.3 and 11.4.

movements of the Jews to and from Transcaucasia, and more than 3,300 for those living in Central Asia.

Some of the Jewish immigrants to Russia were refugees from other parts of the FSU. By the beginning of 1997, the number of officially registered Jewish refugees in Russia exceeded one thousand, a figure that had doubled over the previous two years. Although the issue of the return of ethnic Russians to the Russian Federation from other parts of the FSU has received attention, the estimated rate of Jewish immigration to Russia for 1995—5.5 per 1,000—was about the same as that of ethnic Russians.

We may also assume that official Russian data to some extent under-estimated the actual number of Jewish immigrants from other parts of the FSU because the data were based on Ministry of Internal Affairs registration (with the local police [*militsiia*]), which in turn was dependent on residence permits (*propiska*) or registration. In recent years many immigrants, including Jews, have not been registered, especially in Moscow. This fact is generally known to all who have attempted to study Russian migration.[16]

In 1994–98, Russia had a positive balance of Jewish migration with all other parts of the FSU (except Belarus, with which this balance was about nil), and the unique position of Russia's Jews was dependent on this balance to partially offset their strongly negative vital balance. During this period, the leading input factor of Russia's total Jewish demographic balance was Jewish immigration from other parts of the FSU, and not Jewish fertility.

At the same time, the sizable immigration to Russia of non-Ashkenazic Jews from Transcaucasia and Central Asia has somewhat changed the ethnic composition of the Jewish population in the Russian Federation, especially in Moscow.

Table 11.6.

Percentage of Mixed Marriages among All Registered Marriages involving Jews in Belorussia/Belarus, Latvia, Russia, and Ukraine, 1978–96

Year	Belorussia		Latvia		Russia		Ukraine	
	Males	Females	Males	Females	Males	Females	Males	Females
1978	38.3	26.1	52.9[a]	35.6[a]	59.3	43.0	44.7	34.2
1988	48.3	39.9	...	...	73.2	62.8	54.1	44.7
1990	...	...	59.9	49.1	...	...	...	...
1991	...	...	69.4	57.9	...	...	64.7	55.7
1992	...	...	71.9	60.5	...	...	67.9	57.8
1993	...	...	74.5	61.4	...	...	72.9	63.5
1994	...	...	78.8	67.3	...	...	74.3	66.1
1995	...	...	83.3	70.0	...	...	79.4	70.1
1996	...	...	85.9	82.8	...	...	81.6	73.7

(a) 1980 data.

Sources: Goskomstat SSSR, *Naselenie SSSR, 1988: Statisticheskii ezhegodnik* (Moscow: Finansy i statistika, 1989), 212–13; *Etnosituatsiia v Latvii* (Riga, 1994), 12; Latvia, State Statistics Committee, *Statistical Yearbook of Latvia, 1995* (Riga, 1995), 65; idem, *Demographic Yearbook of Latvia, 1997* (Riga, 1997), 129; Ukraine, Ministry of Statistics, *Naselennya Ukrainy 1992* (Kiev, 1993), 122; idem, *Naselennya Ukrainy 1994* (Kiev, 1995), 131; idem, *Naselennya Ukrainy 1995* (Kiev, 1997), 117; idem, *Naselennya Ukrainy 1996* (Kiev, 1998), 68.

🕮 *The Increase in Mixed Marriages*

Since World War II, the Soviet Jewish population has seen a great increase in the numbers of mixed marriages. This process actually had begun in the period between the two world wars.[17] Unfortunately, Soviet statistics provide little relevant data for the period following the Second World War.[18]

On the eve of the start of the mass emigration in 1988, the frequency of mixed marriages among all marriages involving Jews was as follows: in Russia—73.2 percent for males and 62.8 percent for females (a relative increase of 23 and 46 percent respectively, as compared to 1978); in Ukraine—54.1 percent for males and 44.7 percent for females (an increase of 21 and 31 percent); and in Belarus—48.3 percent for males and 39.9 percent for females (an increase of 26 and 53 percent). In 1990 in Latvia, this indicator was 59.9 percent for males and 49.1 percent for females (a relative increase of 13 and 38 percent respectively, as compared to 1980; see Table 11.6).

In 1988–89 in the Soviet Union as a whole, the frequency of mixed marriages among all marriages involving Jews was 57.9 percent for Jewish males and 47.1 percent for Jewish females; this indicator was higher among previously divorced Jewish persons, where the totals were 61.5 and 48.8 percent, respectively.

Mixed marriage is not merely a consequence of assimilation, but is also the result of demographic realities: the shortage of Jewish marriage partners for Jewish males had, in large part, brought about the spread of mixed marriages in the Soviet Union. The greatest shortage of potential Jewish brides was encountered by Jewish males in Russia where, according to the 1979 census, men outnumbered women among Jews in all age groups under fifty; and according to the 1989 census, even up to age sixty. These numbers are naturally coincident with the character of Jewish migration. In other republics, the sex imbalance was much more moderate.[19] Correspondingly, the percentage of mixed marriages was highest in Russia, and lower in other republics.

A distinctive feature of the age structure of Soviet Jewry during the post-war period is its "regressive" nature; that is, younger generations tend to be consistently less numerous. In view of sex ratios in adjacent age groups of the Jewish population, a male's chances of finding a candidate for marriage within his ethnic community are reduced even further. For instance, in 1989 in Russia the number of Jewish females aged twenty-five to twenty-nine was thirteen less than what was necessary to balance each hundred Jewish males of the same age group, while in the Ukraine and Belarus the imbalance was only three and seven per hundred Jewish males, respectively. For the same age group of males, the imbalance was much greater when it was compared with the adjacent group of females aged twenty to twenty-four: one-third or more in all Slavic republics.

The mass emigration of the 1990s hastened the erosion of the Jewish marriage market. By 1996, according to annual official vital statistics, the frequency of mixed marriages among all marriages in Latvia involving Jews was 85.9 percent for males and 82.8 percent for females, and in Ukraine this indicator was 81.6 and 73.7 percent, respectively—levels much higher than those of Russia's Jews in 1988.

Our assumption that the level of mixed marriage rose as a result of the mass emigration of the 1990s is confirmed by the situation among all currently married Jews in the FSU. Indeed, according to the estimate I made on the basis of the 1994 micro-census data, among all currently married Jews in Russia, 63 percent of males and 44 percent of females had spouses from another ethnic group, an increase of five and four percentage points since 1989, respectively.[20] This estimate coincides with the rise of the Jewish sex imbalance in Russia. Previously, this shortage applied to all those up to age sixty; according to the 1994 micro-census, not only had it advanced to ages sixty to sixty-four, but among all those who were under fifty at the time of the 1989 census, the ratio had worsened over these five years.[21]

In the postwar period in the Soviet Union, rising intermarriage was accompanied by a great increase in the proportion of children born to mixed couples: from 19 percent in 1958 to about 41 percent in 1988. Corresponding to Russia's high percentage of mixed marriages among the Jews of the Slavic republics, the proportion of these children among all children born to Jewish mothers was greater there than in the other republics: 58 percent in 1988, or 2.1 times more than three decades earlier (as noted above, we have no data on the actual number of such marriages). At the same time, it was 42 percent in the Ukraine and 37 percent in Belarus, marking an increase of 2.4 and 2.7 times, respectively (see Table 11.7).

At the start of the mass emigration in 1989, in some small Jewish population groups this indicator was even higher than it was in Russia: 60 percent in Turkmenistan, 63 percent in Estonia, and 75 percent in Armenia. Thus, we see the relevance of the size of a Jewish community to the spread of mixed marriage; this spread may be gauged by the indirect indicator of the proportion of children born to mixed couples among all children born to Jewish mothers.

Following the start of the recent mass emigration, the proportion of children born to mixed couples among all children born to Jewish mothers

MARK TOLTS

Table 11.7.
Percentage of Children of Mixed Origin among All Children Born to Jewish Mothers in the FSU, by Republic, 1958–93

Republic	1958	1968	1988	1993
FSU	19	...	41	...
Russia	27	40	58	68
West				
Ukraine	17	30	42	69[d]
Belorussia/Belarus	14	32	37	71
Moldavia	7	12	17	58
Baltic				
Latvia	14	27	40[b]	48[d]
Lithuania	12	19	32	...
Estonia	34	...	63[c]	67
Transcaucasia				
Georgia	9	13[a]	25[b]	...
Azerbaijan	20	21	28[b]	40
Armenia	27	...	75[c]	100[e]
Central Asia				
Uzbekistan	10	13	13	20
Tadjikistan	13	20	15	18
Kirgiziia	16	...	25[c]	47
Turkmenistan	37	...	60[c]	44[f]
Kazakhstan	35	43	41	65

(a) 1967.
(b) 1987.
(c) 1989.
(d) 1992.
(e) One birth.
(f) Four births to Jewish mothers and non-Jewish fathers.
Sources: Statkomitet SNG, *Demografcheskii ezhegodnik 1994* (Moscow, 1995), 49, 69, 89, 111, 131, 151, 171, 191, 211, 231; Latvia. State Statistics Committee, *Demographic Yearbook of Latvia, 1992* (Riga, 1993), 84; M. Kupovetsky, "Liudskie poteri evreiskogo naseleniia v poslevoennykh granitsakh SSSR v gody Velikoi Otechestvennoi voiny," *Vestnik Evreiskogo Universiteta v Moskve,* no. 2(9) (1995): 147; Mark Tolts, "Demographic Trends among the Jews in the Three Slavic Republics of the Former USSR: A Comparative Analysis," in Sergio DellaPergola and Judith Even, eds., *Papers in Jewish Demography 1993* (Jerusalem: The Avraham Harman Institute of Contemporary Jewry, The Hebrew University of Jerusalem; World Union of Jewish Studies; Association for Jewish Demography and Statistics, 1997), 155; unpublished USSR/CIS statistics; and Appendix 11.5 of this chapter.

in 1993 reached 68 percent in Russia, and it was slightly higher in Ukraine and Belarus. From 1988 to 1993, in Moldavia this proportion rose dramatically, from 17 to 58 percent. These dynamics coincide with the very high level of recent Jewish emigration from the latter three countries. In 1997, in Latvia among all children born to married Jewish females, 65 percent had fathers from other ethnic groups. In 1998, in the Russian Federation the proportion of children born to mixed couples among all children born to Jewish mothers reached 74 percent.

Soviet and post-Soviet vital statistics give no data on the number of children born to couples with Jewish husbands and non-Jewish wives. However, this information is very important to any analysis of the dynamics of the "enlarged" Jewish population. As the number of these births cannot be lower than the figures for children born to Jewish mothers in mixed couples, in order to obtain a minimal estimate, one may assume these figures to be equal.

Approximately twice as many Jewish men in the FSU were currently married to non-Jewish women as were Jewish women to non-Jewish men. Hence, among the proportions of children born to mixed couples as a whole of all newborn children with at least one Jewish parent in the Slavic republics, the greatest proportion was in Russia: about half in the late 1950s, perhaps four-fifths in the late 1980s, and probably as many as nine-tenths in 1998.

In the late 1980s, this proportion was less than 70 percent in the Ukraine and only about 60 percent in Belarus. However, in 1992–93, both countries may have reached the level found in Russia. Moreover, by this time in all three Slavic countries of the FSU (as may be assumed for Jews in the contemporary FSU as a whole), more than half of all children born to at least one Jewish parent had a Jewish father and non-Jewish mother.

The data on offspring of mixed couples collected before the start of the recent mass emigration showed that parents clearly preferred non-Jewish ethnic affiliations for their children.[22] This held true as well for the 1994 Russian micro-census: non-Jewish ethnic affiliation was clearly preferable among offspring of mixed couples. For children under sixteen, the percentage who were declared Jewish was about the same, only 11 percent, regardless of the composition of the mixed couples. Among offspring aged sixteen and older, the percentage was even lower: 6.2 percent for couples consisting of a Jewish husband and a Russian wife, and 4.1 percent for couples consisting of a Russian husband and a Jewish wife.

Thus, there does not seem to be any mass re-affiliation of offspring of mixed couples (nor any influx of crypto-Jews) that could seriously offset the dramatic birth decline in the FSU.

🕎 Dramatic Birth Reduction

Based solely on the different categories of births (to endogamous Jewish couples, to Jewish mothers, and to at least one Jewish parent), one can reconstruct the dynamics of the decline in fertility among Jews in the FSU. However, the figures for each category relate to quantitatively different aspects of internal processes among the Jews.

Births to endogamous Jewish couples form the basis (in Soviet conditions in most of the republics, about the only source) of reproduction of the "core" Jewish population. Births to at least one Jewish parent, by definition, of course include endogamous births, as well as births to Jewish mothers with non-Jewish fathers and births to non-Jewish mothers with Jewish fathers; these birth figures supply the data about Jewish fertility as a whole. Only births to Jewish mothers are considered Jewish according to Jewish religious law (*Halacha*). However, this category of birth had very little specific relevance to secular Soviet society.

All the birth categories showed dramatic decline, but the decline was greatest among the numbers of children born to endogamous Jewish couples, and smallest among those children born to at least one Jewish parent. During the three decades covering the years 1958–88, the decrease in each category of births was different in each republic (Table 11.8).

Between 1958 and 1988, the reduction in the number of births to endogamous Jewish couples was greatest among the Jews in Russia and Ukraine (by 76 percent and 74 percent, respectively), and smallest among the Jews in Uzbekistan (by 37 percent). In the same period, the decline in the number of births to Jewish mothers was more pronounced in Ukraine (by 63 percent), less so in Russia, Belarus, Latvia, and Moldavia (by 56–58 percent), Kazakhstan (by 54 percent), and smallest among the Jews in Uzbekistan (by 35 percent).

A different order applies to the decrease in the number of births to at least one Jewish parent: the greatest decreases were among the Jews in Kazakhstan, Ukraine, and Moldavia (by 49–51 percent); less in Latvia (by 46 percent), Russia, and Belarus (by 41–42 percent); and smallest among the Jews in Uzbekistan (by 33 percent).[23] These differentiations are due to the dynamics of mixed marriages, which have an input into Jewish fertility that varies from republic to republic.

Following the onset of the recent mass emigration, the declines in all categories of births in each republic of the FSU were more intense than during the entire previous three decades. The decrease was greatest among Belarusian and Moldavian Jewry. In Belarus in the short period between 1988 and 1993, the number of births to endogamous Jewish couples was

Table 11.8.

Index Numbers (1958 = 100 and 1988 = 100) of Births among Jewish Population in the FSU, by Republic

Republic and year	Births to endogamous Jewish couples		Births to Jewish mothers		Births to at least one Jewish parent[a]	
	1958 = 100	1988 = 100	1958 = 100	1988 = 100	1958 = 100	1988 = 100
Russia						
1988	24		42		58	
1993	6	23	13	30	19	33
Ukraine						
1988	26		37		50	
1993	5[b]	21[b]	12	32	25[b]	49[b]
Belorussia						
1988	32		43		59	
1993	3	10	9	22	18	30
Latvia						
1988	34		43		54	
1993	8[b]	24[b]	11	26	21[b]	39[b]
Moldavia						
1988	39		44		51	
1993	3	9	8	17	14	28
Kazakhstan						
1988	41		46		49	
1993	9	21	16	35	22	45
Uzbekistan						
1988	63		65		67	
1993	14	23	16	25	18	27

(a) According to two-fold hypothesis (see note (b) to Table 11.10).
(b) 1992 data.
Sources: Tolts, "Demographic Trends among the Jews in the Three Slavic Republics of the Former USSR: A Comparative Analysis," 157; unpublished USSR/CIS statistics; and Appendix 11.5 of this chapter.

reduced by a factor of 10(!). In Moldavia, the number of children born to Jewish mothers fell by a factor of 5.7.

Also between 1988 and 1993, in Belarus and Moldavia the number of births to at least one Jewish parent was reduced by a factor of about 3.3 and 3.5, respectively; however, the decrease of the latter category of births was even more pronounced in Uzbekistan, by a factor of approximately 3.7. This differentiation is due to the different levels of mixed marriage; the input of mixed marriages into Jewish fertility as a whole was lower in Uzbekistan.

In sum, during the thirty-five years between 1958 and 1993, the total number of births to endogamous Jewish couples fell by a factor of 31 in Belarus and by a factor of 29 in Moldavia. During this same period in these republics, the number of children born to Jewish mothers fell by a factor of 10.5 and 13, respectively. The total number of births to at least one Jewish parent fell by a factor of about 7 in Moldavia, and by a factor of 6 in both in Belarus and Uzbekistan.

We may assume that the main reason for the recent dramatic decrease in Jewish birth numbers was actually delineated above: Jewish emigration from, and reduction of Jewish population numbers in, the various republics of the FSU other than Russia. However, despite a greater level of emigration from Ukraine than from Russia, between 1988 and 1993 the decrease in the number of births to Jewish mothers was more pronounced in Russia (70 percent) than in Ukraine (68 percent). Emigration and its consequences were *not* the main cause of decline in the number of Jewish births in Russia.

We arrived at this important conclusion by estimating the expected number of births in 1993–94, assuming that the age composition and absolute number of Jewish women remained steady since 1989 (see Table 11.9). In 1988–89, the number of births to Jewish mothers was 6,895; by 1993–94, this number had declined by 4,662. According to our estimate, if the age composition had remained the same, the decrease in the number of births would have been 3,158. Thus, 68 percent of the recorded actual decrease cannot be attributed to the change of age composition that was a consequence of mass emigration.

Table 11.9.

Dynamics of the Number of Births to Jewish Mothers in Russia, 1988–89 to 1993–94

	Births		
Years	Registered number	Expected number, assuming age composition as in 1989[a]	Expected number as % of registered number
1988–89	6,895	6,895	100
1993–94	2,233	3,737	167
Decrease	4,662	3,158	68[b]

(a) According to actual age-sex fertility rates.
(b) Percent of decrease due to change in fertility.
Sources: 1989 Soviet census and Mark Tolts, "The Jewish Population of Russia, 1989–95," *Jews in Eastern Europe*, no. 3(31) (1996): 11.

There is another cause. In 1988–89, the total fertility rate[24] of Russia's Jewish population was 1.492.[25] For 1993–94, this fertility indicator was estimated at about 0.8; that is, it fell dramatically by 46 percent.[26] This development coincides with the general negative dynamics of fertility in Russia at the time.[27] Between 1988 and 1994, however, the fertility indicator for the total urban population fell by only 34 percent, from 1.9 to 1.25. And in 1994, even in the two major cities of Russia—Moscow and St. Petersburg—the total fertility rate was higher than that of the Jewish population: 1.1 and 1.0, respectively.[28]

One special aspect of the interrelationship between emigration and Jewish fertility in Russia should be noted here. According to Israeli statistics, the level of fertility among immigrants (*olim*) from the FSU was rather high during their first year in the country: some Jewish women obviously preferred giving birth in Israel.[29]

In 1998, the Russian Federation recorded 875 births to Jewish mothers, but only 224 of these children had Jewish fathers. For that year, the total number of births to at least one Jewish parent can be estimated at about 2,200, if we assume the number of children born to non-Jewish mothers and Jewish fathers to be twice that born to Jewish mothers and non-Jewish fathers. As a result, in almost four decades between 1958 and 1998, the total number of births to endogamous Jewish couples in Russia fell by a factor of 29. During this same period, the number of children born to Jewish mothers fell by a factor of 10, and the total number of births to at least one Jewish parent fell by a factor of 6.

✻ *Negative Vital Balances and Aging*

An unfavorable balance of births to endogamous Jewish couples and Jewish deaths, as well as the negative balance of births to Jewish mothers and Jewish deaths, first occurred in Russia in the 1950s. By the 1960s, these two balances were unfavorable in all republics of the European part of the Soviet Union and Kazakhstan. Only in the case of the Jews in Georgia can one link the first negative balances with the mass emigration and *aliyah* of the 1970s (see Table 11.10).

At the same time—also still before the large-scale emigration of the 1970s—the balance of births to at least one Jewish parent and Jewish deaths became negative in Russia and Ukraine. In the 1970s, this balance became negative in Latvia and Moldavia, and only in the 1980s was this noticeable in Belarus, Lithuania, Kazakhstan, and possibly in Georgia. By the end of the 1980s, all these balances were decidedly unfavorable in all republics of the European part of the Soviet Union.

After the start of the recent mass emigration, Jewish vital balances became negative in Uzbekistan: the balance of births to endogamous Jewish

Table 11.10.

Earliest Years when Jewish Deaths Exceeded Jewish Births, by Republic

Republic	Number of children born to endogamous Jewish couples	Total number of children born to Jewish mothers	Total number of children born to Jewish parents	
			Equality hypothesis[a]	Two-fold hypothesis[b]
Russia	before 1958	1959	1963	(1969)
Ukraine	1959	1961	1963	1966
Latvia	1962	1963	1973	1976
Lithuania	1963	...	1980	1984
Moldavia	1964	1965	...	(1978)
Belorussia	1964	1967	1980	1986
Kazakhstan	1964	1967	1983	1985
Azerbaijan	...	1974	...	...
Georgia	1980	1982	1986	...
Uzbekistan	1990	1990	1991	1991
Tadjikistan	1992	1992	1992	1992
FSU	1961	1963	...	...

(a) According to the equality hypothesis the (unknown) number of children born to non-Jewish mothers and Jewish fathers was equal to the (known) number of children born to Jewish mothers and non-Jewish fathers.

(b) According to the two-fold hypothesis the (unknown) number of children born to non-Jewish mothers and Jewish fathers was twice the (known) number of children born to Jewish mothers and non-Jewish fathers.

Sources: Mark Tolts, "The Balance of Births and Deaths among Soviet Jewry," *Jews and Jewish Topics in the Soviet Union and Eastern Europe,* no. 2(18) (1992): 21; idem, "Trends in Soviet Jewish Demography since the Second World War," in Yaacov Ro'i, ed., *Jews and Jewish Life in Russia and the Soviet Union* (London: Frank Cass, 1995), 380; idem, "Demographic Trends among the Jews in the Three Slavic Republics of the Former USSR: A Comparative Analysis," 160; and un-published USSR/CIS statistics.

couples and Jewish deaths, as well as the negative balance of births to Jewish mothers and Jewish deaths first occurred in this republic only in 1990, and the balance of births to at least one Jewish parent and Jewish deaths became negative there in 1991. In Tadjikistan, all three balances were negative for the first time in 1992.

In 1958 in the USSR, the number of births to Jewish mothers exceeded the number of Jewish deaths by 37 percent. However, by 1963 this balance had become negative. By the end of the 1980s, Jewish deaths in the Soviet Union exceeded births to Jewish mothers by a ratio of approximately 3:1. The situation was even more unfavorable in Russia, Ukraine, and Estonia (see Table 11.11).

Table 11.11.

Dynamics of the Vital Index[a] of the Jewish Population, by Republic, 1958–93

Republic	1958	1968	1988	1993
FSU	137	...	37	13[f]
Russia	100	56	27	9
West				
Ukraine	127	59	30	12
Belorussia/Belarus	224	91	52	16
Moldavia	244	94[c]	49	17
Baltic				
Latvia	179	73	49	14
Lithuania	192[b]	100	46	...
Estonia	...	...	31[e]	...
Transcaucasia				
Georgia	260	199	79[d]	...
Azerbaijan	208	116	89[e]	55
Armenia	...	...	67[e]	...[g]
Central Asia				
Uzbekistan	289	181[c]	128	50
Tadjikistan	390	276	191	54
Kirgiziia	...	...	51[e]	19
Turkmenistan	...	...	88[e]	35
Kazakhstan	218	93[c]	59	22

(a) Percent ratio of the number of all children born to Jewish mothers to the number of Jewish deaths.

(b) 1959 data.

(c) 1967 data.

(d) 1987 data.

(e) 1989 data.

(f) Not including Georgia, Lithuania, and Estonia.

(g) Only one birth to a Jewish mother and one Jewish death.

Sources: Tolts, "Trends in Soviet Jewish Demography since the Second World War," 367; unpublished USSR/CIS statistics; and Appendix 11.5 to this chapter.

In the 1990s, the vital crisis of (post-)Soviet Jewry intensified rapidly. By 1993, the ratio of Jewish deaths to births by Jewish mothers in the FSU as a whole had increased to about 8:1 (the data do not cover Georgia, Lithuania, and Estonia); this ratio was 8:1 in Ukraine, 7:1 in Latvia, and 6:1

in Belarus. In the Russian Federation, this ratio had reached 11:1, and was at about the same level in 1998.

From 1988–89 to 1993–94 in Russia, the number of births to Jewish mothers dropped by more than half, from 6.3 to 2.8 per 1,000 Jews. During the same period, the number of Jewish deaths rose by 23 percent from 24.4 to 30. Thus, the negative balance of births and deaths increased by half and reached more than 27 per 1,000 Jews (see Table 11.12). In 1958–59 in Russia, the number of deaths had been only 10.2 per 1,000 Jews.

Table 11.12.

Balance of Crude Birth Rates to Jewish Mothers and Jewish Death Rates, Russia and other Republics of FSU, 1988–89 and 1993–94, per 1,000 "Core" Jews

	Birth rate		Death rate		Balance	
Republic	1988–89	1993–94	1988–89	1993–94	1988–89	1993–94
Russia	6.3	2.8	24.4	30.0	−18.1	−27.2
Ukraine	6.6	3.4[a]	23.4	33.0[a]	−16.8	−29.6
Latvia	7.0	3.1	18.3	24.5	−11.3	−21.4
Moldavia	7.8	5.9[b]	17.1	34.6[b]	−9.3	−28.7
Uzbekistan	13.4	8.7[b]	10.9	17.2[b]	2.5	−8.5

(a) 1994–95.
(b) 1993.
Sources: Tolts, "The Jewish Population of Russia, 1989-1995," 13 (updated); and Appendix 11.5 to this chapter.

In 1988–89, the Jews of Russia had the highest negative vital balance in the FSU. This was not true five years later: the negative balance had become greater among the Jews of Ukraine and Moldavia. This change was due to the fact that the crude Jewish death rates in these states were higher than in Russia. Recent Jewish vital balances in the FSU are much less favorable than in West European countries.[30]

Jewish longevity was among the highest among all peoples of the former USSR, and life expectancy at birth for Soviet Jews in 1988–89 was 70.1 for males and 73.7 for females.[31] In the Russian Federation, Ukraine, and Belarus, the Jewish levels of mortality were very similar.[32] However, in the same period in Central Asia life expectancy was lower: 65.7 for Jewish males and 71.6 for Jewish females.

Actually, the most acute demographic problem in contemporary Russia in general is mortality; the total Russian population has the lowest life expectancy for males among all developed countries. Between 1988 and 1994, the life expectancy of males in the total Russian urban population fell by 7.5 years.

However, the data clearly show that the vital crisis of Jews in Russia is not linked to mortality and longevity levels. For 1993–94, the life expectancy of Russia's male Jews was estimated at 69.6, approximately the same level as at the end of the 1980s (see Table 11.13). Given the demographic situation of contemporary Russia, the life expectancy of Jewish males is relatively high.

Table 11.13.

Life Expectancy at Birth for Jews and Total Urban Population in Russia, and for Total Jewish Population in Israel, 1988–89 and 1993–94

	Males		Females	
	Russia	Israel	Russia	Israel
Russia's Jews				
1988–89	69.7	-	73.3	-
1993–94	69.6[a]	...	73.2[a]	...
Total population				
1988	65.4[b]	74.2[c]	74.2[b]	78.0[c]
1994	57.9[b]	75.9[c]	71.3[b]	79.7[c]

(a) Author's estimates for 1993–94, based on indirect method.
(b) Total urban population.
(c) Total Jewish population.
Sources: Israel. CBS, *Statistical Abstract of Israel, 1998* (Jerusalem: Central Bureau of Statistics, 1998), table 3.20; V. Shkolnikov, E. Andreev, and T. Maleva, eds., *Neravenstvo i smertnost' v Rossii* (Moscow: Signal, 2000), 53, Statkomitet SNG, *Demograficheskii ezhegodnik 1993* (Moscow, 1995), 257; Tolts, "The Jewish Population of Russia, 1989–1995," 12.

In 1994, male life expectancy among the total urban population was only 57.9 years; the difference between the life expectancy of these males and Jewish males grew dramatically to about twelve years. From these figures, we see that the Jewish population has adapted to the recent economic transition in Russia better than the rest of the population.[33]

Nor, as one might have supposed, were the dynamics of Russia's Jewish life expectancy lowered by the selective character of mass emigration. Although unwell people usually are less inclined to migrate, this factor might have raised Jewish mortality levels somewhat. However, this factor was presumably offset by successful Jewish socio-economic adaptation.

At the same time, Jewish life expectancy levels in Russia are vastly lower than in Israel. In the mid-1990s, this discrepancy for both males and females was more than six years. However, during this period in Israel, standardized rates of female mortality were lower for the new immigrants from

Table 11.14.

Jews in the Republics of the FSU, by Age Group, 1959 and 1989, in Percent[a]

Republic and year	All ages	0–14	15–29	30–44	45–64	65+	Thereof 75+	Median age
FSU								
1959[b]	100.0	17.5	18.6	22.7	32.5	8.7	2.4	38.7
1989	100.0	11.6	13.0	20.2	31.6	23.6	10.6	49.7
Russia								
1959[c]	100.0	13.7	18.8	22.8	35.8	8.9	2.3	41.2
1989	100.0	8.4	11.4	19.5	33.8	26.9	12.7	52.3
1994[c]	100.0	6.2	9.9	16.5	35.0	32.4	14.5	56.0
West								
Ukraine								
1959[c]	100.0	17.6	17.9	22.6	32.6	9.3	2.4	39.3
1989	100.0	9.7	12.0	19.8	33.2	25.3	11.5	51.6
Belorussia								
1959[c]	100.0	23.2	20.0	23.0	26.7	7.1	1.6	33.7
1989	100.0	12.5	13.7	21.8	31.8	20.2	8.3	47.0
Moldavia								
1959[c]	100.0	25.6	16.9	24.4	26.2	6.9	1.6	34.6
1989	100.0	16.4	13.5	23.9	26.0	20.2	7.8	42.7
Baltic								
Latvia								
1959[c]	100.0	22.7	16.2	26.3	28.9	5.9	1.5	36.3
1989	100.0	12.4	12.7	22.8	28.8	23.3	9.2	47.1
Lithuania								
1959[c]	100.0	27.3	15.2	27.9	24.9	4.7	1.1	34.2
1989	100.0	15.1	13.7	24.0	26.1	21.1	7.8	43.4
Estonia								
1959[c]	100.0	18.7	18.4	25.9	29.2	7.8	2.2	37.1
1989	100.0	11.3	11.7	23.0	31.4	22.6	8.9	48.7
Transcaucasia								
Georgia								
1970	100.0	28.6	21.2	22.6	19.7	7.9	2.5	30.1
1989	100.0	20.0	20.3	20.9	26.1	12.7	4.6	36.5
Azerbaijan								
1970	100.0	28.5	18.2	20.3	21.8	11.2	3.2	32.2
1989	100.0	22.3	20.7	19.4	23.8	13.8	5.6	34.5
Central Asia								
Uzbekistan								
1970	100.0	26.6	20.2	21.9	21.5	9.8	2.8	31.9
1989	100.0	25.4	20.6	20.2	22.5	11.3	4.5	32.6
Tajikistan								
1989	100.0	28.9	21.1	20.2	21.3	8.5	2.9	30.0

(a) Population of known age.

(b) The data cover Ashkenazic Jews in RSFSR, Ukraine, Belorussia, Latvia, Lithuania, Estonia, Moldavia, and Azerbaijan; Georgian Jews in Georgia; and Central Asian (Bukharan) Jews in Uzbekistan.

(c) Ashkenazic Jews only.

Sources: 1959 and 1989 Soviet censuses and 1994 Russian micro-census.

the former USSR as a whole than for the total Jewish population of Israel, while the indicators for males of both groups were rather close.[34]

However, the level of crude death rates depends heavily on the age structure. Given the condition of stable longevity, the older a population, the higher this indicator will be. According to the 1989 census, Russia's Jewish population was indeed the oldest among the Jews of the FSU; accordingly, the Jewish death rate in Russia was also the highest.

Since World War II, the Jewish population of the FSU has aged substantially, a fact that is linked to the low fertility level. For Jews in 1959, the median age was 38.7 years in the Soviet Union as a whole and 41.2 years in the Russian Federation. But according to the 1989 census, the median age of the Jewish population was 49.7 and 52.3 years, respectively (see Table 11.14). Correspondingly, during the same period the proportion of the group aged sixty-five and above in the total Jewish population rose dramatically from 9 to 27 percent in Russia and from 9 to 24 percent in the Soviet Union as a whole.

Since 1989, the level of emigration from Russia has been much lower than from other parts of the FSU. However, older people usually have a lower tendency to migrate, and according to data from the 1994 micro-census, 32.4 percent of the Ashkenazic Jews in Russia were aged sixty-five and above. At the same time the median age of these Jews had reached 56.0, which was 3.4 years more than the median age in 1989 (which does not appear in Table 11.14). In the entire decade between the 1979 and 1989 censuses, this indicator for total Russia's Jewry rose by only 3.2 years.

To update our knowledge on the process of aging, we used an estimate based on the 1994 micro-census, the 1993–94 life tables, and age–sex migration rates consistent with the observed population decline up to 1999.[35] According to this estimate, by 1999, 35 percent of the "core" Jews in Russia were aged sixty-five and above. At the same time, the median age of these Jews in 1999 reached 58.2.

We have no recent data on levels of Jewish life expectancy in other parts of the FSU,[36] where the mass emigration was much greater than in Russia; however, the rise in the Jewish crude death rates in these countries was clearly coupled with the existence of severe aging, caused in large part by the mass emigration from these countries.

Conclusion

Since 1989, the situation of the Jews has changed dramatically in the FSU. On the one hand, official governmental antisemitism was abolished, even though it was "replaced" by grassroots antisemitic activity. After the break-up of the USSR, Jews in the successor states received rights, and community-building activities were initiated with the help of world Jewry.[37]

On the other hand, together with the total population, the Jews have experienced general political instability, crises, and even wars in some parts of the FSU, as well as critical ecological situations (consequences of the Chernobyl catastrophe and others). All of these exacerbated the already severe difficulties caused by the problems of economic transition in the successor states. At the same time, after the long period of Soviet oppression, free emigration was allowed. Consequently, many Jews were "pushed" in great masses to Israel and to the West.

Given these conditions, in the 1990s a new demographic stage began, characterized by a dramatic numerical decline of the Jews in the FSU and accompanied by a simultaneous concentration of the remaining Jewish population in Russia.

Clearly, the recent mass emigration exacerbated the already existing severe aging and imbalances in the age-sex ratios. Thus, emigration aggravated the negative Jewish vital balance and intensified mixed marriage. Nevertheless, Russia's Jewish longevity remained stable during the mass emigration, despite the dramatic decline in the longevity of the total Russian population.

Since the Jewish population in the FSU is very aged and has already reached the "terminal stage" of demographic evolution, the recent mass emigration actually only accelerated all these negative processes. From our analysis, we see that since 1989 many Jewish demographic indicators (including some of the most important ones) in these countries have worsened more significantly than in the entire previous thirty years. This development is indicative of the demographic collapse of these Jewish populations.

Demography of the Jews in the Former Soviet Union

Appendix 11.1.
*Emigration of Jews and Their Non-Jewish Relatives[a] from the FSU to Israel,
by Republic, 1989–98*

Republic	1989	1990	1991	1992	1993	1994	1995	1996	1997	1998
Russia	3,281	45,522	47,276	24,786	23,082	24,612	15,707	16,488	15,290	14,454
West										
Ukraine	3,575	58,936	39,769	13,149	12,833	22,733	23,556	23,447	24,103	20,083
Belorussia	1,121	23,356	16,006	3,273	2,265	2,906	4,219	4,381	3,369	2,258
Moldavia	1,470	11,926	15,452	4,305	2,173	1,907	2,407	1,953	1,396	1,194
Baltic										
Latvia	294	4,393	1,852	866	1,399	845	541	709	599	447
Lithuania	322	2,737	1,052	369	333	245	353	339	332	194
Estonia	30	391	225	81	110	61	60	99	75	40
Transcaucasia										
Georgia	263	1,346	1,407	2,595	3,750	3,295	2,275	1,493	1,107	944
Azerbaijan	466	7,833	5,676	2,625	3,133	2,285	3,090	2,627	1,876	1,134
Armenia	10	162	108	132	387	370	114	97	82	125
Central Asia										
Uzbekistan	1,544	20,726	14,271	5,533	8,471	6,510	6,172	3,410	2,695	2,399
Tadjikistan	202	2,389	2,736	2,286	1,581	413	455	317	138	97
Kirgiziia	73	992	572	250	449	447	367	347	203	214
Turkmenistan	3	33	0	79	54	59	359	465	400	279
Kazakhstan	67	1,313	998	475	536	699	2,736	2,034	2,350	1,948
Unknown	211	3,177	439	4,289	5,589	692	2,436	843	603	222
Total	12,932	185,232	147,839	65,093	66,145	68,079	64,847	59,049	54,618	46,032

(a) Includes some persons belonging to households with no "core" Jews.

Sources: Israel. CBS, *Immigration to Israel, 1998* (Jerusalem: Central Bureau of Statistics, 2000), 34, 85; Baruch Gur-Gurevitz, *Open Gates: The Story Behind the Mass Immigration to Israel from the Soviet Union and Its Successor States* (Jerusalem: The Jewish Agency for Israel, 1996), 282 [distribution by republic for 1989]; Israel. Ministry of Immigrant Absorption, data for Baltic States for 1990–94.

Appendix 11.2.
Emigration of Jews and Their Non-Jewish Relatives[a] from the
FSU to the U.S., by Republic, 1989–98

Republic	1989[b]	1990	1991	1992	1993	1994	1995	1996	1997	1998
Russia	11,169	...	10,196	10,039	8,654	8,506	5,848	5,277	4,432	2,324
West										
Ukraine	28,875	...	12,398	19,759	13,232	14,278	8,311	8,007	5,903	3,004
Belorussia	9,212	...	3,697	5,755	3,025	3,052	2,042	1,673	1,280	619
Moldavia	2,783	...	3,522	2,484	2,228	1,136	755	665	451	180
Baltic										
Latvia	1,289	...	532	937	620	507	346	318	261	107
Lithuania	461	...	230	338	158	138	97	105	56	15
Estonia	136	...	78	92	86	52	60	53	23	6
Transcaucasia										
Georgia	229	...	163	311	349	350	301	194	84	39
Azerbaijan	1,551	...	794	1,222	1,049	712	583	494	373	188
Armenia	10	...	21	9	50	18	20	11	3	1
Central Asia										
Uzbekistan	2,703	...	3,112	3,807	5,112	3,165	2,834	2,212	1,309	745
Tadjikistan	327	...	336	821	861	580	140	116	47	15
Kirgiziia	75	...	30	46	79	48	44	43	26	19
Turkmenistan	12	...	25	24	54	54	34	68	41	7
Kazakhstan	129	...	95	217	355	302	263	256	230	98
Total	58,961[c]	6,500	35,229	45,861	35,912	32,898	21,678	19,492	14,519	7,369[d]

(a) Include some persons belonging to households with no "core" Jews; distribution for 1991–98 is limited to those assisted by HIAS.

(b) Including all destinations other than Israel for those who emigrated with Israeli visas.

(c) Of these about 56,000 emigrated to the U.S. (see Table 11.2).

(d) Of these, two for whom origin is unknown.

Sources: HIAS data; Yoel Florsheim, "Emigration of Jews from the Soviet Union in 1989," *Jews and Jewish Topics in the Soviet Union and Eastern Europe,* no. 2(12) (1990): 23 [distribution by republic for 1989]; and Sidney Heitman, "Soviet Emigration in 1990: A New 'Fourth Wave'?," 13 [for 1990].

Demography of the Jews in the Former Soviet Union

Appendix 11.3.

Registered Immigration of Jews[a] to the Russian Federation from Other Parts of the FSU, by Republic, 1989–98

Republic	1989[b]	1990	1991[b]	1992	1993	1994	1995	1996	1997	1998
West										
Ukraine	1,184	1,207	855	781	654	879	657	575	439	315
Belorussia	350	347	182	179	110	128	117	82	53	48
Moldavia	141	115	81	115	83	112	77	81	45	31
Baltic										
Latvia	53	51	45	56	64	72	38	31	31	16
Lithuania	15	18	32	42	45	23	9	4	6	3
Estonia	36	35	8	45	30	29	27	13	16	5
Transcaucasia										
Georgia	101	111	133	154	310	363	274	197	148	125
Azerbaijan	228	394	209	217	233	290	257	173	115	114
Armenia	16	14	8	29	34	22	22	13	7	8
Central Asia										
Uzbekistan	171	295	133	242	212	312	238	151	95	96
Tadjikistan	85	29	53	161	161	102	58	58	22	21
Kirgiziia	42	38	18	31	71	76	29	22	9	6
Turkmenistan	21	98	20	35	12	15	16	25	22	9
Kazakhstan	134	195	84	155	134	262	193	94	127	134
Total	2,863	2,947	2,090	2,242	2,153	2,685	2,012	1,519	1,135	931

(a) Not including part of the Mountain Jews ("Tats").

(b) Distribution by republics only for immigrants to urban areas.

Sources: USSR/CIS and Russian migration statistics.

Appendix 11.4.

Registered Emigration of Jews[a] *from the Russian Federation to Other Parts of the FSU,*
by Republic, 1989–98

Republic	1989[b]	1990	1991[b]	1992	1993	1994	1995	1996	1997	1998
West										
Ukraine	1,472	...	1,213	1,243	756	446	354	259	187	140
Belorussia	379	...	298	295	241	130	138	88	49	29
Moldavia	191	...	160	106	73	48	33	34	10	15
Baltic										
Latvia	69	...	57	26	9	13	10	3	5	2
Lithuania	36	...	49	10	14	11	12	6	6	4
Estonia	36	...	37	16	3	3	2	0	0	0
Transcaucasia										
Georgia	109	...	95	31	29	22	19	26	30	29
Azerbaijan	133	...	73	41	20	16	23	17	17	20
Armenia	5	...	10	3	0	2	5	0	1	3
Central Asia										
Uzbekistan	118	...	111	107	63	36	43	38	13	10
Tadjikistan	40	...	46	31	7	4	3	8	4	0
Kirgiziia	13	...	17	7	6	8	3	1	2	4
Turkmenistan	15	...	5	1	2	0	0	4	3	4
Kazakhstan	72	...	91	81	68	37	40	27	13	12
Total	2,973	3,348	2,443	1,998	1,291	776	685	511	340	272

(a) Not including part of the Mountain Jews ("Tats").

(b) Distribution by republics only for emigrants from urban areas.

Sources: USSR/CIS and Russian migration statistics.

Demography of the Jews in the Former Soviet Union

Appendix 11.5.
Dynamics of Jewish Births and Deaths,[a] *by Republic, 1988–93*

| Republic[b] | Total Jewish births | | Thereof, with | | | | Total Jewish deaths | |
| | | | Jewish fathers | | Non-Jewish fathers | | | |
	1988	1993	1988	1993	1988	1993	1988	1993
Russia	3,710	1,121	1,562	361	2,148	760	13,826	12,434
Ukraine	3,515	1,134	2,040	...	1,475	...	11,767	9,123
Uzbekistan	1,358	334	1,183	267	175	67	1,059	664
Belorussia	1,035	226	652	66	383	160	1,975	1,423
Moldavia	578	101	479	42	99	59	1,182	595
Azerbaijan	559[c]	138	401	83	158	55	446[c]	251
Georgia	291[c]	...	219	...	72	...	368[c]	...
Tadjikistan	239	22	203	18	36	4	125	41
Kazakhstan	195	69	115	24	80	45	333	315
Latvia	187	48	128	...	59	...	385	353
Lithuania	97	...	66	...	31	...	213	...
Kirgiziia	53[d]	17	40	9	13	8	103[d]	88
Turkmenistan	30[d]	9	12	5	18	4	34[d]	26
Estonia	27[d]	9	10	3	17	6	87[d]	...
Armenia	12[d]	1	3	0	9	1	18[d]	1
FSU	11,591	...	6,849	...	4,742	...	31,674	...

(a) Not including part of the Mountain Jews ("Tats").
(b) Ordered according to the number of Jewish births in 1988.
(c) 1987.
(d) 1989.
Sources: Vital statistics data.

NOTES

1. This essay is part of a broader research project being carried out by the author at the Division of Jewish Demography and Statistics, the Avraham Harman Institute of Contemporary Jewry at the Hebrew University of Jerusalem. Parts of this study were presented previously in a different form in: Mark Tolts, "Jews in the Russian Federation: A Decade of Demographic Decline," *Jews in Eastern Europe,* no. 3(40) (1999): 5–36; and idem, "Jewish Demography of the Former Soviet Union," in Sergio DellaPergola and Judith Even, eds., *Papers in Jewish Demography 1997* (Jerusalem: The Avraham Harman Institute of Contemporary Jewry, The Hebrew University of Jerusalem; World Union of Jewish Studies; Association for Jewish Demography and Statistics, 2001), 109–39. I wish to express my appreciation to Sergio DellaPergola for his general advice. I am grateful to Evgeny Andreev, Leonid Darsky, Ari Paltiel, Moshe Sicron, Evgeny Soroko, Dail Stolow, Dorith Tal, Emma Trahtenberg, and Sergei Zakharov for providing materials, information, and suggestions. I wish also to thank Judith Even for reading and editing an earlier draft. Responsibility for the content of the paper is, of course, the author's alone.

2. See Sergio DellaPergola, "Modern Jewish Demography," in Jack Wertheimer, ed., *The Modern Jewish Experience* (New York: New York University Press, 1993), 277.

3. Mark Tolts, "Demographic Trends among the Jews in the Three Slavic Republics of the Former USSR: A Comparative Analysis," in Sergio DellaPergola and Judith Even, eds., *Papers in Jewish Demography 1993* (Jerusalem: The Avraham Harman Institute of Contemporary Jewry, The Hebrew University of Jerusalem; World Union of Jewish Studies; Association for Jewish Demography and Statistics, 1997), 164–65. According to the estimate based on the 1994 Russian micro-census, which included in the "enlarged" Jewish population those children of mixed couples who had not identified themselves as Jews and who were living separately from a Jewish parent, the ratio between the "core" and "enlarged" Jewish populations was 1 to 1.93; see Evgeny Andreev, "Jews in Russia's Households (Based on the 1994 Microcensus)," in Sergio DellaPergola and Judith Even, eds., *Papers in Jewish Demography 1997* (Jerusalem: The Avraham Harman Institute of Contemporary Jewry, The Hebrew University of Jerusalem; World Union of Jewish Studies; Association for Jewish Demography and Statistics, 2001), 148.

4. See Mark Tolts, "The Interrelationship between Emigration and the Socio-Demographic Profile of Russian Jewry," in Noah Lewin-Epstein, Yaacov Ro'i, and Paul Ritterband, eds., *Russian Jews on Three Continents* (London: Frank Cass, 1997), 151.

5. In Soviet censuses, not all Mountain Jews were recorded as Jews; others were listed separately as "Tats." The estimates here include the latter. This situation may have changed in the post-Soviet period. According to the preliminary data of the 1999 Azerbaijan census, 10,900 "Tats" were enumerated, but according to the last Soviet census of 1989 there were only 10,200 "Tats" in this republic. We may surmise that some Muslims started to use this ethnic label, and this problem should be studied separately. Thus, our recent estimate for Transcaucasia does not include "Tats."

6. See, e.g., Zvi Gitelman, "'From a Northern Country': Russian and Soviet Jewish Immigration to America and Israel in Historical Perspective," in Noah Lewin-Epstein, Yaacov Ro'i, and Paul Ritterband, eds., *Russian Jews on Three Continents* (London: Frank Cass, 1997), 21–41.

7. For the estimates used here, see note no. 3.

8. Sergio DellaPergola, "The Global Context of Migration to Israel," in Elazar

Leshem and Judith T. Shuval, eds., *Immigration to Israel: Sociological Perspectives* (New Brunswick, N.J., and London: Transaction, 1998), 78.

9. See Mark Tolts, "Recent Jewish Emigration and Population Decline in Russia," *Jews in Eastern Europe*, no. 1(35) (1998): 17–20; idem, "Jews in the Russian Federation: A Decade of Demographic Decline," 19, 21–23.

10. On these statistics see Mark Tolts, "The Jewish Population of Russia, 1989–1995," *Jews in Eastern Europe*, no. 3(31) (1996): 8–9.

11. DellaPergola, "The Global Context of Migration to Israel," 85–87.

12. *Vesti* (Tel Aviv), September 27, 1998, 1.

13. Tolts, "Jewish Demography of the Former Soviet Union," 116.

14. See, e.g., Robert J. Brym, with Rozalina Ryvkina, *The Jews of Moscow, Kiev and Minsk: Identity, Antisemitism, Emigration* (New York: New York University Press, 1994), 82–88; Robert J. Brym and Rozalina Ryvkina, "Russian Jewry Today: A Sociological Profile," *Sociological Papers* (Bar-Ilan University), vol. 5, no. 1 (1996), 1–47.

15. These statistics were published only in part: Goskomstat SSSR, *Demograficheskii ezhegodnik SSSR, 1990* (Moscow: Finansy i statistika, 1990), 592; Goskomstat Rossii, *Chislennost', sostav i dvizhenie naseleniia Rossiiskoi Federatsii* (Moscow, 1992), 442–43; idem, *Demograficheskii ezhegodnik Rossiiskoi Federatsii, 1993* (Moscow, 1994), 402; idem, *Demograficheskii ezhegodnik Rossii* (Moscow, 1995), 424–25; idem, *Demograficheskii ezhegodnik Rossii* (Moscow, 1996), 512–13; idem, *Chislennost' i migratsiia naseleniia Rossiiskoi Federatsii v 1996 g.* (Moscow, 1997), 42; idem, *Chislennost' i migratsiia naseleniia Rossiiskoi Federatsii v 1997 g.* (Moscow, 1998), 78; idem, *Chislennost' i migratsiia naseleniia Rossiiskoi Federatsii v 1998 g.* (Moscow, 1999), 83.

16. See, e.g., Zhanna Zayonchkovskaya, "Recent Migration Trends in Russia," in George J. Demko, Grigory Ioffe, and Zhanna Zayonchkovskaya, eds., *Population under Duress: The Geodemography of Post-Soviet Russia* (Boulder, Colo.: Westview Press, 1999), 126–27.

17. See Mordechai Alrshuler, *Soviet Jewry on the Eve of the Holocaust: A Social and Demographic Profile* (Jerusalem: Centre for Research of East European Jewry, The Hebrew University of Jerusalem, and Yad Vashem, 1998), 66–76.

18. For partial data, see Mordechai Altshuler, *Soviet Jewry since the Second World War: Population and Social Structure* (New York: Greenwood Press, 1987), 26–28.

19. See Tolts, "Demographic Trends among the Jews in the Three Slavic Republics of the Former USSR: A Comparative Analysis," 152–53.

20. Tolts, "The Jewish Population of Russia, 1989–1995," 15.

21. Tolts, "The Interrelationship between Emigration and the Socio-Demographic Profile of Russian Jewry," 154.

22. See A. Volkov, "Etnicheski smeshannye sem'i v SSSR: Dinamika i sostav [Part 2]," *Vestnik Statistiki*, no. 8 (1989): 18; Mark Tolts, "The Balance of Births and Deaths among Soviet Jewry," *Jews and Jewish Topics in the Soviet Union and Eastern Europe*, no. 2(18) (1992): 22.

23. We assume the (unknown) number of children born to non-Jewish mothers and Jewish fathers to be twice that (known) born to Jewish mothers and non-Jewish fathers.

24. The total fertility rate is the average number of children that a woman would bear in her lifetime if current age-specific fertility rates remain stable.

25. Statkomitet SNG, *Demograficheskii ezhegodnik 1993* (Moscow, 1995), 245.

26. Tolts, "The Jewish Population of Russia, 1989–1995," 12.

27. See, e.g., E. Andreev, G. Bondarskaya, and T. Kharkova, "Padenie rozhdaemosti v Rossii: Gipotezy i fakty," *Voprosy Statistiki*, no. 10 (1998), 82–93; Sergei V. Zakharov and

Elena I. Ivanova, "Fertility Decline and Recent Changes in Russia: On the Threshold of the Second Demographic Transition," in Julie DaVanzo, ed., *Russia's Demographic "Crisis"* (Santa Monica, Calif.: RAND, 1996), 36–82.

28. Goskomstat Rossii, *Demograficheskii ezhegodnik Rossii* (Moscow, 1995), 80–81.

29. See Israel, CBS, *Immigrant Population from Former USSR, 1995: Demographic Trends* (Jerusalem: Central Bureau of Statistics, 1998), 79; Moshe Sicron, "Demography of the Wave of Immigration," in Moshe Sicron and Elazar Leshem, eds., *Profile of an Immigration Wave: The Absorption Process of Immigrants from the Former Soviet Union, 1990–1995* (Jerusalem: Magnes Press, 1998), 35 (in Hebrew).

30. Cf. Sergio DellaPergola, "Jews in the European Community: Sociodemographic Trends and Challenges," *American Jewish Year Book* (New York: American Jewish Committee), 93 (1993), 25–82.

31. E. Andreev, L. E. Darsky, and T. L. Kharkova, *Naselenie Sovetskogo Soiuza, 1922–1991* (Moscow: Nauka, 1993), 102.

32. See Tolts, "Demographic Trends among the Jews in the Three Slavic Republics of the Former USSR: A Comparative Analysis," 162.

33. On this problem, for the total Russian population see, e.g., Timothy Heleniak, "Economic Transition and Demographic Change in Russia, 1989–1995," *Post-Soviet Geography* 36, no. 7 (1995): 451–53.

34. See Israel, Central Bureau of Statistics, *Immigrant Population from Former USSR, 1995: Demographic Trends,* 20; Sicron, "Demography of the Wave of Immigration," 36.

35. Mark Tolts, "Russian Jewish Migration in the Post-Soviet Era," *Revue Européenne des Migrations Internationales* 16, no. 3 (2000): 193–94.

36. We note that by the mid-1990s the decrease in life expectancy for the total population was more pronounced in Russia than in other parts of the FSU (Kalev Katus and Sergei Zakharov, "Demographic Adaptation to Socioeconomic Changes in the USSR Successor States," Paper presented at the IUSSP XXIIIrd General Population Conference, Beijing, October 11–17, 1997, 21–22).

37. See Zvi Gitelman, "The Reconstruction of Community and Jewish Identity in Russia," *East European Jewish Affairs* 24, no. 2 (1994): 35–56.

JEWS AND
RUSSIAN CULTURE

Part Four

TWELVE

❦

Judith Deutsch Kornblatt

Jewish Converts to Orthodoxy in Russia in Recent Decades

As a specialist on Russian Orthodox spirituality and a scholar of twentieth-century Russia, I approach the study of Jews in the Orthodox Church with fascination, and find it very revealing of issues of identity and the intelligentsia in the post-Stalinist Soviet Union.[1] As a Jew, I am alarmed. Conversion is always a provocative subject for American Jews, who see assimilation and intermarriage eroding the community of their parents. Mass secularism is one thing, the pull for some toward Eastern religions another, but all the worse is conversion to Christianity. Have we forgotten the Crusades? So much more alarming, then, might be the story of Russian Jews, survivors of the pogroms, who willingly choose baptism in a Church most of us assume to be antisemitic. The Catholic Pope has apologized to the Jews for centuries of the label "Christ killers." Not so the Russian Patriarch. Protestants have purged their liturgy of antisemitic diatribes. Not so the Orthodox. And as even one subject of this study reported: "The first sermon I heard was about the *zhidy* [yids]. In the most negative sense. The Jew as Satan."[2] Yet, Jews in Russia did and continue to become Russian Orthodox. For the most part, these converts are members of the intelligentsia, steeped in Russian culture, and well able to articulate their sense of self within the Soviet society in which they were raised. How do these Jews, now Christians, speak of their Jewish identity, their Russian identity, their religious identity? And what might their self-definition tell us about Russian-Jewish identity in general?

My period of investigation, the 1960s through 1980s, roughly corresponds to the growth of the Zionist movement in the Soviet Union, not to
mention the general anti-Soviet dissident movement, and many of the subjects interviewed for this study had their feet in several ideological circles.
One baptized Jew was actually a regular lecturer on Jewish history for Jews
in Riga who were preparing for *aliyah* in the seventies. He was ultimately
"shut down" by the Moscow Jewish community. As he relates his story:
"Earlier some people had known that I was Christian, and accepted the fact
neutrally. But a rather severe notice came from Moscow. I don't know from
whom exactly, but it stated that if this man continues to read lectures for
you, we will play no more role in your organization. Moscow was always,
well, more 'orthodox'. [He laughs.] Things were more tolerated in Riga.
And even in Leningrad." Another subject of this study, who now serves as
priest to a small parish of mostly Russian-Jewish converts, remembers:
"My Jewish awareness started to grow in 1968.[3] I was networking. Semi-
underground. From the same underground came the dissident movement
and the Zionist movement. . . . I did not hide the fact that I went to
church. For those Jews, in those days, the fact that we were Christian was
not an issue. . . . We were all a minority of outcasts."

My first interview of a baptized Russian Jew took place in 1993, at the
request of a friend's mother, Zoia Krakhmal'nikova, whom I had known for
years, but had not initially realized that Zoia was Jewish. I did know that
she was an outspoken opponent of antisemitism in the Russian Orthodox
Church from within the Church itself, and her stated desire for the interview was to elicit international support for a new Christian, anti-fascist organization.[4] With the tape recorder running, I steered the conversation
from the organizational to the personal, as it became clear to me—if not entirely to her—that her status as Jew in the Church fueled much of her indig-
nation at its at best indifferent, at worst antisemitic, stance toward the Jews
and Judaism.

Krakhmal'nikova often invokes the name of the Russian religious philosopher Vladimir Solov'ev (1854–1900), a Russian, baptized in the Russian Orthodox Church, who placed the Jews, Jewry, and Judaism centrally within his
understanding of the world. In Solov'ev's view, historical Jewry is a model for
the successful integration of national (or ethnic) identity with religious calling, of tying the material fact of their peoplehood with their spiritual chosenness. The Jews, by their very character, are what he calls a paradoxically
"spiritual-national people."[5] But not all Jews, clearly, would define themselves
in this way. As I listened to Krakhmal'nikova, I began to wonder how the reverse would look: How would Jews who now place Russian Orthodoxy cen-

trally within their understanding of the world speak about the relationship of national and religious identities within themselves?

And so I sought out more Jewish converts, both in the former Soviet Union and in their emigrant destinations, all of whom were baptized in the last two decades of Soviet rule. Some of the stories I heard from Jews in the Orthodox Church ring a familiar chord of baby-boomer spiritual and social discontent. Most American Jews of my own generation have acquaintances who entered ashrams, were "born again," and who sought to escape what they saw as a vapid American Jewish upbringing in New Age religions and the like. Context, however, affects our understanding of content; America is not Soviet Russia, as many of the articles in this volume make clear. Russian Jews may share with American or Israeli Jews some, but far from all the assumptions about their own Jewishness. We need only look to the difficulties American Jewish communities have had in integrating the new immigrants for proof of the differences. My goal in the course of this study, therefore, was to listen to *how* the stories were told, to the narrative of their own "spiritual-national" identity recited by these particular Russian Jews.

My original working hypothesis for the study held that Russian Jews enter the Orthodox Church in order to feel more "Russian," that is, less marginalized in the majority, Russian society. This hypothesis turned out to be radically wrong, as I heard over and over how baptism made these Russian Jews feel more "Jewish," but, and this is crucial, now in a positive, rather than negative (marginalized) sense. It is this paradox of identity in the context of, or perhaps in response to, anti-Jewish sentiment in their new religious surroundings, that the following pages will analyze.

🏵 Methods

Between September 1997 and June 1998, I conducted interviews with over thirty people in Moscow, New York, Washington, Haifa, and Jerusalem. The interviews, lasting an average of one to one-and-a-half hours, were taped and later transcribed. On a few occasions, taping was not possible (a chance meeting with a convert inside the walls of the Monastery of the Cross in Jerusalem; or an encounter with a Muscovite who was active in the Church as a young man, and who spoke to me at length of other baptized Jews but was not anxious to be officially interviewed himself). In those cases, I took notes and later typed them for inclusion in the study. My first formal question would be: "Describe for me your path to faith." The interviews were free ranging, but in the course of the hour I would ask about childhood associations with Jewishness and Judaism, whether or not they still feel "Jewish," and how Jewish family and friends reacted to their baptism. For those who had left Russia, I asked about their decision to emigrate, and about how it feels to be a Jewish Christian in their new home. And, finally, I asked about their religious practice now. Some of the interviewees no longer consider themselves part of the Church, and many have decreased their level of commitment. Some, indeed, are no longer Christian. How they described their relationship to Orthodoxy now, as ex-Christians, or as changed Christians, also had bearing on their narratives of faith.

The study is explicitly qualitative, rather than quantitative, and I continued seeking out interviews until the stories became repetitious and I felt I had sufficient justification to speak about patterns, even on a small scale. The individual narratives, and the grand narrative that emerges from their accumulation provide a rich picture of what may not be a "movement," but is certainly a phenomenon of late Soviet society, one that is familiar and yet unique. It is also a story, despite its Christian content, that can tell us much about who the Russian Jews are in this post-Soviet world.

In my search for subjects, particularly in Israel, I was interested only in Jews who had entered the Russian Orthodox Church. It is true that a large number of Russian *olim* [immigrants to Israel] are attracted to Christianity, some because they are in mixed marriages, and some because they are themselves part Russian but had never sought out the Church while still in the Soviet Union. Most Russian Jews in Israel who are drawn to Christianity, however, do not join the Orthodox Church; they turn instead toward various evangelical or messianic Jewish groups. Messianic Jews (sometimes called "Hebrew Christians," in America often known as "Jews for Jesus") proselytize heavily to the new Russian Jews, with numerous pamphlets, meetings, and Passover *Seders* conducted in Russian, and they are not without success. The Christian Embassy in Jerusalem, a fervently Zionist, fundamentalist Protestant group, devotes half of its activities to Soviet, and now post-Soviet Jewry, providing logistical and financial assistance for Jews who wish to emigrate to Israel. An acquaintance now living in Jerusalem recalled for me how warmly he felt toward these "ambassador-missionaries" who approached him in Moscow, and how he attended some of their church services out of gratitude once he had arrived in his new home in Israel.

This study, however, does *not* concern Russian Jews who flirt with non-Orthodox Christianity. The Russian Orthodox Church does not proselytize, perhaps because it still has so much of its own house to put in order, perhaps because it does not really want Jews in its midst. The Jews I interviewed entered the Church with no coercion, and with little proselytizing except from close friends, by their own free, usually intellectual rather than emotional, choice. Furthermore, because I was interested specifically in the *choice* of the Orthodox Church, an institution that requires active ritual as well as abstract belief, I confined my interviews, with one exception, to those who had became Russian Orthodox as adults. They all *chose* to complicate— or explore—their Russian-Jewish national and religious identity with entrance into the nationally Russian Orthodox Church.

🏵 *Background*

Discussion of the "Jewish question" in Russia can be found in many places, and I will not elaborate on the topic here.[6] I will stress only one historical fact that is confirmed by the narratives recorded here: the success of various imperial *and* Jewish intelligentsia efforts to divorce ethnic from religious identity, beginning in the mid-nineteenth century. Some, like one Russian Jew in 1861, sought to make Jews into "Russians citizens of Jewish descent." As he wrote: "Let the new generation, from the cradle, think in Russian, speak in Russian, feel Russian, and be Russian, body and soul." The idea was to become Russian in culture, but "hold firmly to the faith of our fathers," to make of the Russian Jews, along the model of Western enlightenment, "Russian citizens of the Mosaic persuasion."[7] This outcome never materialized in Russia, although it is the prevailing attitude in America, for example, where "Jews are not a recognized ethnic minority; they are members of a religion."[8] According to the classic sociological study of Will Herberg, the "religious community" for Jews, as for Catholics and Protestants in America, has taken precedence over old ethnic lines as the "primary context of self-identification and social location."[9]

Despite the dominant influence of Herberg on contemporary sociologists studying American Jews, some of the latter are indeed finding a more complex pattern of "belongingness" in their subjects, in which religious and national identity (the latter now felt to be perhaps more cultural than ethnic) continue to interact.[10] The Guttman Report, commissioned in 1990 by the Avi Chai Foundation and subsequently creating quite a stir in the Israeli press, indicates that this interaction of religious and national identity remains true in Israel as well, although the relative weight of each pole is still under heated debate.[11] Nonetheless, the bottom line for Americans and Israelis would seem to be religious identity, even among otherwise secular Jews; American researchers Steven M. Cohen and Arnold M. Eisen found repeatedly that their respondents thought the one way to cease being a Jew is to convert to another religion.[12]

Russian-Jewish identity took a different path. Jewish and imperial efforts toward separation of what had been in ancient and medieval times an un-questioned alliance of religious and national identity were amazingly suc-cessful, and continued into the Soviet period. Ultimately, the assertion of national identity took precedence over religious definition, and not vice versa, as religion was systematically repressed on all sides in the new atheist state. Yiddish was favored by the Soviet government as the Jewish national language in the early years, and the Hebrew-oriented intelligentsia (like much of the Russian intelligentsia) had left the new Soviet Union by 1921. "Jewish" became one ethnic category among many. Despite Soviet rhetoric of multinational brotherhood, however, Jewish nationality as confirmed on the passport and by external marks of name and countenance served only to separate Jews from ethnic Russians, even as the Jews lost Yiddish as well as Hebrew culture. Jews were, as Zvi Gitelman has put it, "acculturated with-out being assimilated."[13] They were nationally Jewish, culturally Russian, and religiously nothing.

And this is where we find the Russian Jews of this study, before their baptism. To aid the separation of religious and ethnic/national identity, mod-ern Russian provides its speakers with two separate words: *evrei* and *iudei,* the former having an ethnic meaning: a member of *evreistvo,* Jewry; the latter, a religious one: a follower of the laws and rituals of *iudeistvo,* or *iudaizm.* The two terms for *Jew* were not so distinct in the late nineteenth century, when the so-called "Jewish Question" was so hotly debated. Solov'ev himself wa-vered in his usage, and a Jewish writer in 1881 needed to ask in a Riga monthly: "How Can We More Truthfully Call Followers of the Mosaic Law: *Evrei, Iudei,* or *Izrail'tiane?*"[14] Virtually all of the subjects of this study an-nounce that they are *evrei,* but not *iudei,* and therefore see no problem with being "Jewish Christians."[15]

✺ *Findings*

Contrary to my preconceptions about religious calling, Father Michael, a Russian Jew who had joined the Church in the sixties and was subse-quently ordained as a priest, spoke to me at length not about encounters with Christ or mystical calls to conversion, but about the Soviet society in which he was raised: "It was an issue of how to maintain your difference. How not to be absorbed. It would give you inner power to stay yourself. The intelligentsia was so threatened by this. From all sides. You need some kind of strength from within that gives you the power to survive. And that is exactly what I felt in the sixties. It was the power that I found to *stay my-self*" (emphasis added).

For Father Michael, entrance into the Church was not a way to leave Judaism, but rather a means to escape to somewhere, out of what Simon Markish has called the "mental vacuum" of the Soviet Union,[16] at a time when physical emigration was still impossible. But if not *from*, why not *toward* Judaism, I asked over and over in my interviews. Father Michael's comment was typical of his generation:

> There was one synagogue [in Moscow], and it was under the complete control of the state. The rabbi himself was afraid. It was not at all an option. It became a possibility only later, in the seventies. Only with the possibility of Israel and the emigration. You have to realize that to be a Jew, or to be a Christian in those days, was the way of emigration, a way to leave Soviet society. So if you want to leave Soviet society, better to leave it for real. If you want to be a Jew, be a Jew outside of here. If you want to emigrate, where are you going to emigrate: inside or outside? In the sixties, there was no choice. My way was *inner emigration*. (Emphasis added)

This metaphor of "inner emigration" brings us back to Father Michael's assertion that the Church helped him "stay himself." He did not leave at the time for the physical "homeland" (although he did later, and in Israel met his bride, who was also a baptized Jew). Rather, he looked inward for his spiritual home. Most important, he did not feel he became "different" through baptism, but that he became, or found the strength to remain, "himself."

A Russian-Jewish woman who lived through the late-Stalin and post-Stalin years but did not convert offered this explanation: "It was 'easier' to be Orthodox than to be Jewish." Perhaps even their grandfathers and their grandmothers themselves were unable to explain Judaism to them. And, indeed, a large number of my subjects begin by saying that there was no "Jewish," that is religious, *iudeiskoe*, feeling in their childhood homes, although they might remember the strange customs of a grandfather or great-grandfather. For some, these were good memories. Marina related:

> I come from a good Jewish family, a correct Jewish family. I had a great-grandfather, a man of faith, kind and good and bright. He spoke Russian poorly, with a strong accent and with mistakes, like a character from a Jewish joke. But he is the kind of man whom I will remember forever. When he would pray he would wear a *tallis*, and I would sit by the table and grab onto the fringes. I remember very well how he would sit me on the couch and tell me stories from the Bible and Jewish history. You had the feeling that he was telling stories about one of our relatives.

For some, however, the memories are not so warm. Feliks Svetov writes in his autobiography that once his grandfather became ill, his aunts organized a minyan for him at their home: "Thirty or forty old men and women would fill up the house, toot on their tooters and shout gutturally. I was used to bringing friends home . . . but here would be my grandfather, wrapped in his prayer shawl, muttering prayers. My friends would giggle, and I stopped inviting them home, making up reasons why they couldn't come." For Svetov, the Jew who came to lay out the body of his late grandfather was "old, ugly, and dirty."[17]

Despite scattered childhood memories—positive or negative—any real connection to *iudeskie* roots was lost: "My own Jewish family was very much assimilated into the Soviet structure. Not just Russian. Of course, many of their friends were Jewish. There was a sense of a Jewish community, of Jewishness even without Judaism. My paternal grandmother was the great-granddaughter of a chief rabbi of Lithuania. But in her memory, it was more a sense of a way of life and of community, rather than anything religious. Or maybe it was just the loss of memory. When people secularize, they don't really remember."

Volodya declared: "I grew up in an entirely atheist family. Non-believers. We had absolutely no traditions. Not Orthodox and not Judaic. We didn't even have Yiddish. An average Soviet upbringing." For Volodya, and for many others of his generation, the family had a Jewish national identity, but neither religious nor even strong cultural ties.

To repeat, then, baptism for the generation that came to the Church in the 1960s did not mean a conversion out of Judaism at all. Rather, entrance into the Church meant departure from Soviet ideology, or rather, from the lack of ideology, or idealism, or belief in Soviet society. Misha explained: "For me it was a search for a religious foundation, for a spiritual foundation to get out of this system."

The generation that came to faith as the Soviet Union was falling apart in the 1980s differs in more than age from the generation of the 1960s, and their stories can bring home the uniqueness of this Russian-Jewish phenomenon. Like Father Michael, Volodya, Marina, and others, Russian-Jewish Christians from the 1980s describe their entrance into the Church not as a departure from Judaism (*iudaizm*), and certainly not from Jewry (*evreistvo*), but rather as a response to the vapidity of the Soviet society in which they were raised. The question of Jewish emigration, however, weighed much more heavily on this generation than on the earlier one, and thus the confrontation with their own Jewishness plays a much larger role in their narratives of faith.

In the 1980s, Soviet citizens had more and more access to material on Jewish life, culture, religion, language, and Israel. Many if not most of their friends and relatives had already left. Still, Avraham confessed: "The fact is that we lived in an atheistic society. Young people did not know anything about any religion. We came to it ourselves. I got a copy of the Torah in Hebrew, with Russian translation. When I began to read Torah, I became a religious person. I don't know how much of my feeling was Judaism (*iudeistvo*), but I felt myself part of the Jewish people (*evreiskii narod*). Considering how much cynicism there was then in Soviet society, this gave me the strength to consider myself significant. For me it was both a sort of nationalization and an approach to faith." What we can see here is not simply a thirst for religion, but a way to reconcile spirituality with their already existing, but, as we will see, previously negatively defined ethnic sense of Jewish identity.

For Petya: "You will laugh at this; you won't believe it. In the Soviet Union, I was always shy about being a Jew. Why? Because it carried with it a mass of inconveniences. External ones. . . . But then, after I was baptized, and we began to study Hebrew—because without that you can't understand Christianity—then I began to defend myself as a Jew. And the more I am a Christian, the more I feel myself a Jew."

According to Dmitrii: "Only after baptism did we feel ourselves to be Jews. Before then, to be a Jew was a negative. When someone in Russia calls you a 'Jew,' he means to put you down. It's interesting that in the course of our study of Christianity, of Orthodoxy, we entered deeper and deeper into a different understanding, that Jews are precisely the chosen people. After baptism, we began to feel ourselves more deeply Jewish. Why? It wasn't a kind of pride, but simply an internal feeling."

What we need to note here is the repetition of the internal, as opposed to earlier external feeling of Jewishness—external because it was forced from without, principally by antisemitism. Thus, religion, although not Judaism, brought Jewishness as a positive identification back to these cynical Soviet Jews. And once emigration became not only an option, but an expectation, the question arose for many about whether or not they could continue to be Jews, Christian or otherwise, in Russia. For one Jewish Christian, "I think that without my entrance into faith, I would not have left for Israel so easily. I would have left in any case, but I would have come to that decision much later. I felt that I could fulfill my Jewishness. I didn't need to fear."

Father Alexander, a Jewish priest who did not emigrate, and who now leads a flock of mostly Jewish Christians in a small parish two hundred kilometers outside of Moscow, explained that "The reality is that a Jewish consciousness awoke in practically all the Jews who began to live a Church life, thanks to the Church life, and in connection to the Church life. For many of them, if not for the majority, this became a problem."

I asked my interviewees about their choice specifically of the Orthodox Church, despite its historical connection to antisemitism, for this is the "problem" to which Father Alexander alluded. As I stated earlier, I assumed that I would hear about a desire—unconscious or conscious—to become, finally, Russian. The answer, however, was somewhat different, for baptism into the Russian Orthodox Church did not make these believers more Russian, but more Jewish.

"Why Orthodoxy?" answered Avraham. "Because those personalities that I met were Orthodox; they belonged to the Orthodox Church. Now I see it as a coincidence. Then, I just spoke with those I met, as I am speaking with you."

The question of the Russianness of Russian Orthodoxy *was* important for many of the Russian-Jewish Christians, but in cultural, rather than national terms. Marina called Orthodoxy the "local religion": "Now, I love a lot that is in Orthodoxy. It is my language." Petya explained: "Orthodoxy is closer to our roots. It is in the same language. If Catholicism was served in Russian, and Orthodoxy in Chinese, then of course I would have been a Catholic. [One wonders again about Judaism—JDK.] It is a question of language. But not just of language. Of culture as well. How can you separate language from culture?" And Volodya explained again: "Russian literature was one of the bases of our faith."

Several narratives of Russian-Jewish Christians include discussion of what I call the "aesthetic question." When asked if Judaism had been an option, Mikhail answered: "In everything there is an aesthetic element. The synagogue service itself is not aesthetic. And there were only old men. If in the church there were only old women, at least there was the aesthetic element, a feeling of mystery, perhaps." Why not Protestantism, I asked, especially since many Russians and Russian Jews in Russia and Israel are now attracted to evangelical sects? Ilya answered: "In Protestantism, everything was very simple, and that never attracted me. There was no musical mysticism."

The aesthetic pleasure comes with a price, Marina acknowledged: "But there are also many things that are difficult for me, and always were. It is always a difficult joy for me to be in church. It is an internal requirement, I feel. But, on the other hand, I always feel an internal contradiction."

The contradiction was the very existence of a Jew in the institutional Church as it now stands, but not necessarily as these *intelligenty*—like Krakhmal'nikova whom I discussed in the beginning of this chapter—understood it from their readings of Solov'ev, the Fathers of the Church, and the Gospels themselves. An interviewee who now lives in Israel confessed: "The Christianity that Jesus revealed to me is Jewish at its core. Jesus was a

Jew from the very beginning. With that kind of Christianity I would be fully at home."

Petya recalled the first years after his baptism in the Soviet Union: "We organized prayers at first at home. We prayed in Hebrew. We prayed, as we imagined, the first Jewish Christians prayed." For Avraham: "Of course, the Russian culture makes it easier for Russian Jews to come to Russian Orthodoxy. But I came to Jesus through those gates as to a Jew. As a representative of the Jewish religion. I related to Him as to a Jew. I saw in him a Jew (*iudei*). . . . And the deeper I went into the Church, the more deeply I felt myself belonging to the people of Israel."

🌀 *Conclusions*

In many ways, the quest of these Russian-Jewish Christians is not unique. Conversion, as well as general entrance into religious life from a secular background, occurs around the world. Many researchers connect the modern increase in conversion to the problem of disjunction in contemporary life. A study of American converts to Russian Orthodoxy claims that we are all in a transition period, and are engaged in a search for "belonging, a search for a grand narrative."[18]

The case of the Russian-Jewish Christians I have studied is part of the phenomenon of "belongingness" in our, and especially Soviet, disjointed times, but it is also special, the product of a particular context. The first contextual aspect, as suggested by Father Michael above, relates to the profound ideological crisis created in the Soviet Union after the revelations about Stalin's Terror, to Markish's "mental vacuum." The generation of the 1960s associated entrance into the Church with a resurrection of idealism in general, not necessarily as a religious step. Glasnost in the 1980s did not greatly alter the sense of emptiness among Jews of the intelligentsia. From this point of view, the baptism of Russian-Jewish intellectuals into the Orthodox Church can be seen as a *Soviet,* not a Jewish, and not a Christian, phenomenon.

Second, most of the Russian-Jewish Christians I interviewed felt *more* Jewish after their baptism than before. This feeling is not consistent with what researchers have found among other Jewish out-converts. According to Todd Endelman in *Jewish Apostasy in the Modern World,* "Most Jews who became Christians were eager to leave their Jewishness behind them and worked assiduously to promote their own and their children's absorption into the larger society."[19] Rodger Kamenetz found in American "JUBUs" (Jews who converted to Buddhism) not only the desire to leave Jewishness behind, but smouldering anger at their own heritage.[20] A study of the Messengers of the New Covenant, a sect of messianic Jews, finds that "Much personal testimony centers on alienation from and feelings of anomie toward Jews."[21]

Entrance into the Orthodox Church, however, has brought back to the Russian-Jewish Christians I interviewed a positive correspondence between their religious and national identities. How did this happen? Jewishness had been defined earlier for these people negatively and externally. Virtually everyone reported feeling antisemitism. As Feliks Svetov wrote: "I felt myself to be Jewish only because they reminded me of the fact."[22]

After baptism, however, Jewishness for many has taken on a positive meaning, so that, as Petya told me, "the more I am a Christian, the more I feel myself a Jew." And, claimed Avraham, "The deeper I went into the Church, the more deeply I felt myself belonging to the people of Israel." This new understanding of their Jewishness now connects these Jews to an ancient and spiritually rewarding tradition. The answer to their identity question is both national and religious. Father Michael half-joked: "For me, Judaism was not an issue at all. Until I became a Christian." Ilya announced with a totally straight face: "When I read the Gospels, I understood what it meant to be a Jew. . . . This was the first Jewish book (*evreiskaia kniga*) that I ever read." Ironically, entrance into Russian Orthodoxy gave these Jews a new internal and positive identity, as opposed to the external and negative Jewish identity of their childhoods. They feel now doubly chosen.

Chosenness, however, carries responsibility, and an expression of that responsibility, related to the question of antisemitism, recurred throughout the interviews. Virtually all the Russian-Jewish Christians in this study acknowledged the existence of antisemitism in the Orthodox Church, and, significantly, many used the same metaphor to discuss it. "The Russian Orthodox Church is rather sick," admitted Marina. "The Church is infected with antisemitism," complained Felix. Again, from Ilya: "The Orthodox Church here was suffering from illnesses. The typical illnesses." Or Volodya: "I look on such things in the priests or the parishioners I meet as a kind of illness." And Avraham: "It is infected by antisemitism. . . . It is not just a disease in the Church. It is a genetic disease. It is destroying the Church from the inside."

So what are the Russian-Jewish Christians—at least those who have remained in the Church—doing in this hotbed of infection and disease? One might assume that they, too, would become infected. And, in fact, such so-called "self-hatred" is not unheard-of among acculturated Jews in Russia as well as elsewhere. As Markish points out, not surprisingly, "Russian self-consciousness can lead a Russified Jew even to the point of anti-Semitism."[23] Jewish out-converts to other denominations have been seen to suffer from the "illness." In discussing American Jewish participants in the Messengers of the New Covenant, Natalie Isser and Lita Linzer Schwartz argue that "modern Jews who have converted to 'Hebrew Christianity' or 'Jews for Jesus' groups are not only plagued by the 'ineradicable' Jewishness within themselves, but frequently suffer as well from minority self-hate, often manifested in anti-semitic behavior."[24]

The new, positive, and internal identification of themselves as Jewish, however, alters the relationship of Russian-Jewish Christians to the disease of antisemitism within the Church. Their special status as double heirs to God's chosen people bestows upon them a new mission, a positive and internal role to play within Christianity: that of healer. Not coincidentally, this mission closely corresponds to the work of Father Alexander Men', a major influence on many of those interviewed, who saw himself as helping to heal the division between Church and society, between science and religion, between believers and non-believers, and between the Orthodox Church and other denominations.[25] The very fact that Father Alexander baptized so many Jews, and was himself Jewish by birth, suggested to many of the Russian-Jewish Christians a reconciliation of the unhealthy fracture between Christianity and the Jews.

And thus the diagnosis is made. The physicians are at hand. The murder of Father Men' in 1990 was never solved. Many say it was orchestrated by antisemitic elements within the Church itself, and that suggests that recovery will not be easy. Yet, continued pressure by some factions within the Church, including some Jews, might keep the spiritual body from total decay. Only time will tell.

NOTES

1. Research for this study was undertaken with generous support from IREX and the Vidal Sassoon International Center for the Study of Antisemitism at Hebrew University, Jerusalem. A sabbatical leave from the University of Wisconsin made the research opportunity possible. The present article is part of a book-length study currently under way titled *Doubly Chosen: Soviet Jews in the Russian Orthodox Church.*

2. To respect confidentiality, unless interviewees have also published on the subject of their Christianity, names are here sometimes omitted and sometimes changed. In all cases, only given names are used. Many Jews in the Church are reluctant to identify themselves publicly for fear of discrimination from both Jews and Christians. Jews who converted to Christianity and then arrived in Israel under the Law of Return have legal fears as well.

3. This Russian Jew's awareness of his Jewish identity, like that of so many other Soviet Jews, came on the heels of the 1967 Six Day War, and was reinforced by the general intelligentsia reaction to the 1968 Prague invasion.

4. For more on Krakhmal'nikova, see Judith Deutsch Kornblatt, "'Christianity. Antisemitism. Nationalism': Russian Orthodoxy in a Reborn Orthodox Russia," in *Consuming Russia,* ed. Adele Barker (Durham, N.C.: Duke University Press, 1999).

5. See Judith Deutsch Kornblatt, "Vladimir Solov'ev on Spiritual Nationhood, Russia and the Jews," *The Russian Review* 56 (April 1997): 157–77.

6. There are some excellent studies in English of the growth of the "Jewish Question" in Russia in the nineteenth century. See especially Michael Stanislawski, *Tsar Nicholas I and the Jews: The Transformation of Jewish Society in Russia, 1825–1855* (Philadelphia: The Jewish Publication Society of America, 1983); John Doyle Klier, *Russia Gathers Her Jews: The Origins of the "Jewish Question" in Russia, 1772–1825* (Dekalb: Northern Illinois University Press, 1986); and John Doyle Klier, *Imperial Russia's Jewish Question 1855–1881* (Cambridge: Cambridge University Press, 1995).

7. Cited in Klier, *Imperial Russia's Jewish Question,* 104, 105, 122.

8. Norman Roth, "Am Yisrael: Jews or Judaism?" *Judaism: A Quarterly Journal* 37, no. 2 (1988): 199.

9. Will Herberg, *Protestant-Catholic-Jew: An Essay in American Religious Sociology* (Chicago: University of Chicago Press, 1955, 1960, 1983), 34. As Gitelman states in the present volume, "In America . . . [a] 'good Jew' is one who belongs to Jewish organizations, including synagogues or temples, and contributes to Jewish causes." In contrast, he, Vladimir Shapiro, and Valeriy Chervyakov found that "Jews in the former Soviet Union (FSU) do *not* strongly connect the Jewish religion with being Jewish." The process of separation of religious identity from "Jewishness" began in Russia over a century ago.

10. See, for example, the recent study by Steven M. Cohen and Arnold M. Eisen, *The Jew Within: Self, Family, and Community in America* (Bloomington: Indiana University Press, 2000).

11. For the condensed, "Highlights," version of the Guttman Institute Report, as well as samples of the debate surrounding it, see *The Jewishness of Israelis: Responses to the Guttman Report,* ed. by Charles S. Liebman and Elihu Katz (Albany: SUNY Press, 1997).

12. *The Jew Within,* 27.

13. Zvi Gitelman, "Jewish Nationality and Religion in the USSR and Eastern Europe," in Pedro Ramet, ed., *Religion and Nationalism in Soviet and East European Politics* (Durham, N.C.: Duke University Press, 1989), 67

14. "Kak vernee nazyvat' posledovatelei Moiseeva zakona: evreiami, iudeiami ili izrail'tianami," *Evreiskiie zapiski* (1881): 54.

15. As Gitelman, Shapiro, and Chervyakov found in their recent study, "Judaism is no longer the content or boundary of Jewish identity," and "in Russia and Ukraine, in both years of the survey, only 30–39 percent are prepared to condemn Jews who 'convert to Christianity.'" See also Chapter 4 in this volume.

16. Simon Markish, "Passers-by: The Soviet Jew as Intellectual," *Commentary* 66, no. 6 (Dec. 1978): 31.

17. Feliks Svetov, *Opyt biografii* (Paris: YMCA-Press, 1985), 70, 107.

18. H. B. Cavalcanti and H. Paul Chalfant, "Collective Life as the Ground of Implicit Religion: The Case of American Converts to Russian Orthodoxy," *Sociology of Religion* 55, no. 4 (1994): 442.

19. Todd M. Endelman, ed., *Jewish Apostasy in the Modern World* (New York and London: Holmes & Meier, 1987), 16–17.

20. Rodger Kamenetz, *The Jew in the Lotus: A Poet's Rediscovery of Jewish Identity in Buddhist India* (San Francisco: Harper, 1994), 147–57.

21. See B. Z. Sobel, *Hebrew Christianity: The Thirteenth Tribe* (New York: John Wiley, 1974); quoted in Natalie Isser and Lita Linzer Schwartz, *The History of Conversion and Contemporary Cults* (New York: Peter Lang, 1988), 33.

22. Svetov, *Opyt biografii,* 206.

23. Markish, "Passers-by," 33.

24. See Isser and Schwartz, 34, 154.

25. Almost all the subjects interviewed for this study mentioned Men', describing either a meeting with him, the importance of his writings, or participation in a society established in his name. Alexander Men' (called Alik by his friends) was born in 1935 in the Soviet Union at the outset of Stalin's Terror to two Jewish parents. Together with her sister, Men's mother Elena became attracted to Christianity, and had both herself and her infant son secretly baptized by a catacomb priest after his birth. She later baptized her second son as well. The young Alik, apparently quite precocious, felt drawn to religion throughout his childhood. Although Father Men' was not the only priest who attracted the Russian-Jewish intelligentsia to religion (see Father Dmitrii Dudko, in particular), his intellectual and spiritual influence, and his personal charisma, were crucial. In the words of one subject of this study: "Men' opened the Church for people like me. For intellectuals, for youth, for Jews. And he kept it open as long as he lived. It is precisely that he kept it open for too many that he was killed, you know." For a biography of Men', see Yves Hamant, *Aleksandr Men': A Witness for Contemporary Russia* (Torrance, Calif.: Oakwood Publications, 1995). For an English-language collection of some of his works, see Alexander Men, *Christianity for the Twenty-First Century: The Prophetic Writings of Alexander Men,* ed. Elizabeth Roberts and Ann Shukman (New York: Continuum, 1996).

THIRTEEN

❧

MUSYA GLANTS

Jewish Artists in Russian Art: Painting and Sculpture in the Soviet and Post-Soviet Eras

A Jew with a knapsack in his hand is strolling along a road; the expression of his eyes is sad and cheerful at the same time and a grin is slightly twisting his lips.

This painting, *Yisroelke Wandered and Wandered Throughout Russia in Search of Happiness* (1975) by the Jewish artist Evgenii Abeshaus (b. 1939), has, as any artistic work, a diversity of meanings, both aesthetic and social. It not only shows the development of Jewish art in Russia at a certain period, but also reflects the growing self-consciousness of the Jews during the post-Stalin years and symbolizes their eternal search for peace and home, for equality and respect. At the same time, the overwhelming atmosphere of this painting, its bitter irony, makes the viewer feel that the ever-wandering Jew will never find happiness in Russia. The artist captured the complex and contradictory sentiments of a Russian Jew in a way that allows us to perceive his experience both rationally and emotionally. Such sensibility constitutes a major tenor of the works of Jewish artists. Although the group of artists is relatively small, their art, as a striking expression of their personal and social experiences, has played a distinctive role in the formation of Jewish identity.

In this essay I focus my attention on the unique characteristics of Jewish artistic achievements from the time of the "thaw" (the late 1950s) to

1. Evgenii Abeshaus, Yisroelke Wandered and Wandered Throughout Russia in Search of Happiness, *1975. Oil on pasteboard. The Norton and Nancy Dodge Collection of Nonconformist Art from the Soviet Union, Jane Voorhees Zimmerli Art Museum, Rutgers, The State University of New Jersey, New Brunswick.*

the present day. There has been very little published analysis of Jewish artistic issues and their social importance, in spite of social and political changes in Russia. Yet, in a country where antisemitism persists and art in general has traditionally had a social and moral mission, Jewish art merits special examination.

Defining "Jewish" Art and Artists

I have called Abeshaus a "Jewish" artist. But whom do we actually define as a Jewish artist, and does such a phenomenon really exist? Can an artist be called Jewish just because of Jewish origin or because he or she depicts Jewish subjects? Is there a particular Jewish style in art? These questions have been hotly discussed for more than a century without conclusions. Having examined a great number of works of art created by Jews in Russia in various periods and having considered colleagues' opinions, I conclude that there is no single satisfactory definition of the phenomenon of "Jewish artists." What constitutes a "Jewish artist" varies with social and historical circumstances. If one compares what is meant by "Jewish art," "Jewish artist," and "Jewish artists in Russian art" over the decades, it is obvious that the meaning has continually changed.[1] To be a Jew and an artist at the turn of the twentieth century, at the time of the great sculptor Mark Antokolskii (1843–1902), the painters Isaak Levitan (1861–1900) and Lev Bakst (1866–1924), or later, of Natan Altman (1889–1970) or El Lissitskii (1890–1941), during the flourishing of the avant-garde in the 1920s, was not the same as being a Jew and an artist during the Stalin era. Moreover, even within the Stalin and post-Stalin periods, Jewish art manifested itself in a wide variety of ways.

When defining who is a Jewish artist in Russia, we mean in most cases a Jew who was educated and who worked in a culture not his own, a culture that was a priori regarded as more elevated and more valuable than the vernacular culture. For those artists who came to Russian art at the turn of the twentieth century, entry into Russian culture was an especially complex process because of their close ties to their Jewish background and its traditions. They had to sever those ties and adopt unfamiliar styles of life and art. This was true of Mark Antokolskii, Lev Bakst, and also of Marc Chagall (1887–1985). Hence, these artists always remained people of dual identity, belonging to a certain extent to both Jewish and Russian cultures. After the Revolution, the relation of the artist to traditional Jewish culture virtually ceased. During the Soviet period, persons of Jewish heritage were in most cases brought up in the midst of Russian culture, which they now considered their own. They regarded themselves as not being very different from the autochthonous people among whom they lived. The overwhelming majority did not follow the religion and language of their ancestors and quite often their sense of Jewishness went no further than the *piatyi punkt* ("fifth point") in the passports, where nationality was registered, and their grandmothers' gefilte fish. Nonetheless, their feeling of duality persisted, lingering within them as a sense of incomplete belonging. They shared unspoken feelings of inequality resulting from the regime's policies toward the Jews and the antisemitism of the masses. In each artist's biography this sense of duality was reflected in distinctive ways. What needs to be determined is the correlation between each artist's "Russianness" and "Jewishness." More specifically, how did each individual artist experience self-identity in relation to "Russianness" and "Jewishness?"

Two factors influence my understanding of who may be considered to be Jewish artists in the post-Stalin era. First, those whom I consider Jewish artists had to recognize themselves as Jews. Second, their works had to reflect Jewish issues as well as the complex emotions of the Jewish people.

2. *Tankhum Kaplan,* Mourning for a Dead Child, *from the series*
D. Shostakovich. From Jewish Folk Poetry. *Distemper, gouache.*
Source: B. Suris, Anatolii Lvovich Kaplan *(Leningrad, 1972).*

However, as these artists had been taught in Russian art schools by Russian teachers, they also absorbed Russian styles; hence, these artists were equally part of Russian culture. The "Jewish" works of Natan Altman (1889–1970), Aleksandr Tyshler (1898–1980), Tankhum (Anatolii) Kaplan (1902–80), Gavriil Zapolianskii (b. 1933), Evgenii Abeshaus (b. 1939), or Alik Rapoport (b. 1933) clearly stem from Russian culture and absorb the achievements of various trends—from Romanticism and Realism to the great Russian avant-garde and contemporary post-modernism.

3. *Tankhum Kaplan,* The Golden Wedding. *From the series* Jewish Folk Songs, *1962.*
Color lithography. Source: B. Suris, Anatolii Lvovich Kaplan *(Leningrad, 1972).*

In turn, those artists themselves significantly influenced and colored the
cultural life of Russia. They engendered their own philosophical views,
their choices of artistic subjects, and their interpretations. Their Jewish
identity "manifested itself—at times unperceived by the artists themselves
—in certain deeply rooted attitudes, in a basic mindset handed down via
specific sensibility."[2]

This process of mutual Russian-Jewish influence is not a recent devel-

Jewish Artists in Russian Art

4. Gavriil Zapolianskii, Musicians, *1989. Cardboard, gouache.*
Peter Novisky Gallery of Modern Art, Warsaw.

opment. It has existed since the late nineteenth century, albeit in diversified forms. It may be seen as affecting the particular vision of a human being in Antokolskii's sculpture, in the special emotional atmosphere of Levitan's landscapes, and in the ardor of Bakst's designs. As the Russian Israeli writer Ruth Zernova said about the interdependence of these cross-cultural relations, the "yeast does not function without dough."[3]

Among those who during the last Soviet decades refused to work within the dogmas of Socialist Realism and who strove to achieve political and spiritual freedom both in life and art, Jews played a significant role in establishing original styles and trends. Although most of them—even some who are half-Jewish—sensed their social inferiority deriving from their ethnicity, they reacted in different ways and were not equally interested in reflecting their Jewishness in art. The organizer of the famous "Bulldozer exhibition," Oskar Rabin (b. 1928); the conceptualists Ilya Kabakov (b. 1933) and Eric Bulatov (b. 1933); the founders of the so-called "soc-art," Vitaly Komar (b. 1943) and Aleksandr Melamid (b. 1945); and others—all artists known in the West—were not specifically attracted to explicit Jew-

זקן

5. *Alek Rapoport,* The Elder, *1976. Ink, paper. Collection of
the Rapoport family, San Francisco.*

ish themes and ideas, but aimed at different social and aesthetic goals.[4] The
work of others, such as Felix Lemberskii (1913–70), Ilya Tabenkin (1914–
88) and his son Lev (b. 1952), or Vadim Sidur (1924–86), reflected Jewish
problems and the artists' own relation to them, but mostly in symbolic and
metaphorical forms.[5] Still, there was also a third artistic circle, not a large
one, who conveyed in their works their Jewish national feelings, doubts,
fears, and expectations while expressing their relation to Russia and the
Russians. The high emotional level of their work, their concealed but powerful dynamism and their impressive imagery, became symbols of the Jew-

ish struggle for national roots and rights. My own interest is in the Jewish-related aspects of the works of these artists.

🏵 *Jewish Art and Artists in the Post-Stalin Period*

Stalin's death in 1953 awakened people's hopes and rekindled their search for their national identities. Some Jews also believed in the possibility of a revival of their culture after several decades of enduring its attempted destruction. I remember the joy and excitement of my father and his friends: *"Der rosheh, der vontz hot gepeigert! Me ken lebn und zingn vaiter!"* ("The tyrant, the 'mustache' croaked! We can live and sing again!"), they cried out, and this was undoubtedly the voice of the Jewish majority. Although the following years were marked by significant changes and Stalin's antisemitism (virulent during his last years) was replaced by Khrushchev's and Brezhnev's much less dangerous form, things did not work out for the Jews in the way they had expected. They still remained oppressed more than some other nationalities, and Jewish culture was still not countenanced officially.[6]

By the 1960s, Jewish culture, including Jewish art, had been virtually destroyed by both Hitler and Stalin. The enormous suffering of the Jews during World War II did not alter Stalin's anti-Jewish policies. There had been a short respite granted during the early years of the war, when Jews were officially mentioned and literature in Yiddish was published, but this change was slowed down with the first Soviet military victories. Already by 1943 the writer and war correspondent Vasily Grossman had great trouble publishing his article *"Ukraina bez evreev"* (Ukraine without Jews) in the Yiddish newspaper *Einikayt*.[7] The situation grew worse in the late 1940s and early 1950s when the cream of Jewish culture perished in the basements of the security police.[8] In general, for a Jew to survive at that time as an artist meant to collaborate with officials (or, at least, to appear to do so) and in some cases even to humiliate Jewish brethren openly, as the caricaturist Boris Efimov did, regularly publishing cartoons against Israel and Zionism in the 1940s and 1950s. His images of ugly Jews whose hooked noses were hanging to the floor and whose animal-like fingers dripped blood, were a familiar sight in the Soviet press. Whereas everybody who refused to follow the official requirements of Socialist Realism was doomed to hunger, in the Jewish case even faithfulness to this style could not save those who continued to work on Jewish themes. They could not make a living as artists because they were not ready to succumb to antisemitic forces. In order to survive, Tankhum Kaplan, one of the artists most devoted to

Jewish tradition, was compelled in 1949 to illustrate a book of the anti-semitic writer Vsevolod Kochetov, *On Whom Is the Sun Shining* (*Komu svetit solntse*). Guilty of being both Jewish and "formalist," such artists as Natan Altman, Aleksandr Tyshler, and Rafail Falk (1886–1958) found their last refuge in creating stage designs for the Yiddish Theater, but were literally starving after the theater was closed in 1949.

Nonetheless, there was still a very fragile thread of art stretching out of the past to the present. It consisted of a small group of masters who never stopped working on Jewish themes, striving over the years to preserve and express the Jewish spirit in their works. Kaplan's series *Kasrilovka* (1937–40) and *Kishinev, Chernovtsy* (1940) created an expressive gallery of Jewish characters. Close in spirit were Girsh Inger's (b. 1910) illustrations for Jewish books and the graphics of Mikhail Gorshman (1902–72). Actually, book illustrations and portraits provided a narrow niche in which a Jewish artist could still work. Sometimes the artists resorted to cunning. During the 1930s, Ruvim Mazel (1890–1967) painted biblical scenes, including *Three Angels Visiting Abraham, Cain and Abel* and other works in which he expressed his strong feelings of betrayal, the loss of ideals, and the triumph of cruelty. He got away with it because he painted all of these characters as if they were Turkmen.[9] In the 1960s most of these artists were still alive and were continuing to work on Jewish subjects. While Natan Altman's composition *The Bewitched Tailor* (1963) became a dramatic cry of the artist's exhausted soul, Aleksandr Tyshler's girl with a menorah on the top of her head (*Birthday*, 1962) was a poetic union of fantasy and reality, a celebration of life. Unfortunately, only a very narrow circle of people could see these works, as they were not publicly exhibited. Though the art works were not officially forbidden, the word *evrei,* "Jew," continued to be officially banned and Jewish art was hardly ever on display.

Early in the first post-Stalin decade, it became clear that the attitude toward the Jews in the Soviet Union was not going to change drastically from Stalin's "good, old times." The change that did occur meant only that people were now destroyed more spiritually than physically. Soviet censors kept vigilant watch over the publication of anything with specific Jewish content. Significant was the tragic story of Vassily Grossman's book *Life and Fate* (*Zhizn' i sudba*), the publication of which was literally halted, with all copies destroyed. In 1961, Grossman refused to publish his essay about Armenia in the journal *Novyi mir* (New World) because the publishers asked him to take out a paragraph about Jews.[10] Jewish themes were proscribed in all the media. In 1966–67, the movies *Komissar* and *Interventsia* were banned for more than twenty years because among their main charac-

6. *Aleksandr Tyshler, left,* The Balaganchik, *1966; right,* The Jewish Bride, *1959. State Tretiakov Gallery, Moscow.*

ters were Jews who were portrayed positively. When Nekhama Lifshitsaite, a very popular Jewish singer from Vilnius, performed at overcrowded concert halls—a miracle in itself—her repertoire combined old Jewish folk *lieder* (songs) about the bitter life in the Pale with a few extremely optimistic Soviet songs in Yiddish, such as *"Lomir zogn yezt lekhaim tsu dem lebn tsu dem naiem!!"* (Let's say now *lekhaim*—to life! to our new life!). Jewish cultural life was kept contained within the Yiddish journal *Sovetish haymland* (Soviet Homeland) and was available only to a very limited audience because Yiddish was by then unknown to the majority of Jews. When an album of Kaplan's illustrations to the *Zakoldovannyi portnoi (Bewitched Tailor)* by Sholem Aleichem was published, a great scandal broke out. The people responsible for its publication were accused of paying too much attention to "narrow national details," and the censor's explanation for the criticism was that Sholem Aleichem had been a humanist writer, whose works were deeply international and not just Jewish.[11]

To work on Jewish subjects during the 1960s and later during Brezhnev's period of "stagnation" was to make a political statement that required considerable courage. In 1966, for his illustrations to *Na chem derzhitsia mir* (How the World Lasts) by Itskhokas Meras, about the Jewish ghettos in Lithuania, the sculptor Vadim Sidur got into trouble with the authorities and was soon not allowed to work even on book graphics.[12] Felix Lemberskii, an artist deeply attached to his Jewish roots, dared to express his feelings several times in his last works, but only as vague hints. In such paintings as *By a Wooden Fence* (1961), *A Hardware Store* (1959) and *At a Construction Site* (1964)—topics seemingly remote from Jewish themes—the artist managed to insert religious details. For example, the viewer could glimpse in the painted structure of a building the head of an old man in a *tallis,* a prayer shawl, or perceive the contours of a Star of David in a design of a fence.

At the same time, there was little demand for Jewish culture. People were still afraid to show their attachment to Jewish culture because of their mixed feelings: loyalty to Russia for saving them from the Nazis, tempered by fresh memories of Stalin's persecutions and pain for the Jewish fate. Even more important was the fact that during the years of Stalinism, the chain of cultural continuity had been almost broken and the Jews themselves, especially the younger generation, had lost not only contact with their roots but also interest in them. Zvi Gitelman, Valeriy Cherviakov, and Vladimir Shapiro have noted that urbanization and secular education, the growing number of mixed marriages, and the widespread use of the Russian language had weakened the hold of Judaism, changed the lifestyles of the Jewish people, and moved Jews toward assimilation and Russification.[13] Growing up without a Jewish language, religion, and traditions, the majority of young people tended to acknowledge their Jewishness only as an official designation in their passports or when they were reminded of it by anti-semites. Their assimilation was strongly supported by parents who worried about the future. The older generation was convinced that any interest or involvement in Jewish life was likely to bring trouble and repression.[14]

In addition, Soviet Jews were often still in the grip of the pre-Revolutionary attitudes toward the Jewish past, both religious and cultural, which was perceived as dull, deeply provincial, and worthy of disdain. Traditions of the *shtetls* were considered narrow-minded. Moreover, the *shtetl* mentality, which was called *kleinshtetldikayt* or *mestechkovost',* was used as a synonym for a particularly narrow and unattractive way of thinking, feeling, and behaving. It was also the antonym of intellectuality. Such views were especially common among intellectuals, both Russians and Jews.

In the 1960s, however, it became fashionable for all Soviet nationalities to return to their roots, religions, and folk art. Numerous books were published about life in the villages and the *sol zemli* ("salt of the earth"). The *pros-*

toi chelovek ("simple man") was idealized and Russian icons, woodwork, and samovars were hunted by collectors and admirers. Jewish intellectuals took a great interest in this revival, enthusiastically sharing in the retrieval of Russian, Latvian, Armenian, and other pasts. But at the same time as these young Jews truly admired the Russian village grandmothers of their friends with their oft-cited folk wisdom, they were often ashamed of their own grandparents' broken Russian and the guttural and simultaneously melodious sounds of Yiddish in the house (when such sounds were still being heard). The young artists, Jews of the "thaw" period, who were busy ridding themselves of official strictures in art, were at that moment not thinking at all about their Jewishness. Fascinated with great Russian art and discovering new Western trends that had long been kept underground, these artists were savoring what actually amounted to a mere sip of freedom.

The Jewish intelligentsia sobered up when, together with the rest of the country, they realized that the future was not to be a new "golden age." Starting with bloodshed in Hungary (1956) and ending with Soviet tanks in Czechoslovakia (1968), these were years of bitter disappointments. In the cultural world the situation was not much better. The trial of Andrei Siniavskii and Yulii Daniel and the persecution of Boris Pasternak followed Khrushchev's inveighing against writers and artists at the Manezh art gallery (1962).[15] Still, there were some positive developments for Jews during this period. One important event, the 1967 Israeli Six Day War, not only brought about a sudden surge of Jewish self-consciousness and a search for identity, but also significantly changed the attitude of Russians toward Jews. For the first time in many years, Jews were seen in public places openly and calmly talking about Jewish problems. The notorious and untruthful reproach that "the Jews fought not in the army but in Tashkent" during the Great Patriotic War[16] became less popular. Instead, a newly prized joke was that now the expression "the kike's muzzle" [*zhidovskaya morda*] should be replaced with the repeated official notion from the press—"the face of the aggressor." In the mind of many antisemites, the image of the resigned Jew who was ashamed of being Jewish had turned into a brave and strong Israeli. Moreover, the Six Day War was followed by a period in which Jews were granted the exceptional privileges of emigration. Now virtually any Jew could think of becoming one of those victorious Israelis by leaving the USSR, although there was no massive emigration until March 1971.[17]

The gains of the 1960s were followed in the next decade, however, by bitter desperation when there were no illusions left about "socialism with a human face." People had to confront hard social and political choices. The condition of the Jews was worsened by an official anti-Zionist campaign. Now everything containing the word "Jew" or "Jewish" was considered Zionist propaganda. Books by Jewish writers or about Jews were removed from libraries and people were arrested for studying Hebrew. The private homes of Jewish intellectuals were searched for "Zionist" literature.

Still, the ways in which the Jews were able to deal with the official establishment were expanded. While previously the only option for survival was collaboration with the authorities, now it became possible to protest in different ways. Overt actions still had serious consequences, as in the cases of Anatolii Shcharanskii and the *samoletchiki* group (airplane hijackers) in the 1970s.[18] Covert resistance, nevertheless, was most often left unpunished.[19] Finally, it is hard to overestimate the role of the emergent emigration, which was driven by people's hopelessness, and was a form of protest as well as a means to leave Russia. While pressure on Jews increased and antisemitism continued to be a routine part of life inside the country, emigration was not determined by free choice but by the arbitrary decision of the authorities. Among those who remained in the Soviet Union were Jews who had chosen to stay for a variety of reasons as well as those who, when refused permission to leave, had been stripped of their livelihood. The latter became known in the West as *refuseniks*. All these developments strongly influenced the development of Jewish art.

The Re-emergence of Jewish Art

Several artists, connected socially rather than artistically, were the first to express a search for Jewish identity in the visual arts. Forming a group called *Alef* in Leningrad in 1975, they used art as a tool with which to resist the regime and fight for dignity. In November of that year, the *Alef* group showed their works in the Leningrad apartment of one of their members, Evgenii Abeshaus. Over 4,000 people visited this exhibit. A month later, the art show moved to Moscow, where it attracted 5,000 people. Participating artists were then expelled from the Artists' Union and other official positions. In order to survive, they had to take manual jobs. An American historian writing at the time about the exhibit called it "more than an art show. It is more than a documentary. It is a passionate declaration of faith, a flight of the spirit, an *aliyah*."[20]

The group members did not hide their attitudes in their works. Evgenii Abeshaus's *Adam Ate and Ate of the Fruits That Eve Gave Him but Knew Nothing* (1975) contains a warm, lyrical, and even romantic vision of his people. In this painting, the biblical story is transferred to a realistic, mod-

7. *Evgenii Abeshaus,* Adam Ate and Ate of the Fruits That Eve Gave Him but Knew Nothing, *1975. Courtesy of the artist.*

ern scene. Adam and Eve are kind, loving, simple people. An injection of fantasy and humor—characteristic of Abeshaus's style—accompanied by bright colors and primitive forms intensify the humanity of the scene. A comparison of this *Adam and Eve* to another artwork on the same subject made in 1980 by the non-conformist Jewish artist Vladimir Yankilevskii

(b. 1938) underscores the Jewish emphasis of Abeshaus's painting. Yanki-levskii, in *Adam and Eve,* paints the subjects clad in contemporary clothes, shown from the back at a moment when each tries to pass through different doorways to a house. Their faceless, lonely half-figures, two parts of a whole, unmistakably advise the viewer that the couple is unnaturally sep-arated and has no hope of being reunited. Yankilevskii's idea was to express people's alienation from one another and the difficulty of overcoming such a state—a popular idea at that time. Abeshaus, by contrast, used every pos-sible means to fight isolation, to bring his people together. He was seeking to arouse an appreciation not just of abstract humanity but of specifically Jewish values. His typically Jewish couple sits under a tree of fantasy. They cling to each other and seem to be greeting the obstacles of life with a wise smile and with the well-tried Jewish tool, irony.

Whatever well-known serious subject Abeshaus touched, he turned into something unusual. His new twist, sometimes humorous or naive, sometimes a combination of both, discloses layers of different meanings. His scenes are essentially timeless, although traditional in form. In any case, his approach provided a contemporary atmosphere that would con-nect his subjects to the present life of the Jews. It is as if the artist wanted to say "my contemporaries look different, we live in another age, we are dressed differently, but we are still the same Jewish people and we want others, friends and enemies, to see us as the same Jews."

The search for lost origins and their expression in art was characteristic of other nationalities as well. It was manifested in such works, for example, as Viktor Popkov's *Babka Anisia byla khoroshii chelovek* (The Old Woman Anisia Was a Good Person; 1970s), in portraits of peasants and depictions of moments of village life, and in landscapes with churches and other semi-religious scenes. Artists of Jewish, Russian, and other national origins were moving in similar directions, expressing similar ideas, and using the same styles. They not only shared life experiences, but their outlook was also de-termined to a large degree by Russian culture and Russian traditions in art.

Nonetheless, the Jewish case was especially complicated. Though Jew-ish artists struggled for their spiritual freedom and cultural liberation, they also had to seek acceptance and equality. Wherever Jews lived in the USSR, they were always regarded as a second-class people. Their close bond to their homeland, Russia, their love of Russian culture and life went unrecip-rocated. Moreover, they were often abused and pushed away as unwelcome stepchildren. This treatment reinforced a continued sense of inequality, es-pecially among Jews for whom the Russian experience of life was the only life they knew. Such emotions were powerfully expressed by Jewish artists in

8. *Aleksandr Gurevich,* The Family, *1975. Oil. Courtesy of the artist.*

a number of works that stressed pain and frustration in direct and indirect ways. Aleksandr Gurevich's (b. 1944) *The Family* (1975) is a fine example of such a work. It is unambiguously created in the style of a Russian icon. Its shape, composition, and figures of mother and child explicitly make this first impression. Still, it is easy to see the difference between it and other works of the same genre. The face of the mother is strikingly Jewish. It is shown against a background silhouette of her maimed husband. His ribs stick out of his exhausted figure and his head is split in half. To his right, along his thin and angular arm, is rendered a line of people moving toward an unknown destination, a symbol of the eternal wandering Jew. The incongruous appearance of Jews in an icon creates an impressive sense of incompatibility for the Jews in Russia.

Similar ideas were expressed by other artists. In such paintings as *It Was Quiet and Peaceful in Our Shtetl after the Pogrom* (1975) by Abeshaus, and *In the Red Space* (1982) by Grisha Bruskin (b. 1945), artistic symbols hold strong political meaning. The idea behind both works was to illustrate the persistent impossibility of Jewish life in Russia. In Abeshaus's painting, a gate separates the Jewish cemetery from the rest of the world. Between the cemetery and a Russian Orthodox church with onion domes are a path and a small bridge over a river, details that should symbolically unite the gentile and Jewish worlds. However, these symbols instead reveal the gap between the two. Bruskin's work shows a *golem* (in Jewish legend, a man-made quasi-human) in a Soviet military uniform carrying aloft a synagogue from which people are tumbling down. The background is red. When Bruskin tried to exhibit this picture, he was treated in the classic way. He was invited to a special meeting at the Artist's Union, a meeting that turned out to be more like a trial. "I was ready to go to prison at any time," Bruskin recalled. "This kind of painting was beyond acceptance then, a criminal painting." A conceptualist who considered himself to be a Jewish artist, Bruskin told an interviewer, "I was Jewish and lived in Russia, and to be a Jew in Russia was forbidden. . . . I have a typical Jewish face, and because of Russian anti-Semitism I was made aware of my Jewishness throughout my childhood. I suffered because I felt as everybody else, but at the same time, I knew I was not like everybody else."[21] Bruskin's solo exhibition in Vilnius [Vilna], in 1983, was closed by the authorities after ten days "for Zionist ideology," while his solo exhibition at Moscow's Central House of Workers in the Arts was closed on opening day, in 1984.

In the 1970s and early 1980s, the arbitrary behavior of the authorities, which affected everyone in the country, was aggravated by antisemitism where Jews were concerned. The situation had not changed much from the mid-1940s when a Party boss came to the studio of the great Soviet artist Robert Falk, looked at one of his landscapes, and declared: "This is not a Russian landscape. Our Russian birch trees are tall, straight and well-proportioned while these are birch trees from the *shtetl* (*mestechkovye*) and they are all crooked."[22] Some thirty years later when the first exhibition of non-conformist art was permitted at Izmailovo Park in 1974, troublemakers, hired for the occasion or drawn there by their own rage, gathered at the entrance and asked all would-be visitors if they really wanted to see the "kike exhibition organized by [Jewish artists] Rabin and Glezer."[23] In 1973, two and a half weeks after the artist Leonid Lamm applied for an Israeli visa, he was provoked on the street in an incident organized by the police and the *druzhinniki* (civil police volunteers), then arrested and condemned to three years in the camps for hooliganism.[24]

Under the pressure of obvious and vicious antisemitism, many artists who had felt quite remote from their own Jewishness began to emphasize their official identification as Jews. Lev Kopelev, a dissident writer, cited the words of the Polish Jewish poet Julian Tuwim: "There exists among people a relation by blood, but not by the blood which flows through their veins, but by the blood which came from the veins of many victims."[25] According to this position, such artists as Oskar Rabin, registered in his passport as a Latvian (his mother was Latvian and his father Jewish), and Arkadii Shteinberg, who became a Christian, considered themselves Jews. Vadim Sidur, half-Jewish, wrote: "I am a hybrid flower / Half-Russian and half-kike. / A complicated artist, a rootless 'cosmopolitan' / My time of flourishing is the time of stagnation / . . . . / I am almost suffocated by the spitting in my soul" [*plevkami v moiu dushu*].[26] Among Sidur's many models of victimized people are *Treblinka* (1975), inspired by Vasily Grossman's *Treblinskii ad* (The Hell of Treblinka),[27] and *The Formula of Grief* (1972). *The Formula of Grief* was chosen as a monument for the 10,000 Jews killed in the town of Pushkin, formerly Tsarskoe Selo, and erected there in October 1991.[28]

The Holocaust remained to Jews one of the most important subjects, and yet for years its mention was taboo in the USSR. Although in 1944 poems by Ilya Ehrenburg ("My child! . . . My countless relatives! I can hear your voices from every pit!") and Lev Ozerov about *Babi Yar*[29] appeared in the journals *Novyi mir* (no. 1, 1945) and *Oktiabr* (no. 3, 1946), the topic was completely dropped after 1948. The official line was that Jews were not to be singled out among the Soviet victims of the Nazis. This idea was long hammered into people's heads and the forcefulness of the propaganda was such that, in spite of the tragedies in virtually every Jewish family, many were persuaded by it. In effect, this attitude buried in oblivion the story of Nazi genocide of Jews. From the 1940s to the fall of the Soviet regime, people who displayed interest in the Holocaust put themselves at risk. The Jewish Antifascist Committee, established in 1942, was not only limited in its ability to publish information about the Holocaust but most of its members were murdered between 1948 and 1952. The *Chernaya kniga* (Black Book), a book of documents about the Holocaust, edited by Ilya Ehrenburg and Vasily Grossman, could not be published. Jews around the country, in big cities as well as in small towns and even villages, tried quite unsuccessfully to flout the official prohibition on erecting monuments to those killed by the Nazis. A group of Jews in Odessa who collected money for a monument to victims of the Nazis were arrested and sentenced to eight to ten years in prison for supposedly creating an unofficial nationalist organization. The monument in Ponary (Lithuania), erected in 1945 with money donated by local Jews, was destroyed in 1952 by official order.[30]

9. *Vadim Sidur,* The Formula of Grief, *1972. Aluminum. In 1991,
the sculpture was placed in the town of Pushkin, near St. Petersburg,
as a memorial to Jewish victims of the Nazis. By permission of
the Sidur Museum, Moscow.*

In 1959, when the Russian writer Viktor Nekrasov found out that the
Kiev authorities planned to establish either a stadium or an amusement
park, rather than a monument, at the site of the Babi Yar massacre, he said:
"In Buchenwald a tocsin rings a warning that such a thing must not happen again. But what about Kiev? Will there be dances over the graves of those
executed there?"[31] When the monument was finally completed, it did not
specify that Jews had been massacred. Against this background, the Russian
poet Evgenii Evtushenko's poem *Babi Yar,* which explicitly condemned
Russian antisemitism, made a powerful impression in Russia and abroad.[32]
Soon Evtushenko's poem became a part of the Russian composer Dmitri
Shostakovich's "Thirteenth Symphony" (1962). Evtushenko was seriously criticized for the poem and it was not republished in any of the poet's books for
more than twenty years. At Khrushchev's notorious meeting with the ar-

tistic intelligentsia in December 1962, Leonid Ilyichev, the head of the Ideological Section of the Central Committee, proclaimed that the massacre at Babi Yar involved not only Jews but also Slavs. Why, then, should the Jews be singled out? After the discussion in the Soviet press of Anatoli Kuznetsov's (a Russian by origin) novel *Babi Yar,* published in the journal *Yunost'* (Youth) in 1966, the author was advised to make many changes by reducing the emphasis on the Jews, if he hoped to publish his manuscript as a book. The same was later suggested to the novelist Anatolii Rybakov, a Jew, in connection with his *Tiazhelyi pesok* (Heavy Sand), in 1978. He even had to give up the original title, *Rakhil* [Rachel].[33] Also criticized were Ilya Ehrenburg's memoirs *Liudi, gody, zhizn'* (People, Time, and Life), published in *Novyi mir* from 1960 to 1965. Ehrenburg was accused of not being objective when he stated that among the civilians killed by the Nazis, the majority were Jewish, and that antisemitism still existed in the USSR.[34] Only recently have the full stories of Babi Yar and the Holocaust in general emerged from newly published archival materials.

For an artist to choose to focus on this subject was much more than just an artistic decision. Under these circumstances, it was no wonder that the artist Felix Lemberskii in his painting "Execution" (1950s) showed Nazi soldiers pointing their guns at people, mostly women with children in their arms, at the edge of a deep pit, without any indication of what nationality they might be.[35] "I always felt an obligation and a personal duty to create art about the Holocaust and about Jewish themes," recalled Dmitrii Lion (1925–93), a well-known, non-conformist artist, in one of his interviews. "I was literally shattered by my conversations with Jews who had suffered in the Holocaust. Stalin was still alive when I returned home from the army and began to paint. You can imagine what those times were like! Every day, for many years, I would get up and paint nonstop—no break, no holiday, I could not show anybody what I was doing because it was forbidden." Nevertheless, when he settled in Moscow (1953) as an art student, he posted the figure 6,351,000 (representing the Holocaust death toll) on the wall of his room, and his artwork from the late 1950s shows apocalyptic visions of death, bodies, and gas chambers.[36] Lion's symbolic pictures arrest the attention of the viewer by their expressiveness and sincerity. He was among those artists who believed that only through symbolism might the unimaginable horror of the Holocaust be expressed. It is astounding that only a few works about these crucial and painful themes were known before perestroika. One can only speculate about the reasons, but one may also hope that more works, undiscovered so far, will be found, just as I came across Lemberski's paintings.

Since perestroika, the Holocaust and biblical subjects have been widely used. Artists such as Roman Vainshtock, Gavriil Zapolianskii, Rinat Fridman, and Bentsion Kotliar produced distinctive works on both subjects in the 1980s and 1990s. Often, both themes appear in the same work as, for example, in Anatolii Chechik's painting *Golgotha* (1994) where humanity's suffering and the national Jewish experiences merge into a single human grief. An endless line of shapeless, faceless, and motionless figures seems to drift through the immobile air of the painting. Earthy grays and yellows fuse with a simple but powerful composition, sustaining an impression of absolute hopelessness. Biblical images and Holocaust themes thus became for the artists a way to interpret national or religious issues, and to seek answers to deep philosophical questions.

Many artists adopted hidden symbolic references to Jews, but their messages were unmistakable. Finding their own ways of communicating with the audience, artists came up with personal metaphors to express their emotions and beliefs. Girsh Inger, in his painting *A Dream about a Violin* (1977), managed to catch and express through visual images the typically Jewish mood known as "happy unhappiness," the permanent feature of Sholem Aleichem's writings. Close to Inger in style are Asya Dodina's painting *Strolling* (1993) and Leonid Grolman's *The Stroll in the Night* (1980s). While some artists used specifically Jewish symbolism in their works, a number of others created images whose meanings are universal. The specifically Jewish implication is only barely suggested and exists just as a mood, an undertone. A few sheep in a pen, the simple subject of Lev Tabenkin's painting *Sheep* (1987), convey a sense of the invisible, hopeless human being driven into a corner. A similar existential note is sounded in the works of Solomon Rassin and Adolf Goldman. Their paintings are built on contrasts, such as the fleeting and the eternal, life and death, question and answer, inner unity and superficial disconnection, and the exalted and the vile. In color and shape, these artists seek to express the meaning of these notions.

During perestroika and the years that followed, it was widely believed that interest in Jewish art would be kindled along with the fading away of Russian–Jewish incompatibility. Jewish artists who did not emigrate began working enthusiastically toward a revival of Jewish culture. Soon, however, they realized that such hopes were futile. Only a small number of art patrons and collectors showed any interest, and official cultural organizations and museums provided little encouragement. There were a few important exhibitions of Jewish art in the mid- and late 1990s: a series of shows under the collective name *Diaspora* at the Moscow Central Artist's House in 1992; an exhibition at the Marble Palace organized by the

10. Grigorii Inger, A Dream about a Violin, *1977. Gouache on paper.*
Source: Iskusstvo, *no. 1 (1994).*

11. Leonid Grolman, Stroll in the Night, *1980s. Oil on canvas. Collection of the artist.*

Diaghilev Center; a joint Israeli–St. Petersburg Jewish artists exhibition at the Russian Ethnographic Museum in May 1998; and several occasional shows, such as the exhibit of the oldest masters of contemporary Jewish art, including Gersh Inger at the Tretiakov Gallery (1993) and Moiseii Feigin and Rinat Fridman in 1994. The latter, an artist of the younger generation, had another solo show in 1998 at the St. Petersburg Jewish Community Center that I had the opportunity of seeing. Unfortunately, these shows had little support or publicity.

Since there was no official interest in Jewish art, the activity of those who appreciated Jewish art took on greater importance. One undertaking in Jewish art was the collection of Aleksandr Filtser.[37] In the fall of 1977, Filtser risked trouble with the authorities by opening the door of his own apartment to everyone with an interest in Jewish art. At first, only a few artists and twenty of their works were represented. Still, Jewish artists supported Filtser's idea of demonstrating that despite the constant persecution of the Jews, their art survived and continued to be created. New acquisitions in Filtser's home museum came largely by way of donations from collectors and the artists themselves.[38] In 1992, Valentina and Arnold Bialik opened a gallery of Jewish art, *Novyi kovcheg* (New Ark), in Moscow. For a long time, however, there was no gallery per se and the artwork had to be displayed in diverse locations.

Despite the achievements of Jewish artists during the post-Stalin period, the apex of interest in their subjects came in the first years of the 1990s. The number of artists is diminishing today because of ongoing emigration. The works of those who still remain in Russia give the same impression, as in earlier times, of the art of the suffering and defensive, of those who resist anti-semitism and fight for equality, especially with constantly growing hatred toward the Jews. "If there weren't any anti-Semitism, I would care about my Jewishness much less," said the painter Solomon Epshtein during our conversation in May 1998 in St. Petersburg. His views are supported by others. Interest in the works of Jewish artists still remains limited to a small audience. The Holocaust exhibition held in St. Petersburg in April 1999, with limited attendance, reaffirms this situation. Against the background of continuing emigration, the present interest in Jewish culture, art in particular, consists of the new generation's enthusiasts and those who, staying in Russia, have chosen Jewishness as a form of self-assertion. However, a high proportion of them became religious and, therefore, are not interested either in art in general or in this particular kind of secular work.

On my visits to exhibitions and artists' studios over the last few years, I have observed that certain subjects are repeated again and again, while only a handful of works deal with contemporary themes. I have seen only a few scenes from everyday life, as, for example, in the painting by Solomon Epshtein, *My Fellow Artists* (1970s). There appears to be no interest in portraying the lives of Jews in Russia today: with their humiliations and abuse, and fears of persecution. Why are there no illustrations of the recent past—the heartbreaking farewells at airports and train stations when Jews, departing Russia, leave friends and family behind; the tears, the hopelessness of those who remain?

Why these omissions? The answers are not simple. They involve the natural limits of visual artistic expression, the requirements of the art market, the public's fascination with things exotic, and other considerations. Artists must cater to their principal buyers—foreigners, in this case—who are far removed from all the problems I have described, and indeed are unable to understand or are not very interested in the current life conditions of Jews in Russia. Nevertheless, these potential purchasers are longing for their roots and, therefore, for traditional, recognizable images that were introduced at one time by Marc Chagall, and that brought him his commercial success in the West. This partly explains the endless numbers of violins

12. *Solomon Epshtein,* My Fellow Artists, *1970s.*
Oil on canvas. Collection of the artist.

and goats, bearded Jews wielding menorahs, or *"davening"* [praying], dancing, and singing in current paintings.

Still, there is more to such images than is apparent at first glance. Whereas
for the artists who came of age before or after the revolution and who had a
clear memory of the past (Aleksandr Tyshler, Tankhum Kaplan, M. Aksel-
rod, and so on), the traditional Jewish images represented an effort to keep
their Jewish origin in mind and heart and created a kind of spiritual asylum
from the present, in the art of the younger generations these metaphors be-

came largely a form of national self-assertion. After the demise of Soviet ideology, these images are responding to the still unchanged antisemitism that sustains the position of Jews as unwanted and unwelcome *inorodtsy* (aliens). The most conventionalized Jews in the paintings—with their earlocks, beards, and black felt fedoras—are often opposing the overwhelming post-Communist influence of Russian Orthodoxy and the political power of the Church with its historically anti-Jewish views. Moreover, these images intentionally emphasize the artists' identification with their people. Finally, most importantly, these images constitute in at least this viewer's perception a visual memorial to the physically vanished Jewish world, to the *shtetlekh,* to the Sabbath evenings, to the now-rare sounds of the Yiddish language. It is as if this world that has disappeared is given a second life in the works of the Jewish artist in Russia.

NOTES

1. Avram Kampf, *Jewish Experience in the Art of the Twentieth Century* (South Hadley, Mass.: Bergin & Garvey, 1984); John E. Bowlt, "From the Pale of Settlement to the Reconstruction of the World," in Ruth Apter-Gabriel, ed., *Tradition and Revolution: The Jewish Avant-Garde Art, 1912–1928,* catalog (Jerusalem: The Israel Museum, 1987), 43–60; Seth L. Wolitz, "The Jewish National Art Renaissance in Russia," in ibid., 21–43; Ziva Amishai-Maisels, "Chagall and the Jewish Revival: Center or Periphery?" in ibid., 71–101; "The Jewish Awakening: A Search for National Idenrity," in *Russian Jewish Artists in a Century of Change, 1890–1990,* catalog (Munich and New York: Prestel-Verlag and the Jewish Museum, 1995), 54–71; "Sviaz' vremen" [The Relation of Times], *Zerkalo* [Mirror], no. 1–2 (Tel Aviv, 1996): 166–76. See also Sharon R. Keller, ed., *The Jews: A Treasury of Art and Literature* (New York: Beaux Arts Edition, 1992); Grace Cohen Grossman, *Jewish Art* (New York: Beaux Arts Edition, 1995).

2. Viktor Misiano, "Choosing to Be Jewish," in *Russian Jewish Artists in a Century of Change, 1890–1990* (New York/Munich: Prestel-Verlag, 1995), 89.

3. R. Genzeleva, "Ruf Zernova. Puti evreiskogo samosoznania," *Vestnik Moskovskogo evreiskogo universiteta,* no. 18 (1998): 191.

4. However, as Viktor Misiano pointed out, their art was still related to their Jewish mentality, especially the Sretensky Boulevard group (formed at the beginning of the 1970s). As he noted, "if you were to find yourself, for example, among the Sretensky Boulevard artists—Ilya Kabakov, Vladimir Yankilevsky, Eduard Shteinberg, Viktor Pivovarov, Eric Bulatov—you would always know that those persons present were Jews." He saw it in their striving for isolation from the outside world in, as he called it, the "little ghetto," and believed that these features also influenced the Russian artistic part. See Misiano, "Choosing to Be Jewish," 89–94.

5. "Ancient Church rituals echo within but are not the source of Ilya Tabenkin's world," wrote Bown, not admitting that the sources might be non-Christian. See Matthew Cullerne Bown, *Contemporary Russian Art* (New York: Philosophical Library, 1989), 68.

6. See Misiano, "Choosing To Be Jewish," 89.

7. In Russian, the article appeared first in 1990 in the journal *Vek. Vestnik evreiskoi kultury* [Century. Herald of Jewish Culture], published in Riga in the 1990s. See A. V. Blium, *Evreiskii vopros pod sovetskoi tsenzuroi* [The Jewish Question under Soviet Censorship] (St. Petersburg: Petersburg Jewish University, 1996), 88–93.

8. Aleksandr Borshchagovsky, *Obviniaetsia krov* [Accused by Blood] (Moscow: Izdatelskaya grupa "Progress," "Kultura," 1994); G. Kostyrchenko, *V plenu u krasnogo faraona* [Imprisoned by the Red Pharaoh] (Moscow: "Mezhdunarodnye otnoshenia," 1994); A. Vaksberg, "Stalin protiv evreev" [Stalin against the Jews], *Detektiv i politika,* no. 3 (1992); R. Ganelin, "Evreiskii vopros v SSSR" [The Jewish Question in the USSR], in *Evrei v Rossii. Istoria i kultura* [Jews in Russia: History and Culture] (St. Petersburg: Petersburg Jewish University, 1995), 36–43.

9. Ruvim Mazel worked for a time, from 1915 to 1923, in the Turkmen region of Central Asia and had become artistically involved in the life of the Turkmen.

10. Blium, *Evreiskii vopros pod sovetskoi tsenzuroi,* 122–23.

11. Ibid., 120–21.

12. G. Farber and A. Frenkel, eds., "Vadim Abramovich Sidur (1924–1986)," in *Formula skorbi* [The Formula of Grief] (St. Petersburg: Gruppa issledovania Katastrofy, 1991), 25.

13. Z. Gitelman, V. Cherviakov, and V. Shapiro, "Iudaizm v natsional'nom samosoznanii rossiiskikh evreev," *Vestnik Moskovskogo Evreiskogo Universiteta,* no. 3(7) (1994).

14. When Golda Meir visited the Moscow synagogue in 1948, most of those who welcomed her were people of the older generation; this is because the establishment of the state of Israel had not weakened but had even intensified the persecution of Jews. When in the 1950s I became a university student in Riga, where Soviet policies were milder, my father, in order not to get me in any trouble, gave up his seat in the synagogue and forbade me to come near the synagogue ever after. I remember families of my friends whose parents would not speak Yiddish in the presence of the children and who refused to discuss any Jewish issues.

15. Andrei Siniavskii (1925–97) and Yuli Daniel (1925–88), Russian writers and scholars who published their works abroad under the pseudonyms Abram Tertz (Siniavskii) and Nikolai Arzhak (Daniel). Daniel was the Jewish son of a Yiddish writer. For these publications they were sentenced to seven and five years, respectively, in forced labor camps in 1966. Boris Pasternak (1890–1960) was a Russian poet of Jewish origin who received the Nobel Prize for his novel *Doktor Zhivago* in 1958.

16. Tashkent is the capital of Uzbekistan in Central Asia, to which many people were evacuated during World War II.

17. Very limited emigration had begun in 1965–66 and was almost completely stopped for half a year or more after June 1967.

18. Anatolii (Natan) Shcharanskii (now Sharansky, b. 1948) was arrested in 1978 for defending the political rights of refuseniks. In 1970, a group of young Zionists, led by Eduard Kuznetsov, tried to hijack an airplane from Smolnii, a small airport near Leningrad. All of them were arrested and sentenced.

19. I am referring, for example, to the quite open and frequent gatherings of great numbers of Jews, mostly young people, to celebrate Hanukkah or Passover in somebody's apartment and the tumultuous crowds of youth, dancing and singing outside the synagogues. The militiamen generally just observed, but did not detain, them.

20. Ruth Rishin, "The Twelve: Art as an Aliyah," in *12 From the Soviet Underground,* catalog (San Francisco: Bay Area Council on Soviet Jewry, 1976), 7. See also in the same

catalog Mikhail Borgman, "The Twelve: The First Leningrad Exhibit," 4–6. Borgman, a young art historian from Leningrad, lost his job at the Leningrad Theater Institute at the time of the exhibitions and became an elevator operator. In 1989 the group *Alef* was represented in the United States at the Louisville Art Festival. See Regina Solovieva and Aleksandr Mansurov, "Snova 'Alef'" [Again about 'Alef'], *Vek,* no. 2 (1989): 49–51.

21. Under pressure, the authorities agreed to send Bruskin's works to Sotheby's to be auctioned in 1988; he achieved great success. See Renee Baigel and Matthew Baigel, eds., *Soviet Dissident Artists: Interviews after Perestroika* (New Brunswick, N.J.: Rutgers University Press, 1995), 317–18; *Russian Jewish Artists in a Century of Change, 1890–1990,* 154.

22. Tatiana Levina, *Robert Falk* (Moscow: Slovo, 1996), 56.

23. Aleksandr Glezer, "Svobodnye liudi nesvobodnoi strany" [Free People in an Oppressed Country], *Evreiskaya gazeta,* Number 16 (April 1998), 3.

24. Matthew Baigel and Renee Baigel, eds., "Leonid Lamm," in *Soviet Dissident Artists,* 109–10.

25. Lev Kopelev, "Sami o sebe," *Noii. Armiano-evreiskii vestnik,* no. 5 (Moscow, 1993): 163.

26. Vadim Sidur, "Sami o sebe," ibid.

27. Shaken by what he saw at the Nazi extermination camp Treblinka in Poland, Vasily Grossman wrote *Treblinskii ad* in 1944. It was first published in the journal *Znamia* in 1945 and once more in 1945 as a small brochure poorly printed on rough yellow paper. Sidur's sculpture *Treblinka* stands in Berlin in front of the courthouse that held all the files of Jews sent to the concentration camps. See Julia Sidur, "Pamiatniki Vadima Sidura," in Farber and Frenkel, *Formula skorbi,* 28.

28. The sculptor Aleksandr Pozin enlarged Sidur's original plaster model and the architect Boris Beider designed the memorial. Farber and Frenkel, *Formula skorbi,* 32, 36.

29. *Babi Yar* was on the outskirts of Kiev. There, thousands of Jews were killed in September 1941. *Babi Yar* became a symbol of Jewish suffering from the Nazis.

30. About the restrictions placed by the authorities on research and discussion of the Holocaust, see Blium, *Evreiskii vopros pod sovetskoi tsenzuroi,* 125; Zvi Gitelman, ed., *Bitter Legacy: Confronting the Holocaust in the Soviet Union* (Bloomington: Indiana University Press, 1997); Aleksander Frenkel and Leonid Kolton, "Muzhestvo pomnit'" [The Courage to Remember], in Farber and Frenkel, *Formula skorbi,* 4–11.

31. Blium, *Evreiskii vopros pod sovetskoi tsenzuroi,* 125.

32. Evgenii Evtushenko, "Babi Yar," *Literaturnaya Gazeta,* September 19, 1961.

33. Blium, *Evreiskii vopros pod sovetskoi tsenzuroi,* 126.

34. A. Rybakov tells the story in his *Roman-vospominanie* [A Novel of Reminiscences] (Moscow: Varguis, 1998), 239–40.

35. When Ehrenburg's memoirs finally appeared in 1967 as volumes 8 and 9 in a collection of his writings, references to Jews had been heavily cut. See Blium, *Evreiskii vopros pod sovetskoi tsenzuroi,* 128.

36. According to Lemberski's daughter, Galina Lemberski, her father repeated to her more than once that he had devoted the painting to the memory of the victims of Babi Yar and of the Jews in his hometown of Berdichev, where his parents were also killed.

37. See Baigel and Baigel, *Soviet Dissident Artists,* 45–46, 51; *Russian Jewish Artists in a Century of Change, 1890–1990,* 194.

38. About Aleksandr Filtser and his museum, see Aleksandr Rapoport, "Korni i vetvi 'Ets-Khaim,'" *Iskusstvo,* no. 1 (1994): 61–63; Aleksandr Filtser, *Jewish Tradition in the Russian Empire and Soviet Union* (Moscow: Izdatelstvo "MACAU & Co," 1993). I was told that Filtser emigrated and the fate of his collection is unknown.

FOURTEEN

❧

Mikhail Krutikov

Constructing Jewish Identity
in Contemporary Russian Fiction

❧ The Soviet Legacy and Jewish Resilience

"Jews were almost the most guarded secret of the Soviet Union. It was perhaps only sexual life that was concealed with more zeal. Both things could exist only in the zone of bashful suppression, only as a euphemism."[1] This perceptive observation made by Vail' and Genis, two Russian-Jewish émigré journalists, helps to locate the subject of our discussion within the cultural context of the late Soviet period. In the Russian parlance of the 1960s through the 1980s, *Evrei*—Jew—had a peculiar status, somewhere between a dirty word and a state secret. Each time a character with a Jewish name appeared in a work of fiction, the appearance was charged with a cluster of wide-ranging connotations and implications.[2] A *Evrei* in print would immediately alert attentive readers, especially among the Russian-Jewish intelligentsia and foreign observers, and would sometimes become a subject of wide-ranging speculations and heated discussions in Moscow and Leningrad kitchens and on the pages of foreign publications. Works as different in their style and artistic quality as the poem *Babi Yar* by Yevgenii Yevtushenko; the memoirs of Il'ia Ehrenburg, *People, Years, Life;* the novels *Babi Yar* by Anatolii Kuznetsov and *Heavy Sand* by Anatolii Rybakov; and the novella *Oh, Sabbath!* by Dina Kalinovskaya immediately became not just literary but also political events.[3]

The period of the Khrushchev thaw from the late 1950s through the early

1960s extended the limits of freedom of expression tolerated by the Soviet authorities. The era saw, among other things, the renewed publications of Yiddish literature, both in the original and in Russian translations. Another considerable achievement was the cautious rehabilitation of the writers who had perished during Stalin's purges, among them the Russian-Jewish writer Isaac Babel. Nevertheless, a number of important texts dealing with Jewish issues, and inspired by the thaw—most notably Vassily Grossman's magisterial novel *Life and Fate*—remained beyond the allowed limits and had to wait until the new wave of liberalism brought them into the focus of literary discourse in the late 1980s. The thaw of the early 1960s and the glasnost of the late 1980s frame the duller two-decade "period of stagnation," during which many hopes were frustrated and the largest part of Jewish creativity in Russia was forced underground. However, the period of stagnation was also the time when the new phenomenon of emigration began to play an increasingly important role in the life and imagination of Russian Jews.

The relatively few works published during the late Soviet period were merely the tip of the iceberg of Russian-Jewish writing actually produced in those years. A number of writers, some of them quite established in the Soviet literary hierarchy, wrote works that, for ideological reasons, were not publishable in the Soviet Union. Some of these texts were published abroad, but many others remained in the drawers of the authors' writing desks. These works began to appear in the Soviet periodicals after 1987. At first, the situation resembled that of the thaw, with the Communist Party trying to control the stream of potentially subversive publications, but around 1990 the system of ideological supervision collapsed. With some caution, one can assume that the period of discoveries of so-called "white spots" (suppressed materials and information) has ended, and we now possess a relatively complete corpus of the Russian-Jewish writing produced during the late Soviet period.

The Jewish presence in the Russian literature of the 1990s has been quite strong. The word *Evrei* is no longer taboo and is used liberally in contemporary fiction, along with other traditionally shunned "non-normative" words. The process of revision affects not only words but also concepts, styles, and literary personalities. Many of yesterday's outcasts have become today's cult figures, among them such émigré writers as Joseph Brodsky and Sergei Dovlatov. The transitional decade composed of the *piatiletka* [five-year plan] of glasnost (1986–91) and the *piatiletka* of freedom of speech (1991–96), in the words of the critic Natalia Ivanova, has been followed by a new period, for which the very concept of *piatiletka* is inappropriate. Current Russian fiction is no longer dominated by the urge to liberate itself from the Soviet mentality and sensitivities, even though the Soviet experience continues to serve as primary material for most of the writers.

When discussing the post-Soviet period of Russian literature, it is sometimes difficult to distinguish between texts actually written in the 1990s and those written before 1991 but published only after that year. It will be the task of future literary historians to establish the chronology and to put everything in order. From my vantage point of contemporary observer, I can only attempt to single out the most important themes and motifs, and to suggest a classification of the ample and diverse corpus of texts by Jewish authors in which Jewish characters and issues figure prominently.

My analysis focuses on the search for Jewish identity in Russian-Jewish writing during the past thirty years. In the absence of Jewish communal, religious, and social life in the Soviet Union, Jewish identity could be expressed in only a limited number of ways. The most natural way to acquire a positive Jewish identity in the Soviet Union was to have been raised in a family with strong Jewish identification. The most natural role model in this case would be an older relative. This "authentic Jew" was usually male, an elderly father or a grandfather, who had grown up in the *shtetl,* received some religious education, could speak some Yiddish, but most importantly had had an unusual life experience that made him different from the ordinary Soviet mass. Such a figure makes a cameo appearance as a "token Jew" in many different texts by Jewish authors, but it occupies a more central position in the Soviet-Jewish *Bildungsroman,* the novel about the formation of a distinctly Jewish personality under the Soviet conditions. A number of fine novels were written in this genre during the Soviet period, but only one, Grigorii Kanovich's *Candles in the Wind,* was published at that time. The publication of other novels, most notably *The Life of Alexander Zilber* by Yurii Karabchievskii and *The Fifth Corner of the Room* by Israel Metter, had to wait until the 1990s.

Another, more radical, way to realize one's Jewishness was to try to make use of the right to leave the country, the only privilege granted to Jews in the final two decades of the Soviet Union. The mere act of applying for an exit visa to Israel would immediately intensify the applicant's feeling of alienation from the mainstream society. The experience of emigration and adaptation to another society supplied abundant material for a narrative to focus on the search for a new identity. Russian-Jewish immigrants in Israel, America, and, to a lesser degree, Germany, have created a diverse literature that, until the late 1980s, was unknown to the wide Russian audience. Today the process of reunification of all branches of Russian literature has been by and large completed, and new works of émigré fiction are arguably more likely to be published in Russia than abroad.

Most of the fiction that deals with personal development or emigration is written in the traditional Russian style of psychological realism. It is not, however, the only style represented in contemporary Russian-Jewish writing. Seeking to interpret the historical experience of Jews in Russia in philosophical or religious terms, some writers use more experimental techniques. In fiction of this kind, Jewishness appears not as a specific configuration of social and psychological characteristics, but rather as an existential condition, a mark of election that an individual is bound to bear. Individual fates are treated as historical paradigms or philosophical parables, not as stories of real people of flesh and blood in concrete circumstances. One of the first works of this kind, Friedrich Gorenshtein's novel *The Psalm,* was written in 1975, but was published in Russia only in 1991–92.

✡ *The Russian-Jewish* Bildungsroman *and the Problem of Identity*

Forming the new Soviet man was perhaps the most important task of the propaganda and education system in the Soviet Union. From 1917 onwards, the system worked hard to eliminate religious elements from the cultural legacy of pre-Revolutionary Russia. After 1948, the intolerance of Jewish national culture was added to the intolerance of Judaism. It is not surprising, therefore, that any realistic novel with a Jew as the central character would be perceived as subversive by the vigilant ideological overseers and most likely would be banned from publication.

One example of the Russian-Jewish *Bildungsroman* is *The Life of Alexander Zilber* by Yurii Karabchievskii, written in 1974–75 but not published in book form until 1991.[4] It is the story of a Jewish boy growing up in postwar Moscow, narrated in a traditional nineteenth-century psychological manner. The protagonist Alexander Zilber recalls his childhood and adolescence from the secure perspective of the adult writer. As a dreamy and sentimental Jewish boy, he feels vulnerable in the rough environment of fatherless teenagers. Neither does he find much comfort in his family: after the death of his father in the war, his mother has remarried a man active in the shady business of so-called "industrial cooperation," a semiprivate form of production tolerated by the state for a brief period of the reconstruction. Alexander loves his tender mother, but is terrified by his greedy and boorish stepfather. To resist the cruel reality, the boy escapes into a fantasy world where he feels strong and confident. The main source of his inspiration is classical Russian literature, and particularly the novels of Ivan Turgenev.

At first Jewishness appears as yet another factor that makes Alexander's life miserable. His Jewish looks and name instantly single him out to be the victim of bullying. He is not the only Jew among his peers, but he does not feel solidarity with other Jewish boys, and each of them is doomed to endure his suffering alone. This experience restrains Alexander's ability to relate to the outside world and turns him into an introvert. The isolation is encouraged by his stepfather, who is always suspicious of strangers in whom he sees potential informers. The stepfather's circle is limited to a few trusted business associates and is almost as unattractive to Alexander as the community of teenagers.

The change in Alexander's attitude to his stepfather comes about when the latter gets arrested and then returns home, apparently thanks to a bribe. This episode coincides with the brief period of fear and uncertainty that preceded Stalin's death in 1953. The newspaper story about the Doctors' Plot unleashes a ghastly wave of popular antisemitism, and this makes Alexander realize that Jewishness is a not an individual problem but a mark that can suddenly determine the fate of many people who otherwise have nothing in common.

Karabchievskii carefully avoids open political declarations. The adult narrator explains that his family belongs to the milieu that was not "eligible" for political repressions. When people like the stepfather were arrested, it was not for any political "crimes" but for corruption, fraud, or embezzlement. The stepfather and his associates were card-carrying Party members who combined sincere loyalty to the Communist ideology with the practical business activities that were condemned as criminal by this ideology. As the narrator reconstructs the child's experience, he is surprised by the selectivity with which the adults around him see reality. The antisemitic campaign of 1953 is the first incident that puts Alexander's family into direct confrontation with the system. To his astonishment, the stepfather withstands the pressure with his usual calm and resilience.

The only person who refuses to compromise with the regime is Alexander's paternal grandfather. Looking back at this man from an adult perspective, the narrator sees in him almost a prophet. However, as a teenager Alexander, along with everybody else, regards the grandfather as an old fool. The old man has absolutely no respect for the Soviet way of life and cannot be bothered to conceal his attitude. He attends synagogue regularly, and his system of values is dominated by God and *Yiddishkuyt* [Jewishness]. But as the narrator realizes later, the grandfather is the pillar of the whole family. Every Passover he is transformed from a miserable old man into a king presiding over the shabby *Seder* table in his little room.

Alexander's Jewish identity is formed by two main factors. As a boy, he feels estranged from the outside world. This isolation contributes to the development of his imagination and character, but it cannot help him to form any positive Jewish identity. Positive impulses come from his grandfather and stepfather, each of whom in his own way shows an example of resistance to the pressure of the regime. These non-heroic, even pathetic characters, become Alexander's Jewish role models. His newly discovered internal freedom forms the core of Alexander's Jewish identity, and is based on the opposition to all forms of coercion and suppression of the individual personality.

· While Karabchievskii looks back to the childhood of his character from the perspective of the mid-1970s, the St. Petersburg writer Alexander Melikhov presents a similar situation from a post-Soviet vantage point of the early 1990s. Lev Katsenelenbogen, the protagonist of the novel *Expulsion from Eden: A Confession of a Jew*,[5] is a half-Jewish boy growing up in a small industrial town in north Kazakstan. The dominating desire of Lev's childhood and adolescence is his hope to blend in with the "simple folk" around him. Gradually he comes to the realization that because of his Jewish name, his father's past experience in the Gulag, and his psychological type he will never be accepted as an equal by his Russian peers. Lev formulates this in a maxim: "A Jew can become almost anybody—a hero, a saint, a world's savior—but he can never become an ordinary person." Jewishness is not an identity that one can share with others; it is a mark of a stranger. Andrei Sergeev, the recipient of the 1997 Russian Booker Prize for his book of memoirs about his Soviet childhood, pointed to this purely functional use of the protagonist's difference as a Jew. Melikhov "pulled for his Jewishness as if for a tail, and unraveled a most complicated network of the Soviet social structure on many levels."[6]

In Kazakstan, where Lev's father has been exiled after ten years in prison, Lev lives among different ethnic groups, each of which has its own strategy for survival. The Russians naturally assume that they represent the "norm," but prefer not to get involved with the Ingush, a small nation exiled to Kazakstan from the Caucasus by Stalin for their alleged collaboration with the Germans. The Ingush can be friendly neighbors, but they become fierce and brutal if they feel that one of them is in danger. Family and national solidarity are their main values. The Kazaks, by contrast, are disorganized and ready to accept the inferior status of "natives," although the few who, using ethnic quotas, manage to make their way up the social ladder quickly become arrogant, suspicious, and incompetent.

There are no Jews in the town, apart from Lev's father. His figure dominates Lev's world. He is superior to everybody else not only morally and mentally, but also physically, a fact that destroys the stereotype of a Jew as a weak intellectual. And yet the father is not accepted by any ethnic group as an equal. Lev realizes that he too is doomed to have the same fate of an outsider. But Lev's situation will be even worse because, unlike his father, who grew up among the Jews in a *shtetl,* he will never have memories of belonging to a community. The idea of a Jewish community does not appeal to him. He feels even further removed from the Jewish way of life, customs, and Yiddish or the Hebrew language than he does from Kazak culture.

The novel is written from two perspectives, that of the boy and that of Lev as an adult man. The adult Lev is nervous and insecure, even though he is successful in life. As he analyzes his childhood, he sees the roots of his present distress in the childhood split between the Jewish and the Russian halves of his personality. The objective reality of life forces the growing boy to become Jewish, even while he desperately tries to escape his fate on the subjective level. The biblical image of Eden in the novel's title represents the grim little town of Lev's childhood as a lost paradise, while all his later life, including his move to St. Petersburg, his successful career, and his happy marriage to a Russian woman, are seen as part of his continuous exile from this paradise.

Jewishness is the stigma that will always make Lev a stranger in his own eyes and in the eyes of everyone around him. He notices with alarm that he passes his Jewishness on to his children, even though they are only one-quarter Jewish. His son feels "a Russian among Jews, a Jew among Russians." This feeling of living in a "little Jewish house of glass" intensifies during the 1970s and 1980s. Interestingly, Lev feels his alienation most intensely not among the ethnically polarized, poor working class population in Kazakstan, but within the ordinary homogeneous environment of a St. Petersburg office.

The Jewish identity constructed in both novels is purely an individual feeling for these characters; it has no roots in Jewish cultural identity, religious tradition, or historical awareness. Lev and Alexander instinctively distrust any idea of community, which they perceive as a threat to their personal autonomy that has been achieved through the long and exhausting struggle against the pressures of the Soviet reality. For them, a collective identity is an instrument of manipulation and a result of the loosening of the individual's sense of responsibility. Lev sums up his philosophy in these words: "A nation is always right and blameless. What would be qualified as paranoia in an individual's case, is a necessary condition of greatness and glory of a nation."

Emigration as Reality and Fiction

For Russian Jewry, emigration has an altogether different meaning than for most other active Jewish communities in the world. While the majority of Jews living today in Israel, Anglo-Saxon countries, France, and Latin America are children or grandchildren of immigrants, and have some family memories of the "Old Country," most Russian Jews have been living in their country for generations. For them emigration is not a part of their past but a future possibility for themselves or their children. To be sure, the difficult process of modernization that Russian Jews underwent during the Soviet period involved massive migrations from the *shtetl* to the city, but it was confined to the same country. Most of the foreign Jews who became Soviet citizens in 1939–40 did so involuntarily and without movement in space.

Until the late 1960s, the very idea of leaving the Soviet Union was nothing more than a dangerous dream. But in the course of the 1970s, the possibility of emigration became a fact of life for many Soviet Jews and eventually developed into an important and distinct feature of Soviet Jewish identity. The fiction created by the Russian-Jewish emigrants is usually based on the intense personal experience of coming to terms with the new reality, and the recovered Jewish identity often plays a significant role in this process. Unlike the slowly developing *Bildungsroman,* the narrative of emigration is usually fast and dramatic and confessional. It deals not with an organic development of the character moving from childhood to adulthood within the same relatively stable environment, but with a sharp break in the life of a mature person caused by his or her voluntary decision to change environments.

The real experience of emigration is by no means uniform. Some make the decision to start a new life and erase the old one from memory, thus completely reinventing an identity. Another strategy is to confront the new reality and to try to represent it in the categories of the old culture. The choice of the Russian language for writing about the new experience and of a Russian medium for publication is an indication of the author's attachment to the old culture and his or her need to share experiences with former compatriots. At the same time, the audience in Russia, or at least part of it, sees an emigration story as a realization of a dream about a new life.

❀ *The "Great* Aliyah" *Comes to Israel*

Russian-Israeli literature already has a history of its own. This is not the place to discuss whether it belongs to the broader Russian or to the Israeli literary context, but one remark can help to clarify the current situation. During the Soviet period, Russian writers in Israel were cut off from a mass audience in the Soviet Union. They could reach only the émigré readers and a few Jewish activists in the Soviet Union. Nowadays a Russian writer in

Israel, as indeed anywhere else, is free to publish his or her works in Russia or elsewhere. Moreover, Jews no longer constitute the largest Russian-speaking diaspora, since after the demise of the Soviet Union millions of ethnic Russians found themselves living outside Russia.[7] The opportunity to leave Russia is not an exclusively Jewish privilege anymore, although Jews are more privileged when it comes to receiving immigrant status in the United States, Germany, and obviously Israel.

Dina Rubina is one of the most popular Russian-Israeli writers in Russia today.[8] She began her literary career before emigration and has successfully overcome a difficult period of transition. In her novels and short stories, she focuses on the predicament of the Russian intelligentsia in Israel as it tries to have its cake and eat it too; that is, as it strives to become part of the new society and retain its cultural identity at the same time. Rubina's characters are usually connected with the numerous Russian cultural institutions in Israel. Russian immigrants in Israel develop a strong sense of community that is based on their shared experience in the Soviet past and on common problems they face in Israel, even though the ideological and religious differences among them can be profound.

Rubina's most comprehensive work to date is the novel *Here Comes Messiah*. Two protagonists in the novel can be viewed as two parts of the author's split personality. One of them is Zyama, a former musicologist turned journalist, who in Israel recovers her Jewish identity through the reconstruction of her late grandfather's personality in the course of a series of meetings with his former lovers. The grandfather, a Red Army commander and an irresistible womanizer, was far from a traditional Jewish ideal, but the vitality and authenticity of his character make him a role model for his granddaughter in Israel. Zyama, who is named after her grandfather and looks like him, becomes a convinced Zionist and comes to live with a community of settlers on the West Bank, from which she commutes to her work in the south Tel Aviv editorial office of an "intellectual" Russian weekly.

The other part of the author's alter ego is the self-obsessed female writer N., who struggles with the problems of immigrant life in Israel in order to concentrate on her literary work. The main cause of her troubles is her son Shmulik, who is pathologically unable to take care of himself. Shmulik is the reverse of the ideal Russian-Jewish child. He is thick, lazy, not ambitious, and has a sole talent—the ability to shoot extremely well. N. is forced to live in a state of constant neurosis created by the tension between her desire to write and her inability to free herself from life's pressures.

The novel is constructed as a series of sentimental, hilarious, and some-

times absurd episodes that portray the reality and dreams of the "Great
Aliyah" in a rather unflattering light. In the words of the Russian critic Lev
Annenskii, Rubina peels off one illusion after another until nothing is left.[9]
Among the shattered dreams are the comfort of homecoming, the security
of the state, and the sense of purpose of Zionism. Rubina's bitter and grotesque irony is close to that of Philip Roth, particularly in his novel *Operation Shylock.*

Forming the social background of the novel is the consolidation of political and cultural resources of the Russian *aliyah* that eventually led to the
formation of the *Israel ba-Aliyah* party and its electoral success in 1996.
Isolated episodes constitute the picture of growing political awareness
among Russian immigrants, who begin to realize that only political repre-
sentation will enable them to retain their group identity in Israel. The
ironic and slightly skeptical tone of the novel can be deceiving, as the author's attitude toward the depicted events is very serious. The seemingly
comic novel has a tragic end that forces the reader to rethink the whole
story. On the night after Yom Kippur, when all the characters of the novel
come together in a Jerusalem restaurant to break the fast, Shmulik, the
shlimazl son of the writer N., kills Zyama by mistake, shooting her while
trying to save her from an Arab assassin.

The tragic death of the heroine makes no moral or ideological sense if
one reads the novel as a purely social satire. The reader is suddenly forced
to recognize that Russian *aliyah* has a metaphysical significance that tran-
scends individual existence. This impression is supported by the deliber-
ately eclectic style that mixes elements of social satire reminiscent of Soviet
literature of the 1920s with a Bulgakovian mysterious vision of Jerusalem
as the Holy City. Within this context, Zyama's death becomes an equivalent of the Yom Kippur sacrifice: the innocent woman is chosen to atone for
the sins of her people. One cannot miss the parallels with Bulgakov's treatment of Jesus in the novel *Master and Margarita.*

In her next novel, *The Last Wild Boar from Pontevedra Forest,* Rubina
uses a similar device of correlation between the plot and Jewish calendar.
The grotesque culmination of the complicated intrigue involving two
Spanish men and two women, all working in a "Palace of Culture and Sport"
in a small town in Israel, takes place during the routine Purim carnival, in
which all characters come together as part of their job. The novel is less
Jewish in character than *Here Comes Messiah*; one possible reason may be
that the author wanted it to be accessible to a wider Russian readership, and
therefore chose to use Jewish elements merely as functional tools for organizing the plot.

❧ Love and Death in Manhattan

Death and loss are important motifs in another novel about emigration, *A Merry Funeral* by Ludmila Ulitskaya.[10] The scene is a loft apartment in Manhattan's Chelsea neighborhood, where the Russian-Jewish immigrant artist Alik is dying from an undiagnosed disease. The development of his disease determines the pace and the boundaries of the novel. Former and current friends and lovers, casual acquaintances, and complete strangers gather around Alik, attracted by his magnetic personality. This community is depicted as an autonomous organism that exists in almost complete isolation from its American environment. The feeling of Russian exclusivity and superiority is symbolically expressed by Alik's rejection of American medicine and by his wife's refusal even to touch American money, not to mention earning it. Alik is treated by one of his friends, a brilliant doctor who is unable to learn English and cannot pass the American licensing exam. Alik's wife, a former Russian fashion model, continues to live in a dream world as if she has never left Moscow. These attitudes of Alik's family defy the two most sacred aspects of the Russian-American dream: health and money.

The rejection of the bourgeois American dream by no means implies the rejection of real America. Alik is a passionate admirer of New York City, a place he knows intimately. Ulitskaya's depiction of downtown Manhattan—with its ethnic restaurants on the Lower East Side, art galleries in Soho and Greenwich Village, the fish market at South Street Seaport in the small hours, the morning rush on Wall Street—belong to the best portrayals of New York in Russian literature. As an artist, Alik loves the picturesque diversity and vitality of New York, but as a bohemian, he hates its complacency and vulgarity.

Alik and his friends also have a peculiar love-hate attitude to their motherland. In their conversations, they reiterate over and over again the supremacy of Russian culture and spirituality over American mercantilism and egoism. The Americans, they say, hate suffering and always try to eradicate it from their life, whereas the Russians traditionally value pain and misery as the means of perfection of the human personality. In stark contrast to this theoretical statement, all immigrants dread going back to Russia even for a short visit. All Russian immigrants in America are sooner or later haunted by the same nightmare in which they go back and then, for some mysterious reason, cannot leave Russia. Alik's practical ex-wife Irina, the only successful character in the novel who has made her way up from a tightrope acrobat in a Russian circus to a successful American lawyer, sums up this émigré reconstruction of Russia as follows: "Alik has re-created Russia around himself. This is a kind of Russia which does not exist anymore, and nobody knows whether it ever existed at all."

The most problematic aspect of emigrant literature is the question of continuity. The Israeli way is impossible in America; the Russian immigrant community is too small and weak to build a viable institutional framework, let alone a political party. As a distinct linguistic and cultural group, the group has no future beyond the first generation. With Alik's passing away, his circle will almost certainly disappear. The author can only try to find comfort in the humanistic tradition of Russian literature.

Ulitskaya attempts to go further and create a broader picture of the immigrant community. The construction of *A Merry Funeral* resembles that of Leo Tolstoy's novella *The Death of Ivan Il'ich,* although Ulitskaya treats the situation differently. The tragedy of the gradual estrangement of a dying man from everyday reality is set in the situation of exile, where the sense of separation is part of everyone's experience. Alik's death is not just a death of an individual, but also represents an unrecoverable loss for the community. The notion of community as an organism that provides meaning for the individual's existence is perhaps the most Tolstoyan element in Ulitskaya's novel. But unlike Tolstoy, who believed in the idealized peasant commune, Ulitskaya believes in the spiritual power of the Russian-Jewish intelligentsia, a community that is sustained by people like Alik.

🏵 *Longing for the* Ordnung

Olga Beshenkovskaya's provocative autobiographical narrative *Viehwasen 22: The Diary of an Angry Emigrant,*[11] is not comforting reading for those who believe in the high moral values of Russian-Jewish intelligentsia. The intertextual references send the reader not to Leo Tolstoy but to George Orwell (*Viehwasen,* the name of the street where the heroine lives, is, according to her explanation, German for "Animal Farm").[12] In the opening declaration that sets up the tone of the entire narrative, Beshenkovskaya openly proclaims her utter disgust with Russian Jews (as indeed with almost everybody else): "My God, how I hate people! Especially the Germans and the Jews. Or rather the Jews and the Germans. . . . However, the Russians weren't better either. But the Jews and the Germans. . . ."

Viehwasen 22 is a story about the travails of a refined Russian-Jewish woman from St. Petersburg who suddenly finds herself in the middle of the Russian-Jewish "*shtetl*" in Germany. In Russia she belonged, at least in her view, to the crème de la crème of Russian intelligentsia and lived on the cultural diet of Pushkin's and Blok's poetry. Her Jewish origin provided her with a status of an outcast, which gave her the aura of a sufferer, but did not cause much trouble. She could not become part of the official literary establishment, but instead was accepted by the unofficial elite of "genuine" writers and artists. Her troubles began only after the collapse of the Communist system, which unexpectedly destroyed the security of the low-income life of the anti-establishment cultural bohemia. When it came to the choice of her future home, Germany was the only attractive option: Israel seemed too Jewish, America too vulgar.

The author's first encounter with Germany in Frankfurt airport is shocking. She finds herself among crowds of Jewish families from Ukraine and Moldova talking all at once with horrible *shtetl* accents. She fears that the entire life effort of her parents, who worked hard to leave the *shtetl* behind, has been in vain. The author admits that she cannot stand the Yiddish language and has never liked Yiddish literature, which she finds pathetic and pitiful. Whatever sense of Jewish identity she possesses comes not from the Torah or Sholem Aleichem's stories, but from Thomas Mann's novel *Joseph and His Brothers*.

Germany creates many problems for the sensitive new immigrant. She is haunted by the memories of her father's war experience in Germany. At that time, her mother could not force herself to cross the German border when she tried to find traces of her lost husband. Now Germany seems to bear the war memories everywhere. The Germans welcome the newcomers with contempt: "The victors are coming!" The officials, including the rabbi of the local Jewish community, as well as ordinary people with whom she tries to establish contact, are often openly hostile. The painful adaptation to the new life causes her to develop an incurable psychological disorder. In a moment of despair, the author admits that the decision of a Russian Jew to emigrate to Germany amounts to a double betrayal of two homelands, Russia and Israel.

Surprisingly, the story has a happy ending. The author finally finds her social niche. She is accepted as an equal by the world of the German academia that is represented as a model intellectual community. She learns German so well that now she can even write poetry in the new language, and joins the elite group that is separated from the plebs by invisible but strict barriers. She achieves a social status similar to the one she once had in the Soviet Union, but her status is now more stable and respected, something that it could not be in Russia. Having secured her position in the new society, she can afford to be ironic about herself and other immigrants.

🏛 *Jewish Fate in Russia: Historical and Metaphysical Perspectives*

Grigorii Kanovich is arguably the only Russian writer for whom the Jewish theme had been central during Soviet times.[13] Sheltered by the Lithuanian literary establishment, he managed to publish three Jewish novels during the 1970s and 1980s. In these works, he avoided dealing with the Soviet reality directly: his best book of that period, the three-part autobiographic novel *Candles in the Wind,* is safely set in the prewar "bourgeois" Lithuania, while the two other novels depict Jewish life in Lithuania during tsarist times. This time setting not only allows, but even obliges the Soviet author to criticize the vices of capitalism, including antisemitism. Kanovich picks up his characters from among the poor artisans, the milieu he knows best, and rarely ventures in his narrative beyond the class boundaries of the proletariat and petty bourgeoisie. In his novels of the Soviet period, he manages to recreate the atmosphere of the Lithuanian *shtetl* without placing too much emphasis on its Jewish aspect. His main characters are of course Jewish and speak Yiddish, but the Jewish atmosphere is so natural as to not require reiteration.

Already in his Soviet period, Kanovich demonstrated a penchant for historical generalization. With his move to Israel in the early 1990s, his tendency to meditate on the fate of the vanishing Diaspora became dominant in his works. His most recent novel, *The Park of Forgotten Jews,*[14] is apparently one of the concluding links in his saga about Lithuanian Jewry. The narrator assumes the role of the last chronicler of a disappearing culture. The Park of Forgotten Jews, as the author calls the Bernadine Garden in the center of Vilnius, is the leading metaphor as well as the physical locus of the novel. In the summer, this is the meeting place of the last Jews of Vilnius. They come to sit on a bench and dream in silence about their past. The actual time is 1990–91, the last year of the Soviet Union. The historical moment shows the contrast between the optimistic enthusiasm of the Lithuanians busily preparing for the restoration of their independence after the fifty-year Soviet rule, and the despair of the last remnants of the once famous Jewish community who seem to have forgotten to leave the stage in time. They are left alone with their dreams, which for them are more real than their surrounding life. These dreams, rather than reality, constitute the content of the novel.

The main character is the former Red Army officer Yitshak Malkin, who is a tailor in peacetime. His dreams revolve around the war, which was the central event in his life. Comedy and tragedy are mixed together as he remembers the most important episodes, such as his honorary assignment to make a new parade uniform for the legendary Soviet Marshal Rokossovski and his postwar visit with his wife to their old *shtetl* and the farm where she was saved by Lithuanian peasants from the Germans. Sometimes an irritating reality disturbs the slow flow of Malkin's dreams. The young Lithuanians rally in the park against the Soviet rule, or the curator of the newly founded Jewish museum brings yet another American visitor who is eager to meet the last of the rare species of *litvakes,* the Lithuanian Jews, *in situ* to hear their authentic stories. "Why should we know about our troubles more than we already do?" Malkin philosophically asks the visitor, Professor Joseph Fishman from Columbia University.

All of Malkin's friends on the park bench have had controversial and uneasy experiences during the postwar years. Leah Staviskaya worked for the Soviet secret police helping to catch Lithuanian partisans who were fighting against the Red Army. Now completely destitute and senile, she is frightened to death by the Lithuanians' threats to kill her for her past crimes against their independence. In contrast to her, Moshe Gershenzon made several unsuccessful attempts to escape from the Soviet Union. In 1956 he married a terminally ill woman who was eligible for repatriation to Poland. To his horror, she died on the train just before they reached the Polish border, and he was ordered to stay. Ironically, he is now one of the few last Jews remaining in Vilnius after almost everybody else has left. These physically and mentally broken people will die in a few years and with them will end the long history of Lithuanian Jewry.

Kanovich's sense of irony is sharp and bitter, especially when he writes about the attempts to preserve the memory of the past. In his novel, Germans want to organize a photography exhibition, "Ponar in Photographs and Documents." It turns out that the person in charge was once a prisoner-of-war in Russia, and Malkin saved him from execution. This encounter makes Malkin dream about future instead of past. He envisions an official closing ceremony of the Vilna Park of Forgotten Jews, in the presence of the heads of states Helmut Kohl, George Bush, Margaret Thatcher, and Mikhail Gorbachev. After the speeches, the remaining Jews sing the Israeli anthem *Hatikvah,* the Soviet anthem, and the Lithuanian national song, and finally walk away. How much better would it be, Malkin fantasizes, if all superfluous Jews in the world could just fly away like birds and not bother other nations with their senseless existence. This motif appears already in the first part of Kanovich's autobiographic trilogy titled *Birds over the Cemetery.*

The days of the Park of Forgotten Jews are numbered, as Lithuania's independence will sweep away this community of shadows. One by one, the old Jews leave the stage. One follows his Russian wife back to Russia, another joins his son in Israel. Malkin makes his final journey to his native *shtetl*. There, on the riverbank, he sees his last dream: past, present, and future merge before his eyes in one dark spot. The symbolic comeback is also the end. Kanovich not only does not believe in the future of Jews in Lithuania, but he also doubts the ability and the will of future generations to preserve the memory of that community. In the interview following the publication of the novel, he poses a rhetorical question: "Who needs Jewish museums and monuments in Lithuania, when even the young generation in Israel does not care about Jewish past?"

Unlike most of today's Russian-Jewish writers, Kanovich has a distinct Jewish identity that links him to many generations of Lithuanian Jews. To some degree, he identifies his own life with their fate: "I shall finish it [the saga] with the same conclusion as, I believe, I have finished my own way. . . . my sons have gone in different directions, the elder one to Canada, the younger to Israel. Now I have also come to Israel."[15] As shown in the first part of this analysis, the sense of Jewish identity of writers who grew up in the Soviet Union is more problematic. Their feeling of uncertainty is clearly expressed by Yurii Karabchievskii in a newspaper article:

> It is too late for me to change my identity, one just cannot become a new man out of the blue. Moreover, I have no identity that would connect me with the past, I have no genealogy and will never have one. But the most important thing is—I do not need it, and if someone wants to offer it to me—I will not take it. . . . My whole identity is in the present and in the immediate past. And if it suddenly disintegrates, dissolves in the global Russian chaos, I will be left alone, outside history and geography.[16]

Another strategy of dealing with the problem of uncertain Jewish identity is to try to create an imagined identity out of familiar cultural elements. One of the earliest and most powerful experiments of this kind is attempted in Friedrich Gorenshtein's controversial novel *The Psalm* (finished in 1975 and first published in Germany).[17] In Russia it appeared in journal publications in 1991–92 and was met with mixed critical response. The book's subtitle, *Reflection about God's Four Punishments*, establishes it in the genre category of a metaphysical novel-parable. The protagonist is the Antichrist, who comes to the Soviet Union in the guise of an ordinary Jew, Dan Yakovlevich. Apart from being a namesake of the biblical patriarch Dan, son of Jacob, this man is also the last biblical prophet whose mission is to expose the sins of Christian civilization. On the surface he is an inconspicuous Soviet citizen, who eventually gets married and settles with his family in the provincial city of Gorky. Each part of the novel deals with an episode of his life, as well as a parable representing each of the punishments that God sends to the Russian people. At first Dan's function seems to be purely instrumental, but as the novel progresses, his personality acquires almost superhuman dimensions, superseding all other characters.

The fifth and final part of the novel contains a most grotesque caricature of the Christian "renaissance" among Moscow intelligentsia that began in the 1960s. The author mixes realistic pictures of Moscow life with horror fantasy. Passionate discussions of Dostoevsky in Moscow kitchens are followed by the scenes of a homunculus preaching from a retort and a witches' orgy in a winter forest. Gorenshtein treats the Russian Neo-Christian movement as the most dangerous variety of fascism that combines the rampant violence of Russian nationalism with the fanaticism of Orthodox Christianity. Seen from that historical perspective, German Nazism and the Soviet Communist regime are merely preparatory steps, a training school for the emerging apocalyptic Russian fascism. The young people who seek the truth in religion are represented as degenerate products of many years of barbarism, oppression, and misery, but it is for the Jews among them that Gorenshtein saves his most bitter venom and anger. Incidentally, a novel on the same theme was written at the same time by another Jewish author, himself a Christian convert. *Open Me Doors* by Felix Svetov' (Fridland) presents a detailed, although obviously a very apologetic, portrayal of Moscow's Jewish and Christian intelligentsia of the 1970s.[18] In his recent review of the novel, Alexander Solzhenitsyn underlines the centrality of the Jewish theme in the novel and calls it an "encyclopedia of stories and quests of [Jewish] emigration."[19] Particularly interesting is the penetrating psychological analysis of a midlife crisis that transforms an alienated Jewish atheist into a believing Orthodox Christian. Both novels are saturated with references to Dostoevsky, highly polemical in *The Psalm* and reverential in *Open Me Doors*. It remains an open question, however, to what extent Gorenshtein's *The Psalm* was a response to Svetov's novel.

Gorenshtein's narrator speaks in the authoritative voice of a religious teacher. He alone knows God's intentions and can interpret God's actions. Historical Christianity is for him a product of pagan distortion of the stern and unsentimental teachings of Judaism. The Judaism of *The Psalm* is based exclusively on the Old Testament, which is evoked in order to refute Christianity. According to the author, the degradation of the biblical religion started when the apostles conspired to kill Jesus in order to be able to represent him as equal to God. Thereafter, the Greeks, and later the Europeans, contributed to this process by adding their pagan myths of resurrection and salvation to the Christian tradition. The Russian people, with its unstable spirit swaying easily between the extremes of piety and sin, usher in the final phase of the degradation of Christianity. Antichrist is the last Jewish prophet who is sent to the Russian people, not to call them to repent but to dispel their Christian illusions.

In Gorenshtein's theological system, Jews will always remain the chosen people, and the triumph of antisemitism in the twentieth century is the definite, albeit negative, proof of this basic historical fact. This does not mean, however, that modern Jews are morally superior to the gentiles.[20] As one critic observed, Gorenshtein might be obsessed with Judaism, but he is completely uninterested in the historical situation of Jews in Russia or elsewhere.[21] In fact, his obsession with Judaism has very little to do with historical Judaism either. The author seems to be unaware of post-biblical Judaism, and his interpretations of the Bible have nothing in common with those accepted in Jewish tradition. The closest thing to Gorenshtein's "Judaism" is perhaps the inverted medieval Christian image of Jewish religion.

One angry Russian critic of liberal-Christian orientation pronounced Gorenshtein the founder of the new trend of "philosophically intoxicated" literature, a result of many years of religious and philosophical illiteracy. Vladimir Sharov, according to the same critic, is currently the main representative of this trend in Russian literature.[22] Most of Sharov's novels published in the 1990s were written during the 1980s. Jews figure in almost all of these novels, but their presence as a group is most prominent in his historical fantasy *Rehearsals*.[23] These Jews are not Jewish according to any definition of Jewish identity. They are Russian peasants who were once assigned the roles of the Jews in a strange Passion play and then passed these roles on to their children for generations. The story begins in the seventeenth century in the court of the patriarch Nikon, who orders the start of the rehearsal of the Passion play. The actual performance never takes place due to the abrupt dismissal of Nikon, and the whole company is exiled to Siberia. The director, an itinerant Breton actor, dies on the way, and the rest of the story takes place in the remote Siberian village where the company eventually settles down.

The actors continue to rehearse the play, which acquires for them a religious significance. Eventually the village community is permanently divided into three casts: Jews, Romans, and Apostles. Each generation brings a new interpretation to the play, and the actors firmly believe that, when they finally achieve perfection, Jesus will miraculously appear and bring about the end of history. Periodically the Apostles, frustrated by the long wait, give way to their antisemitic feelings and make up their minds to kill the Jews and thus to hasten the end. Frightened Jews run away, the Apostles chase them through the woods and marshes, murdering those whom they can catch, but in the end, having made a large circle in the woods, the exhausted Jewish survivors always come back to the village, only to begin a new cycle a few years later.

It seems that nothing can affect the peculiar customs of the remote Siberian village. But the establishment of Soviet rule causes serious changes in village life. To preserve the ritual, the villagers voluntarily transform the village into a prison camp, and continue to perform their play secretly every Easter. However, it becomes increasingly difficult to keep the ritual since the old actors cannot train the new generation. The story ends when the last Jew, Isai Kobylin, refuses to maintain the traditional "hide-and-seek" ritual and in the last moment runs away instead of coming back to the village.

Rehearsals is another complex parable of Russian history. Jewish identity is completely arbitrary, but once a person is marked as Jew it becomes his fate. Jews can be defined only in their relationships to the Russians, however painful these might be. Once on their own, Jews simply cease to exist, as in the case of Kobylin, "the last Jew." Sharov's imagination builds bizarre constructions from ordinary reality intermingled with wild fantasy, which grows, like a wild bush, in all thinkable and unthinkable directions.[24] Like Gorenshtein, Sharov is not interested in the concrete social and psychological aspects of Jewish life in Russia, but only in its metaphysical dimension. Jews as an entity have a special mission in Russian history and will always find themselves in the forefront of history. Antisemitism is a core element of the Russian collective identity, but at the same time, life without Jews is unimaginable to the Russian mentality.

The biblical layer of Sharov's prose is deeper and subtler than Gorenshtein's. Sharov is familiar not only with the Old Testament in Russian, but also with some Jewish interpretations. Some of his texts can be read as extended midrash-type commentaries to the books of the Old and New Testament. His novel *Should Not I Care?*[25] has intertextual references to the Book of Jonah, while in his most recent novel, *An Old Girl,*[26] Sharov transforms the parable of Job into a story about a devout Communist woman who loses her faith in Stalin after the senseless arrest of her husband, who is accused of absurd crimes. Sharov's worldview can be perhaps described as a postmodern, post-Soviet variety of Christian Gnosticism. For him, Judaism and Christianity can take on different cultural guises, but they continue to remain the main forces in the Russian historical drama, from which they can never be separated.

Constructing Jewish Identity in Contemporary Russian Fiction

🕎 *Russian-Jewish Writing Today and Tomorrow*

The Jewish content of even the most openly Jewish works of modern Russian literature is informed neither by Jewish culture (Yiddish or Hebrew), nor by Judaism, but by Russian literary tradition. The texts of Turgenev, Dostoevsky, Tolstoy, Bulgakov, and even of the New Testament, rather than those of Mendele, Sholem Aleichem, Dubnow or Bialik, let alone Rashi or Maimonides, serve as major points of reference for Russian-Jewish writers' search for their Jewishness. In this sense, the works of Russian-Jewish authors are different from works of their American-Jewish counterparts, in which Jewish cultural (religious and/or secular) connotations fulfill a more significant literary role (good examples are the most recent novels of Allegra Goodman and Allen Hoffman).

When "authentic," Yiddish-speaking *shtetl*-bred Jews occasionally do appear in Russian-Jewish fiction, their images bear no cultural connotations. A grandfather may even cut a heroic figure morally superior to Soviet reality, but he is never able to represent a culture in the same sense as Russian culture. Most Russian-Jewish writers (with the notable exception of Kanovich) construct their Jewishness from Russian elements, sometimes turning them upside down. Judaism is imagined as an Old Testament religion, defined through its "non-Christian" character in a manner somewhat reminiscent of medieval Christian stereotypes of the "Synagogue" as the opposition to the "Church," but, of course, much more positively. A Jewish hero is often a cosmopolitan intellectual who negates narrow-minded Russian nationalism, but who asserts at the same time the true universal values of Russian intelligentsia. Yurii Karabchievskii represents what one perhaps can call the "assimilationist" position: "When I contemplate the historic fate of the Jewish people, when I show lives of my Jewish characters, write about anti-Semitism—all this for me is part of Russian life." Russian-Jewish creativity, Karabchievskii asserts, eventually contributes to Russian, not to Jewish culture.[27] On the other side of the spectrum, one finds outspoken Zionist Maya Kaganskaya, who, surprisingly, also asserts the centrality of Russian cultural heritage for her new Israeli identity: "I owe my Israel neither to anti-Semitism nor to the 'founding fathers' of Zionism, but to Dostoevsky, Leontiev, Slavophiles and back-to-soil movement . . . my Zionism comes from them."[28]

Current Russian fiction is not rich in distinctly Jewish characters. Jewish "markers" appear frequently in works of Mark Kharitonov, Sergei Gandlevskii, Anatolii Naiman, and other leading Russian writers of Jewish or partly Jewish origin, but the Jewish theme is never more than a minor one in their writing. Jewishness has become a mere fact of life and no longer alerts the reader. This difference between the Soviet and post-Soviet perceptions of Jewishness is well captured by one author: "For a long time the life story of Rabinovich corresponded to his name."[29] In other words, during the Soviet period it was enough to give a literary character the name of Rabinovich, and his image would have to be shaped according to a limited number of schemes. Nowadays, as the same author demonstrates, the old stereotypes no longer work.

At this point, one reservation needs to be made. Recent political and social developments seem to confirm the apprehension that antisemitism will remain an important factor of Russian life in the foreseeable future. The presence of stable antisemitic currents in political, social, and cultural spheres cannot leave the artistic imagination unaffected. A study of the image of the Jew in works of Russian nationalist writers is beyond the scope of the present chapter, but I am convinced that these works, too, will contribute to the future development of the Jewish theme.

It is hard to resist the temptation to speculate about the possible future development of Russian-Jewish writing. The realist trend of Russian literature will probably become less interested in reproducing the Soviet reality. Along with this loss of interest will fade away the last images of Yiddish-speaking, *heder*-educated wise "old Jews," as well as acute sensitivity to Soviet-style antisemitism, the excitement of emigration, and the novelty of life abroad. So far, there are no indications of nostalgia for the *shtetl* as a "lost paradise," a trend currently fashionable with some Jewish writers in English. Israel and America will probably still retain their attraction for Russian writers and readers, and we can expect a new panoramic novel depicting the past two or three decades of Russian-Jewish Diaspora experience.

Finally, the "metaphysical" trend seems to have good prospects in Russian postmodernist literature. By now, Russian Jews have already almost completely lost the ethnic component of their identity. Most of them live in the modern urban environment, speak Russian as did their parents and grandparents, and are fully at home in Russian culture. As I have tried to demonstrate, Jewish identity in contemporary Russian fiction is constructed predominantly from Russian cultural elements including Turgenev, Tolstoy, Dostoevsky, Bulgakov, as well as the Russian Orthodox translation of the Bible. Russian-Jewish identity is increasingly defined not by the memory of the *shtetl* but by the eclectic gamut of contemporary forms of religious, cultural, and political life. The new generation of authors lives in an atmosphere that not only enables a free exchange of information and ideas, but also encourages the most daring artistic experiments. So far Sharov seems to be the

Constructing Jewish Identity in Contemporary Russian Fiction

only writer consistently dealing with Jewish themes in the postmodernist key, but his example is likely to become contagious.

NOTES

1. Peter Vail' and Alexander Genis, *60-e: mir sovetskogo cheloveka* (Moscow: Novoe Literaturnoe Obozrenie, 1998), 298.

2. Sergei Lezov discusses this phenomenon in his essay "'Evreiskii vopros' v russkoi intellektual'noi zhizni" (The "Jewish Question" in Russian Intellectual Life), *Znamia* 6 1996): 181–87.

3. A good example of this approach is the study by Jakub Blum and Vera Rich, *The Image of the Jew in Soviet Literature: The Post-Stalin Period* (New York: Published for the Institute of Jewish Affairs, London, by Ktav Publishing House, 1984).

4. In the collection *Toska 'po domu* (Moscow: Slovo, 1991).

5. *Izgnanie iz Edena: Ispoved' evreya, Novyi Mir* 1 (1994).

6. Interview on Radio Liberty, 8 December 1998.

7. An indication of the growing interest in this phenomenon is the new academic journal *Diasporas* (Moscow), which began to appear in 1999. Not surprisingly, the first issue is devoted almost exclusively to Jewish Diaspora.

8. Apart from frequent journal publications, a number of Rubina's books have been published in the past few years. Among them are *Vot idet Messiya* (Moscow: Ostozhye, 1996); *Angel konvoinyi* (Moscow: Medzhibozh, 1997); *Poslednii kaban iz lesov Pontevedra* (St. Petersburg: Symposium, 2000). The first book has appeared in English as Dina Rubina, *Here Comes the Messiah,* tr. Daniel M. Jaffe (Brookline, Mass.: Zephyr Press, 2000).

9. Foreword to *Vot idet Messiya,* 5.

10. "Veselye pokhorony (Moskva—Kaluga—Los-Andzhelos)," *Novyi Mir* 7 (1998); in book form: *Veselye pokhorony* (Moscow: Vagrius, 1999), 7–124. The English version is Ludmila Ulitskaya, *The Funeral Party* (New York: Schocken, 2002).

11. "Viehwasen 22: Ispoved' serditogo emigranta," *Oktiabr'* 7 (1998).

12. None of the German speakers whom I consulted knew this word; neither could I find it in a dictionary.

13. *Svechi na vetru* (Vilnius: Vaga, 1979); *Slezy i molitvy durakov* (Vilnius: Vaga, 1983); *I net rabam raia* (Vilnius: Vaga, 1984).

14. "Park zabytykh evreev," *Oktiabr'* 5, no. 6 (1997).

15. *Tsomet/Perekrestok,* no. 2 (Moscow/Tel Aviv, 1995): 51.

16. Quoted by Benedict Sarnov in ibid., 144.

17. Friedrich Gorenshtein, *Psalom* (Munich: Strana i mir, 1986). In Russia: *Oktiabr'* 9–12 (1991), 1 (1992).

18. *Otverzi mne dveri* (Paris: Les éditions réunis, 1978).

19. "Felix Svetov—'Otverzi mne dveri,'" *Novyi Mir* 1 (1999): 166–73.

20. In his play *Berdichev,* Gorenshtein presents a highly unflattering portrait of three generations of Russian Jews and exposes their greed, opportunism, and lack of morality.

21. Lev Annenskii, "Fridrikh Gorenshtein: miry, kumiry, khimery," *Voprosy literatury* 1 (1993).

22. Irina Rodnianskaya, "Gipsovyi veter," *Novyi Mir* 12 (1993).

23. *Repetitsii. "Mne li ne pozhalet' . . ."* (Moscow: Nash dom, 1987).

24. This simile belongs to Dmitrii Bavilskii, one of few contemporary Russian critics who appreciate Sharov's talent. His review "Nishi Sharova," *Novoe Literaturnoe Obozrenie* 28 (1997), presents a penetrating analysis of Sharov's writing, but remarkably does not mention its Jewish aspect at all.

25. "Mne li ne pozhalet' . . ." Published in the same volume as *Repetitsii* (Moscow: Nash dom, 1997).

26. "Staraia devochka," *Znamia* 8, no. 9 (1998).

27. Yurii Karabchievskii, "Ya—russkii pisatel'," *Shofar* (Lvov/Lviv) 8 (1990): 12.

28. Quoted by Alexander Voronel in "Filosofskoe myshlenie kak atribut etnicheskogo sushchestvovaniia," in *Evrei v kulture russkogo zarubezh'ia,* ed. M. Parkhomovskii, vol. 5 (Jerusalem, 1996), 448. Konstantin Leontiev (1831–91), conservative nationalist Russian writer and thinker.

29. Mikhail Belen'kii, "Za stolom, za chistoi skatert'iu," *Znamia* 10 (1996): 110.

Contributors

ROBERT J. BRYM is Professor of Sociology at the University of Toronto. His works include *Intellectuals and Politics* (1980), *The Jews of Moscow, Kiev, and Minsk* (1994), and *Sociology: Your Compass for a New World* (forthcoming, 2003). He has served as editor of *The Canadian Review of Sociology and Anthropology, Current Sociology,* and *East European Jewish Affairs.* He is currently analyzing the results of the 2000 World Values Survey and doing research on the Russian civil service.

VALERIY CHERVYAKOV is a Senior Researcher at the Institute of Sociology, Russian Academy of Sciences, Moscow. He has worked on major research projects on the Soviet style of life, Jewish ethnicity in Russia and Ukraine, and sexual behavior of teenagers in Russia and the United States. The author of many scholarly articles, he is the director of the Transnational Family Research Institute. He has co-authored (with Zvi Gitelman and Vladimir Shapiro) several articles on the ethnicity of Russian and Ukrainian Jews.

ALANNA COOPER received her Ph.D. in cultural anthropology from Boston University. Her dissertation was based on fieldwork among Bukharan Jews in Uzbekistan, and among Bukharan Jewish immigrants in Israel and New York. Her current research interests include the study of other Central Asian Jewish communities and the connections between them, as well as the study of contemporary and historical Jewish emissary work.

THEODORE H. FRIEDGUT is Professor Emeritus of Russian and Slavic Studies of the Hebrew University of Jerusalem. Professor Friedgut is the author of the two-volume *Iuzovka and Revolution* (1989). His current research includes the renaissance of the Jewish community of Russia, Jews and violence in the Russian revolutionary movement, and structural problems of normalization of Russia's society in the second decade of independence.

ZVI GITELMAN is Professor of Political Science and Preston R. Tisch Professor of Judaic Studies at the University of Michigan. He is the author or editor of several books on Russian, East European, and Israeli politics, most recently *A Century of Ambivalence: The Jews of Russia and the Soviet Union, 1881 to the Present* (Indiana University Press, 2nd ed., 2001). He is currently working on ethnic identities of Russian and Ukrainian Jews and on oral histories of Soviet Jewish war veterans.

MUSYA GLANTS received her doctoral degree from Leningrad State University, and is an Associate at the Davis Center for Russian Studies, Harvard University. She specializes in painting and sculpture of nineteenth- and twentieth-century Russia and has taught Russian art at Tufts and Harvard Universities. She has published numerous articles on Russian and Russian-Jewish art. With Joyce Toomre, she edited *Food in Russian History and Culture* (Indiana University Press, 1997) and was the American consultant for the television series *The Hermitage: A Russian Odyssey,* which was nominated for an Emmy Award. Glants is working on a book about the Russian-Jewish sculptor Mark Antokolskii.

MARSHALL I. GOLDMAN is the Kathryn W. Davis Professor of Russian Economics, Emeritus, at Wellesley College and the Associate Director of the Davis Center for Russian Studies at Harvard University. He has just completed a new book entitled *The Piratization of Russia: Economic Reform Gone Awry.*

MARTIN HORWITZ has worked closely with newly reviving Jewish communities in Russia and Ukraine since 1990, when he was director of the Moscow office of the World Union for Progressive Judaism. Since 1992 he has traveled extensively in these communities as director of the Jewish Community Development Fund in Russia and Ukraine. He previously taught Russian literature and language for eighteen years at Cornell University and Bennington College.

JUDITH DEUTSCH KORNBLATT is Professor of Slavic Languages and Literature at the University of Wisconsin–Madison and author of *The Cossack Hero in Russian Literature* (1992). She is also co-editor with Richard F. Gustafson of *Russian Religious Thought* (1996), and is currently completing a manuscript on which the current chapter is based, titled *Doubly Chosen: The Question of Jews in the Post-Stalinist Russian Orthodox Church.*

MIKHAIL KRUTIKOV was a Lecturer in Yiddish Literature at the University of London School of Oriental and African Studies, and is European correspondent of the Yiddish *Forverts.* He is the author of *Yiddish Fiction and the Crisis of Modernity, 1905–1914* (2001), and co-editor of *Yiddish and the Left* (2001).

YOHANAN PETROVSKY-SHTERN lectures in comparative literature and history at Tufts University and in Judaic Studies at Hebrew College (Boston). He is the author of a forthcoming monograph *Evrei v Russkoi armii (1827–1914)* [Jews in the Russian Army, 1827–1914]. He is preparing a book titled *Through the Military to Modernity.*

YAACOV RO'I is professor of history at Tel Aviv University and Senior Research Fellow and Director of the Cummings Center for Russian and East European Studies. His recent publications include, as editor, *Jews and Jewish Life in Russia and the Soviet Union* (1995); as co-editor, *Russian Jews on Three Continents: Migration and Resettlement* (1997); and as author, *Islam in the Soviet Union from World War II to Gorbachev* (2000), and *Islam in the CIS: A Threat to Stability?* (2001).

VLADIMIR SHAPIRO is Director of the Jewish Research Center, Head of the Ethnic Sociology Center "Diaspora," Institute of Sociology, Russian Academy of Sciences. He is the author of *Chelovek na Pensii* (1980) and several articles, co-authored with Valeriy Chervyakov and Zvi Gitelman, on the ethnicity of Russian and Ukrainian Jews.

SARAI BRACHMAN SHOUP is the former program director of the Charles and Lynn Schusterman Family Foundation, Tulsa, Oklahoma, where she worked on programs that seek to enrich and expand Jewish communities in the United States, Israel, and the former Soviet Union. She is currently based in Ann Arbor, Michigan, where she is an independent consultant for foundations and nonprofits. She is also the author of "The Modern Zaddik: Jiri Langer as Architect of a New Jewish Identity," *Review of Rabbinic Judaism* IV, no. 1 (August 2001).

MARK TOLTS is Senior Research Associate at the Avraham Harman Institute of Contemporary Jewry at the Hebrew University of Jerusalem. He has written widely on the demography of the former Soviet Union, and on Soviet and post-Soviet Jewry in particular.

Index

INDEX